WHO'S WHO IN THE OLD TESTAMENT

221.92
Som

WHO'S WHO IN THE OLD TESTAMENT

DONALD SOMMERVILLE

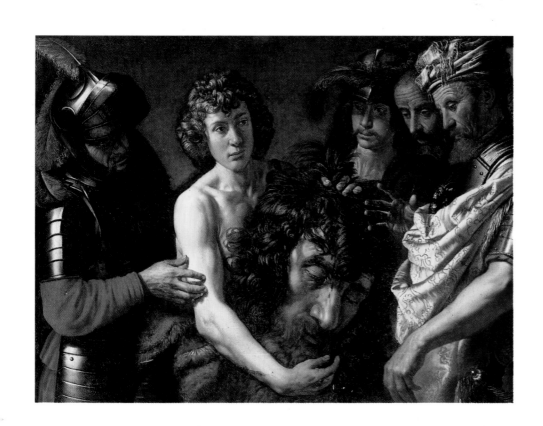

WITHDRAWN

Crescent Books
New York/Avenel, New Jersey

JOHNSTON PUBLIC LIBRARY
JOHNSTON, IOWA 50131

Copyright © 1995 Brompton Books Corporation

All rights reserved. No part of this publication may be reproduced, stored in a retrieval system or transmitted in any form by any means, electronic, mechanical, photocopying or otherwise, without first obtaining the written permission of the copyright owner.

This 1995 edition published by Crescent Books, distributed by Random House Value Publishing, Inc., 40 Engelhard Avenue, Avenel, New Jersey 07001

Random House New York · Toronto · London · Sydney· Auckland

Produced by Brompton Books Corporation, 15 Sherwood Place, Greenwich, Connecticut 06830

ISBN 1-517-14022-5

8 7 6 5 4 3 2 1

Printed and bound in The Czech Republic

The Scripture quotations contained herein, unless otherwise attributed, are from the New Revised Standard Version Bible © 1989 by the Division of Christian Education of the National Council of Churches of Christ in the U.S.A., and are used by permission. All rights reserved.

Page 1, top: Statues of Melchizedek, Abraham and Isaac, Moses, Samuel, and David at Chartres Cathedral.

Page 1, bottom, from left to right: Elijah, Jonah and Obadiah.

Page 2: The Sacrifice of Aaron, by Francesco Fontebasso.

Page 3, top: Moses striking the rock; detail from a fourth-century A.D. Christian sarcophagus.

Page 3, bottom: David with the Head of Goliath, from the circle of Matthias Stomer.

Below: Lot and his Daughters, by Jan Massys.

Right: Deborah prepares to go to war against Sisera and his army.

Below right: David kills Goliath; a twelfth-century stone bas-relief at Angers Préfecture.

Contents

INTRODUCTION

This book has the title *Who's Who in the Old Testament*. In order to understand the book properly and to make best use of it, it is important to appreciate the implications of that title. "Old Testament" is specifically a Christian description, applied to a collection of Israelite or Jewish sacred writings and designed, as such, to be considered alongside an exclusively Christian work, the New Testament. No single Jewish collection of writings is equivalent to what Christians know as the Old Testament. Within the Christian community there is also some disagreement as to exactly which writings belong in the canonical Old Testament and which should be regarded as apocryphal: not with the authority of scripture, but, in the famous phrase of Martin Luther, "good, and useful for reading."

The Jewish scriptures are divided into three sections: the Law or *Torah*, the Prophets or *Neviim*, and the Writings or *Ketuvim*. Of these three sections the *Torah* is regarded as the most important, with the other books being in some senses subsidiary, interpreting and expanding upon the essential core of the Law. This is one respect in which Jewish and Christian interpretations differ. In Christianity the Prophets are seen in large part as pointing the way toward Christ, whereas in Judaism they comment on the Law and how its true observance may be restored. The Hebrew word *nabi*, usually translated as prophet, does not have the same sense of foretelling as the Greek *prophetes*, via which the English usage developed. The division of books in Jewish scripture is according to the list below (in the usual Jewish order, but using the English names). Traditionally, there were said to be 24 books in the Hebrew Bible, since Samuel, Kings, Chronicles, Ezra-Nehemiah, and the Minor Prophets were each counted as a single book.

Above: A terracotta figure of the Babylonian goddess, Astarte, dating from *c.* 2000-1600 B.C.

The Law
These books are also known to Christians as the Pentateuch.
Genesis
Exodus
Leviticus
Numbers
Deuteronomy

The Prophets
"The Former Prophets"
Joshua
Judges
Samuel
Kings

"The Latter Prophets"
Isaiah
Jeremiah
Ezekiel

"The Twelve Minor Prophets"
Hosea, Joel, Amos, Obadiah, Jonah, Micah, Nahum, Habakkuk, Zephaniah, Haggai, Zechariah, Malachi

The Writings
Psalms
Proverbs
Job
Song of Solomon (Song of Songs)
Ruth
Lamentations
Ecclesiastes
Esther
Daniel
Ezra-Nehemiah
Chronicles

These various books became accepted as works of scripture, in something at least very close to their present form, by Jewish rabbis over a period probably from the fourth to the first century B.C. They were carefully copied and preserved over the centuries, and the oldest complete version (known as the Masoretic Text) of the Hebrew Bible that now exists dates from the tenth century A.D. The Dead Sea Scrolls, found near Qumran in the 1940s and 1950s, include a virtually complete copy of the Book of Isaiah, and parts of almost every other Old Testament book. The Dead Sea Scrolls are certainly much older than the Masoretic Text, but the Qumran Isaiah is almost identical to the received version. There are more substantial differences in the other books, which are similar to the differences between the Masoretic Text and the Septuagint translation.

Beginning in the early part of the third century B.C., translations of the Hebrew Bible into Greek were made in Alexandria in Egypt for the Jewish people living there. These are known as the Septuagint, from the word for 70, the supposed number of learned translators employed in the task. The process of translation probably took two centuries, and was evidently, from the results, based on different editions of the Hebrew Bible than those which later formed the Masoretic Text. The Septuagint translation also includes books based on Hebrew originals which have since been lost or, like Sirach, have only been recovered in Hebrew in modern times. Virtually complete

Above: The Shrine of the Book in Jerusalem.

copies of the Septuagint survive from the fourth and fifth centuries A.D.

In 382 A.D., St. Jerome was commissioned by Pope Damasus to make a translation of the Bible into Latin, which had become an important language in the Christian church. Jerome's Old Testament was produced between approximately 390 and 405. He based his work not on the Septuagint, but on original Hebrew sources, although he did unwillingly include books not found in Hebrew, but with less careful translations. Over time Jerome's translation became known as the *versio vulgata* – the common version – leading to its modern designation, the Vulgate. This Latin Bible, in corrected editions, is regarded as the authentic text by the Roman Catholic Church. The books not found in Hebrew originals by Jerome are described as being deuterocanonical, but are regarded as being of equal spiritual worth and authority, not as being of lesser value, as is implied by their alternative designation of apocryphal, used by many Protestant churches.

From the time of the Reformation, "Protestant" translations of the Bible have usually placed the Apocrypha in a separate section to the books originally found in Hebrew. In additional to the apocryphal/deuterocanonical books normally translated in this way, there are other ancient books and writings accepted as being scriptural by some Christian denominations, but rejected as wholly apocryphal by most others.

The Old Testament books officially defined as scriptural by the Roman Catholic Church are as listed below, with asterisks marking those regarded as apocryphal by most Protestant denominations. This book discusses personalities from all of these in a single, broad, alphabetical sequence.

The Old Testament

Genesis
Exodus
Leviticus
Numbers
Deuteronomy
Joshua
Judges
I & II Samuel
I & II Kings
I & II Chronicles
Ezra
Nehemiah

Tobit*
Judith*
Esther
I & II Maccabees*
Ruth
Psalms
Proverbs
Job
Lamentations
Ecclesiastes
Song of Songs
Sirach*
Wisdom of Solomon*
Isaiah
Jeremiah
Ezekiel
Daniel
Hosea
Joel
Amos
Obadiah
Jonah
Micah
Nahum
Habakkuk
Zephaniah
Haggai
Zechariah
Malachi
Baruch*

JOHNSTON PUBLIC LIBRARY
JOHNSTON, IOWA 50131

In addition to these, sections included in the canonical Books of Daniel and Esther by Roman Catholics are regarded as being apocryphal by Protestants.

Areas of difference in biblical studies not only cover which books should be accepted as having full scriptural authority, but also range across a wide variety of detail within the various books themselves. Older religious traditions, maintained today in the more "fundamentalist" or "orthodox" varieties of faith, lay stress on preserving traditional biblical texts and maintaining their divinely-inspired authority. Most modern religious scholars tend to take a rather different view, studying and criticizing biblical texts in the same ways as with other religious, philosophical and historical literature. The belief here is that, while the Old Testament (and other scripture) may be the word of God, it is expressed in

Left: An interior view of the Shrine of the Book in Jerusalem.

Below: Enoch and Elijah, as sculpted in stone on the west front of Modena Cathedral, *c.* 1100 A.D.

human terms, and understanding it and its context will help develop an understanding of its essential message. This book discusses the personalities named in the Old Testament within this style of study.

Such biblical students are agreed that the material in the present Old Testament has been assembled from a great variety of sources and, particularly in the case of the early books, over many hundreds of years. Considerable revision and editing has also taken place, and these have combined to leave gaps, inconsistencies, and evident contradictions in many places. It would be misleading, however, to think that out of all this some "correct" or "original" version can be constructed or conceived. It would, perhaps, be better to think in terms of different but equally valid descriptions of events combining to give a more complete image – in effect a three-dimensional view rather a single viewpoint.

Scholars studying the Pentateuch have developed a range of theories regarding the sources used by the ancient compilers of these books,

which are thought to have reached their modern form in around 400 B.C. From the eighteenth century the texts have been examined with increasing sophistication, noting at the simplest level that different sections of Genesis, for example, use different names for the deity: *Yahweh* at some points, and *Elohim* at others. Detailed study has now identified four broad strands of tradition incorporated into the Pentateuch. These are conventionally identified by initial letters in order of their suggested ages, the oldest first: J, E, D, P. All were probably based in turn on older written and oral material, and it would be incorrect to think of any as being more or less valid than any other. Details of the assessment of the sources of the various sections of the Pentateuch, and their precise dating and attribution, are the subject of continuing scholarly debate, but certain broad conclusions can be stated.

The J source is usually described as dating back to the ninth century B.C., or perhaps earlier. It gets its name from the initial letter of the German spelling of *Yahweh*, which is the title

Left: The Tower of Babel, by Verhaecht.

Above: A Swedish woodcarving depicting Adam and Eve.

it uses for God. Its editor or editors were members of the tribe of Judah, and were possibly from Jerusalem. E (from *Elohim*) is of a later date, perhaps from the eighth century, and is written more from the perspective of the northern tribes of the Israelite kingdom. D is later still, emphasizing observance of the Law and suppression of the worship of other gods. An early form of Deuteronomy, from which D derives its initial, may have been the book of Law discovered in the temple in the reign of Josiah, *c.* 621 B.C. The Priestly, or P source probably dates from the fifth century, and was therefore incorporated into the Pentateuch at a late stage in its development. It includes much material on temple ritual and extensive genealogies. Genesis 1 is in P. Some scholars also believe that Deuteronomy is only the first of several books by a single author or group of authors. They trace common elements from all the books, from Deuteronomy through to II Kings, and describe these as being the Deuteronomic history.

This book outlines the descriptions of the various Old Testament characters as they are given in the Old Testament. In addition to people, it also includes pagan gods and holy angels who are treated in the Old Testament accounts in the same way as the human characters. Many characters are also placed in a historical setting established from non-biblical sources.

This book includes entries on some 300 of the most important personalities named in the Old Testament. Several thousand people in all are mentioned by name in the Old Testament, many of them only very briefly in genealogical lists or similar material. It is frequently difficult to tell for some of these, and also for more significant persons, exactly which one is meant at a particular point. There is also often some confusion between individuals, groups or tribes, and geographical locations or political divisions all bearing the same name. Such problems and any contradictions in the account are discussed under the individual entries. Cross-references between entries are shown by the use of *italics* for the first mention of the other name in a personality's entry. Where more than one person share the same name, these are distinguished by a number, e.g., Ahaziah (1).

Quotations from scripture made in this book, unless otherwise attributed, are taken from the New Revised Standard Version Bible, whose copyright is more specifically acknowledged on page 4. Other quotations are taken from the New American Bible (acknowledged where they occur as N.A.B.), the Revised English Bible (R.E.B.), and the New Jerusalem Bible (N.J.B.). That slightly different readings are given by each of these highly respected translations only confirms the value of careful study of the biblical texts, and affirms the necessity for such study to be informed by prayer and faith if it is to be fully rewarding.

Aaron

As the first high priest Aaron was a very important figure in Israel's early history. He was the son of *Amram* and *Jochebed*, and the elder brother of *Moses*, but younger than their sister *Miriam*. Aaron's wife was Elisheba and they had four sons: *Nadab (1), Abihu, Eleazar*, and *Ithamar*. Aaron figures extensively in the Books of Exodus, Leviticus and Numbers, and also appears in the New Testament in Hebrews where the priesthood is discussed. He is believed to have lived around the thirteenth century B.C. or perhaps earlier, but the chronology within the Bible is not consistent, and non-Biblical historical sources do not provide a clear answer either.

There are many inconsistencies and contradictions in the descriptions of Aaron, which reflect the many sources from which the present text of the Old Testament must have been collected. Aaron is given a more prominent role in certain sections of the account than in others, where his relationship with Moses or his priesthood may not be specifically mentioned. The more extensive accounts are believed to originate from the so-called P source, which stresses the importance of religious ritual and observance. The J and E sources do not give Aaron an important role, and do not mention his position as priest.

The first mention of Aaron in the Old Testament occurs when the Lord instructed Moses to return to Egypt to free the Israelites. Moses complained that he was not a fluent enough speaker to achieve this, and the Lord told him to take Aaron with him as spokesman. After Moses had met Aaron and explained what was to be said, they went to see *Pharaoh (4)*. Pharaoh refused their plea to "Let my people go," and instead increased the labor burden required of the Israelites, who were accordingly angry with Moses and Aaron.

The Lord explained to Moses that he had hardened pharaoh's heart in order to have the opportunity to demonstrate to him his divine power. They went to see pharaoh again, and Aaron's staff was turned into a snake which swallowed the snakes generated by the staffs of the Egyptian magicians. Moses and Aaron then joined in using the staff to kill all the fish in the Nile and turn the river into blood.

This was still insufficient to convince pharaoh to let the Israelites go, and so a series of plagues was next inflicted on the Egyptians. Aaron's rod was used to bring on the first plagues, of frogs and gnats, and he and Moses worked together later in the series, inflicting the boils and the locusts. Moses alone was responsible for the others. Each time, when the plague was at its height, pharaoh wavered in his determination to keep the Israelites in Egypt, but each time, once the plague had been removed, he "hardened his heart."

The final punishment of the Egyptians was the killing of all their first-born children and the first-born of their livestock. At the same time, the Lord instructed Moses and Aaron in the rituals by which the Passover feast commemorating this event was to be observed.

Aaron's next role was in the battle with the Amalekites once the Exodus was well under way. *Joshua* was sent out to lead the troops in battle, and was successful for as long as Moses, assisted by Aaron and Hur, held his (Moses's) arms up in the air.

There are different versions of Aaron's role during the time when the Lord was giving the Ten Commandments to Moses. Exodus 19 mentions that he alone accompanied Moses onto the mountain. Exodus 24 explains that Aaron, two of his sons, and 70 elders

Left: Aaron Staying the Plague; an engraving by H. Moses that conveys the drama of Aaron's action.

went with Moses, and then later in the same chapter says that Aaron and Hur were left behind in charge of the people in Moses's absence. In this final version, continued in Exodus 32, Aaron agreed to make a god for the people to worship when they became restive during the long delay before Moses returned from the mountain. The Lord sent Moses down from the mountain, and when he returned to the camp and found the people worshiping the golden calf, he was outraged and destroyed the idol. Aaron simply blamed the people's wickedness for what had transpired. Aaron was not punished for this episode, although others were, and Deuteronomy 9 explains that this was because Moses had interceded for him.

Exodus 28 & 29 describe the selection of Aaron and his sons as priests, give detailed instructions on the vestments that they were to wear, and explain how they were to be consecrated for their office and the duties of sacrifice. Leviticus 8 & 9 include similar material. Leviticus 10 relates the consequences of failing to observe such rituals properly. It describes how Nadab and Abihu burned incense illicitly and were consumed in a divine fire; Moses told Aaron that he should not mourn for his sons. Throughout the Book of Leviticus many of the instructions on legal and ritual matters issued to the people are given with the formula, "The Lord spoke to Moses and Aaron, saying to them: 'Speak to the people of Israel, saying: . . .'"

After the extensive description of law and ritual in Leviticus and the first section of Numbers, the narrative history is resumed. Aaron and his sister Miriam quarreled with Moses because of Moses's marriage to a Cushite woman and, more importantly, because of the leading position Moses had taken up. "'Has the Lord spoken only through Moses? Has he not spoken through us also?'" As they were confronting Moses with this, the Lord formed a pillar of cloud around them, and explained Moses's unique position: "'With him I speak face to face.'" As a consequence of this protest, Miriam was made leprous for a time.

Right: Shadrach, Mesach and Abednego in the fiery furnace, as portrayed on an early Christian sarcophagus.

Aaron stood by Moses during the rebellion of *Korah* against their rule. After Korah and his followers were swallowed up in the ground, Aaron made atonement for the people who protested at this outcome, and this stopped the plague with which the Lord was punishing them. After these incidents Moses decided that it was necessary to have his and Aaron's authority confirmed, and this was done when Aaron's staff miraculously sprouted buds.

When the wanderings of the Israelites reached Mount Hor, the Lord spoke again to Moses and Aaron, and told them that Aaron would not be allowed to enter the Promised Land. Instead, Moses, Aaron, and Aaron's son, Eleazar, climbed up the mountain.

Below: Abel offers a lamb as a sacrifice in a sixth-century A.D. mosaic in San Vitale, Ravenna.

Aaron died there, and his priestly vestments were given to Eleazar. "When all the congregation saw that Aaron had died, all the house of Israel mourned for Aaron thirty days."

Abednego

Abednego is the Babylonian form of the name *Azariah*. With three companions, *Daniel, Hananiah* and Mishael, also respectively known by their Babylonian names Belteshazzar, Shadrach and Meshach, the Book of Daniel tells how Abednego was taken to Babylon from Jerusalem on the orders of King *Nebuchadnezzar*, to be educated at his court.

All four began by refusing to eat the food provided for them by the king, but became healthier by eating only vegetables. Shadrach, Meshach and Abednego then incurred the king's anger by refusing to worship him, and were thrown into an especially hot furnace as punishment. The fire was so hot that it killed those who threw the three in. They were unharmed, but seemed to the Babylonians to be joined in the furnace by a fourth man with the appearance of a god. Nebuchadnezzar therefore called them to come out and thereafter worshiped the true God. A part of the story known as the Prayer of Azariah appears only in Greek sources, and is regarded as being apocryphal/deuterocanonical. This section specifically mentions the intervention of an angel of the Lord in saving the three men in the furnace.

Abel

Abel was the second son of *Adam* and *Eve* and appears with his elder brother, *Cain*, in Genesis 4. Abel became a shepherd while his brother was a tiller of the ground. When the time came to make an offering to the Lord, the lambs that Abel brought were preferred to the produce brought by his brother. Cain was jealous and offended and, although warned against sin by the Lord, he killed Abel in the field.

Abel is mentioned in the Gospels of Matthew and Luke as being an innocent murder victim, and in Hebrews his faith is praised but the spilled blood of Christ is said to speak more eloquently.

For a more extensive discussion of the significance of the Cain and Abel story, see the entry on Cain.

Abiasaph

See *Ebiasaph*.

Abiathar

Abiathar was the son of *Ahimelech* and a descendant of *Eli*, and was an important priest and member of the royal council of King *David*. After *Saul* discovered that the priests of the town of Nob had helped David, he ordered them to be killed. Abiathar escaped and went to join David, taking with him his ephod – the priestly garment containing the oracular Urim and Thummim – which David consulted (I Samuel 22 & 23).

Below: The Meeting of David and Abigail, by Guido Reni. The couple married after the death of Abigail's first husband, Nabal.

Abiathar remained in David's service during his time as a guerrilla, and came to Jerusalem, where he is named with *Zadok* as being one of the principal priests in various lists of David's officers and servants. During *Absalom*'s revolt the two priests first carried the Ark out of Jerusalem, but returned with it on David's orders to act as spies in concert with *Hushai* the Archite. Zadok's son and Jonathan, Abiathar's son, were to be the messengers for any information.

In other passages Abiathar is said to have a son called Ahimelech, which may occur because of a confusion with the name of his father.

When David was nearing death and *Adonijah* and *Solomon* were rivals for the throne, Abiathar supported Adonijah. After Solomon became king and had Adonijah killed, he decided to spare Abiathar because of the good service he had done for David, and banished him instead to his estate at Anathoth (I Kings 1 & 2).

Abigail

When *David* went into exile in the wilderness to escape from *Saul*, he heard of a rich man named *Nabal*, and sent men to him asking for help. Nabal refused, and when David learned of this he decided to attack Nabal's household and kill all the men there. Nabal's wife was Abigail, who was "clever and beautiful," and when she heard of the refusal she realized that this would anger David. Therefore, without telling her husband, she took food supplies to David and his men and persuaded him not to attack. When she returned, she found Nabal drunk at a party and so did not immediately tell him what she had done. In the

morning, when he was sober, she told him, and he had a seizure and died ten days later.

David then sent servants to Abigail to ask her to marry him, which she did. She followed him to Gath during his service with *Achish*, and was taken prisoner for a time by Amalekites after they attacked Ziklag when David was away on campaign. After David came to the throne following Saul's death, Abigail bore him his second son, who is named as Chileab in II Samuel, and alternatively as Daniel in I Chronicles.

A second **Abigail** is mentioned, principally in II Samuel 17, who was one of David's sisters and the mother of a commander in *Absalom*'s army.

Abihu

Abihu was the second son of *Aaron* and was, like his father and brothers, a priest. Abihu and his elder brother, *Nadab*, burned incense before the Lord when they should not have, and they were themselves burned to death. Aaron and their surviving brothers were forbidden to mourn for them.

Abijah

Abijah appears principally in II Chronicles 13. He was the second king of Judah and succeeded his father *Rehoboam*. He is believed to have reigned from 913-911 B.C. Abijah features in I Kings 14 & 15, where his name is given as Abijam, and in I Chronicles 3 and II Chronicles 11 & 12.

Abijah fought with *Jeroboam (1)*, king of Israel. In Kings he is criticized for repeating the sins of his father, but in the more extended account in II Chronicles, a speech he gives before an important battle cites his strict religious observance and descent from David as the justification for his cause. Abijah's victory in this battle enabled him to extend Judah's territory to include Bethel and other important cities. After his brief reign Abijah was succeeded by his son *Asa*.

Abijah is a name also borne by six other personalities in the Old Testament. Two of these are fairly well known: one was a corrupt son of the prophet *Samuel*; while the other was a son of Jeroboam (1), who died young and was widely mourned.

Right: Abimelech and Sicol meet Abraham; an illustration from a Paduan Bible.

Abimelech

Abimelech was one of the sons of *Gideon*, by a Canaanite concubine. He became ruler of Shechem after his father's death by persuading the local people, to whom he was related, to give him funds from the temple of a local god. With this money he hired men who helped him kill 70 of his brothers. His youngest brother, *Jotham*, escaped to criticize Abimelech's supporters for this crime. Abimelech ruled for three years but died during a campaign to suppress a rebellion. He was injured when a millstone was dropped on him from a fortified tower by a woman, and he had his armor-bearer finish him off rather than be killed by a female. This is stated to have been divine punishment for his fratricide. Abimelech's story appears in Judges 9, and the manner of his death is also alluded to in II Samuel in the story of *David* and *Uriah*.

The name **Abimelech** also appears for two personalities in Genesis in the stories of *Abraham* and *Isaac*.

Abishag

Abishag was a young and beautiful woman brought to King *David* in his old age to help him keep warm in his bed. She became his attendant, but we are specifically told that they did not have sexual relations. After David's death she became involved in the final quarrel between *Solomon* and *Adonijah*. Adonijah asked to be allowed to marry her, but Solomon refused and had him executed because such a

marriage with a close royal attendant would have strengthened Adonijah's claim to the throne.

Abishai

Abishai was the brother of *Joab* and *Asahel*, sons of *David*'s elder sister Zeruiah. He was the leader of the Thirty, the "mighty men" who formed David's bodyguard, and in the lists which set out their names he is credited with having killed 300 enemy soldiers.

Abishai is first named during the time when David was an outlaw. He was one of David's two companions in the raid into *Saul*'s camp at Hachilah, and wanted to take the opportunity of killing the sleeping Saul. David refused to allow the Lord's anointed to be struck. Abishai is said to have helped his brother Joab in the murder of *Abner*, although Joab carried out the deed. In a later campaign he and Joab successfully commanded sections of the army in battles with the Ammonites and Aramaeans. On another occasion Abishai killed a giant Philistine, Ishbibenob, who had threatened David.

During *Absalom*'s revolt Abishai and Joab remained loyal to David, commanding divisions of his army. Abishai was also with David when the king was cursed by Shimei, but David would not allow him to kill Shimei as he wanted, and repeated the prohibition when Shimei came to apologize after Absalom's defeat. Abishai's final service was as one of the leaders who helped crush the revolt of *Sheba*, after which David again became king of the whole of Israel.

Abner

Abner was the commander-in-chief of *Saul*'s army. He was the son of Ner and was Saul's cousin. When *David* killed *Goliath* it was Abner who was in command of the army and who was sent to find out who David was. Abner was also in command of the army during David's rebellion, when David and two companions came into the camp by

Left: The death of Abimelech, shown in a woodcut by Gustav Doré.

Right: Doré's interpretation of Abishai saving the life of David.

night to steal Saul's spear, and was reprimanded by David for allowing this to happen.

After Saul's death Abner took service with Saul's son, *Ishbaal*, against David. He commanded Ishbaal's army at the battle of Gibeon, and was forced to kill *Asahel* in his retreat from there. The war did not go well for Ishbaal, and he then compounded his problems by criticizing Abner for having taken *Rizpah*, one of the women of Saul's harem, for himself. Abner then decided to make peace with David, and forced Ishbaal to agree that *Michal*, Saul's daughter and David's former wife, should be returned to David. Abner and other leaders had a meeting with David to confirm the peace.

Joab, Asahel's brother, tried to make David change his mind and, without the king's knowledge, had Abner return to a private meeting at which Joab murdered him. David had Abner given a state funeral and himself publicly mourned his death, but did not punish Joab.

Abraham

Abraham is regarded as the founder of the Israelite nation. He is respected in Jewish, Christian and Muslim tradition as a father figure, loved and protected by the Lord, and the first true believer. He is the earliest biblical character who is also placed in some form of historical context, his life coinciding with the reigns and activities of various named kings, and his movements seeming to follow what are known to be ancient trading routes. The description is not sufficiently precise to date his life more exactly than to some time during the period 2000-1500 B.C., and most scholars would certainly accept that the events described in Genesis 12-25, in which Abraham chiefly appears, are likely to be an amalgam of many different folk legends rather than

Above: Abraham's tomb in Hebron in Israel.

strictly the biography of a single individual. The incidents in Abraham's life are traced variously to the J, E and P sources of the Old Testament. He also appears in the Muslim Koran.

Abraham's father, Terah, moved the family, including Abraham, his wife, *Sarah*, and his nephew, *Lot*, from Ur near the Persian Gulf to Haran in modern Syria, where Terah died. The Lord then appeared to Abraham and instructed him to go "'to the land that I will show you'" where "'I will make of you a great nation, and I will bless you'".

Abraham, Sarah, Lot and their dependants first traveled to Canaan, where the Lord told Abraham that the land would be given to his descendants, and in thanks Abraham built altars at Shechem and Bethel. He traveled on in stages to the Negeb and, following a famine, to Egypt. Sarah, who had been passed off as Abraham's sister (see her own entry), was taken into pharaoh's [*Pharaoh (1)*] harem, and Abraham was given slaves, herds and other possessions. The truth about Sarah was discovered because the Lord afflicted pharaoh and his house-

hold with plagues, so pharaoh sent Abraham and all his family away. A similar episode appears later, with Sarah being taken into the household of King *Abimelech* of Gerar, but he was warned in a dream of the harm he was about to do, and returned her.

Abraham and Lot returned to Canaan, but had by this time become so wealthy that there was competition between their herdsmen for access to the grazing land. Abraham settled the dispute by giving Lot first choice of where to settle, which Lot did at Sodom. Lot was then caught up in the wars of Sodom with other local kingdoms, and was taken prisoner, but Abraham mobilized his war band, freed Lot and recovered much booty besides. On his return Abraham met *Melchizedek*, the priest-king of Salem (i.e., Jerusalem). Abraham was blessed by him, and in return Abraham paid him a tithe.

Abraham was now troubled that he had no children, but was again promised by the Lord that he should have many descendants, and that they would be given the land between the Nile and the Euphrates. Sarah was also concerned that they had no children,

and so she suggested to Abraham that he should try to have children by her slave, *Hagar*. Hagar and Abraham had a son, *Ishmael*, when Abraham was 86 years old.

When Abraham was 99 years old, the Lord again appeared to him, promising him that he would have many descendants and that they would be given the land of Canaan. As a token in return, the custom of male circumcision was to be instituted. Abraham duly had himself, his son, Ishmael, and all males in his household circumcised. (To this point in Genesis the spellings Abram and Sarai are used, but from here the more familiar Abraham and Sarah are employed. The Genesis text describes this as a change of name to match the new dispensation, but more likely it results from a linguistic confusion between the various biblical sources.) In his dialogue with the Lord, Abraham found it laughable that he and his wife, who was 90 at the time, could expect to have a child.

Abraham next gave generous hospitality to three visitors (who were, in fact, angels), one of whom again told him that he would have a son. This time Sarah overheard and was amused, but the Lord reminded them that nothing is impossible. The Lord then told Abraham that he intended to destroy Sodom and Gomorrah. The Lord and Abraham debated whether a whole city should be destroyed if a few righteous people lived there. The Lord agreed that he would spare the cities if ten righteous people could be found. In the event, only Lot and his family were spared when the cities were destroyed.

Sarah became pregnant and had a son, *Isaac*. As Isaac grew, Sarah, who had had Hagar briefly expelled from the household when she was expecting Ishmael, again became jealous, and persuaded Abraham to send Hagar away once more. Abraham's greatest test followed when the Lord instructed him to make preparations to sacrifice Isaac, only to stop him proceeding with the final stages. This incident is also recounted in the Koran. In this case the son to be sacrificed is not named, but Muslim tradition suggests that it was Ishmael.

The final events recorded of Abraham's life all concerned domestic matters. Sarah died, and Abraham bought land for her burial. He then sent servants to search for a suitable wife for Isaac (*Rebekah* was chosen), and finally, before his death aged 175, Abraham took a second wife, Keturah, and had six additional children.

As well as the principal narrative in Genesis, there are numerous other references to Abraham in both the Old and New Testaments. Among the many interesting aspects of the story of Abraham are that the great rewards offered to him are above all for his unquestioning obedience and faith; the considerable approval for his hospitality to strangers; and, especially when compared to other sections of the Old Testament, that his religious observances are not specifically described to be monotheistic (although, of course, they are assumed to be so).

Absalom

Absalom was the third son of King *David*. He appears in a genealogy in I Chronicles 3 (his mother was Maacah, daughter of Talmai, king of Geshur), but the various stories of his life and rebellion against his father are in II Samuel.

Absalom's full sister, *Tamar (2)*, was raped by their half-brother, David's eldest son, Amnon. Nothing was done for two years, until Absalom persuaded David to allow Amnon and David's other sons to attend a sheepshearing feast, and killed Amnon while he was drunk. David was at first concerned that all his sons had been killed but, although they were not, Absalom still had to go into exile and live with Talmai.

After Absalom had been away for three years, *Joab* persuaded the king to allow him to return to Jerusalem. Nonetheless, David still refused to let Absalom see him, and only after Absalom had forced Joab to press his case further were the king and his son publicly reconciled. However, on Absalom's part, this reconciliation was more apparent than real. He collected a retinue, and curried popular favor by offering to give judgment in legal cases when David was clearly becoming lax in his administration of justice. Eventually he felt strong enough to rebel openly, allied by now to *Ahithophel*, who had been one of David's leading advisers.

Faced with this rebellion, David decided to retreat in the first instance, but sent back the high priests *Zadok* and *Abiathar*, along with *Hushai*, another adviser, as spies in Absalom's camp. To symbolize his total break with his father, Absalom had sexual relations with the women of David's

Below: An illustration from a fourteenth-century Paduan Bible showing Abraham circumcising his son, Isaac.

harem who had been left behind in the palace. This step was particularly advised by Ahithophel, but Absalom rejected his next piece of advice, which was to pursue David immediately with such military forces as could be quickly assembled. Instead Absalom listened to Hushai, who advised a slower and more systematic mobilization and, when this had been accepted, took steps to warn David what was planned.

In due course Absalom's army and David's forces fought near Ephraim, across the Jordan, and Absalom was defeated. Absalom had been described in an earlier passage as being handsome and having particularly fine long hair. During the battle he was riding on a path among woods, and became caught by his hair in the branches of an oak. David had ordered before the battle that Absalom was not to be harmed, but Joab disobeyed and killed him. When news of the victory was brought to David, who had not participated personally in the battle, his first question was about Absalom, and he was overcome by mourning when he heard that his son was dead.

Below: The death of Absalom, as shown in the *Kölner* (Cologne) Bible of 1493. His long hair was the indirect cause of his demise.

Achan

Achan appears in the story of *Joshua* and in the events following the capture of Jericho (Joshua 7). While Jericho was being besieged, the Lord had forbidden the people to take any loot for themselves. Achan disobeyed this instruction. The Lord's displeasure was made clear by the defeat of the next expedition, against the city of Ai. Joshua asked what he should do, and was told to assemble the tribes and, by casting lots, seek out the guilty family. When Achan was selected he confessed to having silver, gold and a beautiful mantle hidden under his tent. After these items were recovered, he and all his family were stoned, and they and their possessions were then buried in the valley of Achor. In texts drawing on Hebrew sources this verse includes the fact that they were burned.

Achan also appears under the name Achar in a genealogy in I Chronicles 2.

Achish

Achish was the ruler of the Philistine city of Gath in the time of *David*.

There are two versions of the story of Achish and David. After David fled from *Saul* he came to Achish and, in I Samuel 21, was recognized, decided to

feign madness, and was thrown out. In the second version David and his men joined Achish's service, supposedly to fight for him. They were given the town of Ziklag to live in, and were instructed to raid into Judah. Instead, the account has David making attacks on other tribes, enemies of Israel. When the Philistines then gathered an army to fight Saul, David was ready to serve with them until the other Philistine leaders objected, fearing treachery from David. Achish therefore asked him to leave.

These versions of the story probably represent ways in which different strands of tradition have apparently tried to gloss over aspects of the life of David that might seem less creditable – i.e., suggesting that he does not go over to the Philistines at all, or saying that he does, but does not fight against Israel, which would have been hard to do while preserving the good opinion of Achish, as I Samuel 29 clearly states he does.

Adah

Two personalities of the name Adah appear in the Old Testament. One, in Genesis 4, was the mother of *Jabal* and *Jubal*. The other, also known as *Basemath*, was a Hittite wife of *Esau*.

Adam

According to traditional translations of the Old Testament, Adam was the first human being. The story of the creation given in Genesis 1, in which humankind (i.e., the whole species, including male and female) is created on the sixth day, is believed by biblical scholars to be a later account than the

Below: Adam and Eve – an engraving by Albrecht Dürer. The first man and woman have been tirelessly depicted over the centuries, usually at the moment of temptation, as here.

Above: Edvard Munch's painting of Adam and Eve gives the characters a more modern incarnation than is usually seen.

material in Genesis 2, which describes the creation of an individual man and woman and of the Garden of Eden.

The naming of this individual as Adam is now generally believed to have been a mistranslation of the Hebrew word *adam*, meaning "man," which may be connected linguistically to the Hebrew word *adama*, meaning "earth," and with the word meaning "red." Together these may relate to the description in Genesis 2 of "Adam's" creation from the clay or the soil. Such a story of the creation of the first man or men out of clay appears in the traditions of many tribal groups around the world, including various native North American and Australian peoples.

Some modern translations of the Old Testament scarcely use the proper name Adam at all in their main description of his doings. These include the Revised English Bible, the New American Bible, and the New Jerusalem Bible, while the New Revised Standard Version mentions the name only in footnotes as an alternative reading. Instead, such translations use the anonymous form "the man."

Various activities of this man are, of course, described in Genesis 2-4. He was created "from the dust of the ground" and "has breathed into his nostrils the breath of life" by the Lord God. He was established in the fruitful Garden of Eden, but was forbidden to eat of the tree of knowledge. Woman, unnamed at this point, was then created from one of the man's ribs while he slept.

In Genesis 3 the woman was tempted to eat the forbidden fruit, also giving some to the man. The first effect of this was that they realized their nakedness and clothed themselves. This is usually taken as meaning that they became aware of their sexuality. The Lord then told the man that in future he must work hard for his living and would then die, "'By the sweat of your face you shall eat bread until you return to the ground, for out of it you were taken; you are dust and to dust you shall return.'" The woman and the serpent were also punished. The man was then expelled from the Garden of Eden and prevented from returning by cherubim and a flaming sword. After the expulsion the man had sexual relations with the woman (who has now been named as *Eve*), and they had three children, who are named in the Old Testament: *Cain, Abel* and *Seth*. According to Genesis 5, Adam lived for a total of 930 years, and had other children also.

Adonijah

Adonijah was the fourth son of *David*. His mother was Haggith. He appears principally in I Kings 1 & 2.

In David's old age Adonijah was his eldest surviving son, and decided that he wished to succeed to the throne. He collected a retinue of chariots, cavalrymen and other guards, and persuaded

Abiathar, a leading priest, and *Joab*, the general, to join his party. He then tried to confirm his status by making ceremonial sacrifices and inviting leading officials and members of the royal family to a feast. When this was made known to David, he gave instructions for *Solomon* to be anointed immediately. This frightened Adonijah and his supporters, who deserted him, leaving him to take refuge at the altar. Solomon decided not to kill him if he proved to be worthy.

After David's death Adonijah, using *Bathsheba* as an intermediary, asked Solomon if he could marry *Abishag*. Since she had been one of David's personal attendants such a marriage would have strengthened Adonijah's claim to the throne. Solomon therefore sent *Benaiah* to kill Adonijah.

Two other Old Testament personalities also bear the name **Adonijah**.

Agag

Agag was a king of the Amalekites and appears in I Samuel 15. The prophet *Samuel* instructed *Saul* that the Lord wished the Amalekites to be destroyed utterly. Saul duly attacked them, but spared Agag's life and carried away as booty for later sacrifice many of their sheep and cattle. Samuel fiercely reprimanded Saul for this disobedience: " 'Surely to obey is better than sacrifice, and to heed than the fat of rams. For rebellion is no less a sin than divination, and stubbornness is like iniquity and idolatry.' " Samuel then "hewed Agag in pieces" as punishment for his brutality in earlier days. This quarrel was the cause of the final break between Saul and Samuel.

Another **Agag** is mentioned in a verse in Numbers 24. In part from a reading of the context there, it is possible that Agag is not a personal name but a type of royal title.

Ahab

Ahab succeeded his father *Omri* as king of Israel. As well as the information about him contained in the Bible, more also appears on the Moabite stone (see *Mesha*), and in Assyrian inscriptions from the reign of Shalmaneser III. Ahab reigned approximately 873-51 B.C. His wife was *Jezebel*, a Phoenician princess, and the daughter of Ethbaal.

Like all of his predecessors as king of Israel, Ahab is condemned in the Old Testament accounts for encouraging idolatrous practices. According to I Kings 17, "Ahab did more to provoke the anger of the Lord, the God of Israel, than had all the kings of Israel who were before him." This was because, under the influence of his wife, he worshiped *Baal*, and built a temple and altar to Baal in his capital of Samaria. These religious policies produced a number of dramatic confrontations with prophets, especially the prophet *Elijah*.

Initially Ahab and his people were punished by three years of drought, foretold by Elijah. Elijah then arranged a meeting with Ahab, using *Obadiah (1)* as a go-between. When they met, Ahab described Elijah as the " 'troubler of Israel.' " Elijah told Ahab that he would prove the superiority of the true God over Baal in a contest with 450 of Baal's prophets. The false priests were duly exposed in the contest and put to death. Elijah then sent Ahab home because, he told the king, the drought was breaking in a great storm. When Ahab arrived home he told Jezebel what had happened, and her subsequent threats to Elijah made him flee for his life.

Ahab was twice attacked by *Benhadad (2)*, king of Aram-Damascus. On the first occasion Ben-hadad laid siege to Samaria, but was defeated when Ahab, urged on by an unnamed prophet, made a sortie and routed the attacking army. Ben-hadad attacked

Below: Samuel prepares to kill Agag; a woodcut by Gustav Doré. The death of the king of the Amalekites was a violent one, for Samuel hewed him into pieces.

again the next year, but was beaten in open battle near the town of Aphek and cornered. Ahab then made a treaty with him and allowed him to return to Damascus. Another unknown prophet admonished Ahab for allowing Benhadad to go free.

Ahab had a further encounter with Elijah following his seizure of *Naboth*'s vineyard, after Jezebel had arranged for Naboth to be falsely accused of blasphemy. Elijah came to the king and pronounced a comprehensive curse on him and on Jezebel. Ahab was contrite, and the Lord told Elijah that, because of Ahab's repentance, the punishment of his family would be postponed.

Following Ahab's victories over Benhadad, there were three years of peace between Israel and Aram. Modern commentators have suggested that this period corresponds with the time (thought to be 853 B.C.) when Israel and Aram-Damascus allied against Shalmaneser of Assyria, as recorded in Assyrian sources.

Next Ahab summoned his ally, King *Jehosaphat* of Judah, to join him on a campaign to recapture Ramoth-gilead, which presumably had not been returned by Ben-hadad as required by the earlier treaty. Jehosaphat asked to be reassured that the venture had

Below: King Ahab's Coveting; Naboth Lies Dead and Elijah Delivers God's Curse on the House of Ahab, by Thomas Matthews Rooke.

divine approval. Four hundred prophets were assembled, and all advised that the attack would succeed, but Jehosaphat asked for further confirmation. Ahab agreed to consult *Micaiah*, although he hated the prophet, and had always had unwelcome predictions from him in the past. Micaiah first gave a favorable response but, when challenged to speak candidly, foretold a terrible defeat for Ahab. Micaiah explained that the prophecies from the other seers had been inspired by a lying spirit sent by the Lord to tempt Ahab to disaster.

Despite this information, Ahab and Jehosaphat went on their campaign, but, when it came to battle, Ahab took the precaution of fighting in disguise. However, he was fatally wounded by a stray arrow and died at the end of the day. Jehosaphat retreated home safely.

A second **Ahab**, a false prophet, appears in the Book of Jeremiah.

Ahasuerus

Ahasuerus is the name given in the Bible to the Persian king better known as Xerxes. He reigned from 486-65 B.C., and in 480 and 479 attacked Greece, only to be defeated at Salamis and Plateae. In the Bible he appears principally in the Book of Esther, in both the Hebrew version and in the more extensive and slightly different deuterocanonical/apocryphal version preserved in Greek.

In the third year of Ahasuerus's reign he gave a great banquet for all his officials and generals. After a period of heavy drinking he sent for his queen, Vashti, so that she could show off her beauty before the gathering. She refused to come and, greatly angered, he divorced her and sought a suitable replacement. He eventually chose a beautiful young Jew called *Esther*, who was the adopted daughter of *Mordecai*, who worked at the royal court at Susa.

Although Mordecai had been instrumental in foiling an assassination plot, Ahasuerus appointed another man, *Haman*, as his chief minister. Haman disliked Mordecai, and contrived to have Ahasuerus agree to kill all the Jews living in his realms because of this. Esther managed to have Haman disgraced instead, and Ahasuerus then appointed Mordecai to head his government.

Ahaz

Ahaz, also known as Jehoahaz, succeeded his father *Jotham* as king of Judah, and reigned *c.* 736-16 B.C. He is condemned in accounts in both Kings and Chronicles for his religious policy, and is even said to have revived the practice of human sacrifice and to have used some of his own sons as victims. To this, Chronicles adds that he "sacrificed to the gods of Damascus," while Kings adds the detail that he had the priest *Uriah* install in the temple a copy of an altar that Ahaz had seen in Damascus, and had the altar built by *Solomon* moved to accommodate it.

His reign was a time of decline and defeat for Judah. Ahaz lost battles against the Edomites and the Philistines, both thus regaining territory that had been won from them by *Uzziah*. *Pekah* of Israel and Rezin of Aram-Damascus allied against Ahaz and also inflicted a major defeat. Ahaz appealed to the dominant power in the region, Assyria, for help in this war: "Ahaz sent messengers to King Tiglath-pileser of Assyria, saying, 'I am your servant and your son. Come up, and rescue me from the hand of the king of Aram and from the hand of the king of Israel, who are attacking me.'" The Assyrians needed little encouragement since, as other records show, they were already expanding in that

Ahaziah

direction anyway, capturing Samaria and Damascus in 734-732 B.C. It was when visiting Damascus to pay tribute to *Tiglath-pileser* that Ahaz saw the altar mentioned above. Chronicles additionally tells us that many of the valuables that he paid over to the Assyrians came from the temple.

1. Ahaziah was the son and successor of *Ahab* as king of Israel. He is thought to have reigned from 851-849 B.C. He was associated in some capacity with *Jehosaphat* in an unsuccessful attempt to build a fleet on the Red Sea. At the

Above: The Wrath of Ahasuerus, graphically painted by Jan Steen.

Below: The Story of Elijah and Ahaziah; Stothard's watercolors from the Painted Chamber at Westminster.

end of his short reign Ahaziah was injured in a fall in his palace. He sent servants to consult with the prophets of *Baal* to see if he would recover. They met the prophet *Elijah* on their way, and he told them that, because Ahaziah had not attempted to consult the true God, he would die. Two companies of soldiers that Ahaziah had sent to arrest Elijah for this unwelcome prediction were consumed in fire before Elijah agreed to go and see the king personally, only to repeat the oracle which he had already given. The king died shortly afterward.

2. Ahaziah was the youngest son of *Jehoram (2)* and *Athaliah*, and succeeded his father as king of Judah, reigning for roughly a year: *c.* 843 B.C. During his reign he was allied with King *Jehoram (1)* of Israel, and joined him on a campaign against Aram-Damascus. Jehoram was wounded and returned to his palace at Jezreel. One of his officers, *Jehu*, who remained in the field with the army, took the opportunity to begin a coup. When he arrived at Jezreel, the two kings, Ahaziah and Jehoram, went out to meet him and were attacked. Jehoram was killed immediately, and Ahaziah died shortly after. According to Chronicles, he was captured while hiding in Samaria, was brought before Jehu and killed, whereas, according to Kings, he was wounded in the first encounter with Jehu, fled to Megiddo and died there.

Ahikar

Ahikar was the nephew of *Tobit*, and appears in the book of the same name. Ahikar was royal finance minister to the Assyrian kings, *Sennacherib*, and his successor, *Esar-haddon*. Ahikar managed to have Tobit, who had been disgraced late in the reign of *Sennacherib*, permitted to return to his home in Nineveh. Tobit later went blind and was cared for for two years by Ahikar, until Ahikar moved away to another town. Ahikar and his nephew, *Nadab*, returned later to share in Tobit's happiness when his sight was restored, and to join the celebrations of the marriage of Tobit's son, Tobias.

In the final chapter of the book there is an obscure reference to a quarrel between Ahikar and Nadab. This and other episodes in the book may relate to another ancient work, known as "The Wisdom of Ahikar."

Ahimelech

Ahimelech was the leading priest in Nob, a town of priests near Jerusalem. When *David* first fled from *Saul* he came to Nob and asked Ahimelech for food, pretending that he was traveling alone because he was on a secret mission from Saul. Ahimelech could only offer some consecrated loaves, which David accepted. David then asked him for a sword, and was given the only one available, which was the sword of *Goliath*. This incident of a lay person eating consecrated bread is alluded to by Christ in the Gospels, when he refutes criticism that his disciples have picked and eaten grain unlawfully on the Sabbath.

These transactions had been observed by *Doeg*, Saul's chief shepherd, and he later told Saul what had happened. Ahimelech protested that he thought he was helping one of the king's servants, and was not conspiring against him. In this second passage Ahimelech was also accused of consulting the Lord on David's behalf. Saul ordered that he be killed, but his soldiers refused to attack priests, and Doeg carried out the execution instead, killing 85 priests and all the other inhabitants of Nob. Only Ahimelech's son *Abiathar* escaped, and went to join David (I Samuel 21 & 22).

Ahithophel

Ahithophel is an important character in the story of *David* and the rebellion of his son *Absalom*. Ahithophel had been one of the king's leading advisers, well known for his particularly wise advice: "Now in those days the counsel that Ahithophel gave was as if one consulted the oracle of God; so all the counsel of Ahithophel was esteemed both by David and by Absalom" (II Samuel 16).

Ahithophel was persuaded to join Absalom in his rebellion after seeing how lax David's government had become. After they had captured Jerusalem, Ahithophel advised Absalom to have sexual intercourse with the concubines that David had left behind in the palace, as a symbolic act confirming that his break with his father was irrevocable. He also offered to lead an immediate pursuit of David to defeat him before he had time to reorganize. Ahithophel's advice was rejected on this second point, largely because

David had left his friend *Hushai* behind to join Absalom's camp under false allegiance. Ahithophel then realized that the cause was lost, went home, put his affairs in order, and hanged himself. This is one of very few suicides, other than in battle or its immediate aftermath, mentioned in the Old Testament.

Amalek

Amalek was descended from *Eliphaz*, the eldest son of *Esau*. He was traditionally regarded as the ancestor of the Amalekites, the desert tribe which fought against the Israelites during the Exodus and at various later times.

Amaziah

Amaziah was the son and successor of *Joash (1)* as king of Judah. He reigned *c.* 798-783 B.C. Joash had been murdered in a conspiracy led by some of his court, and once Amaziah was established on the throne he had the culprits executed, but was careful to obey the law and only kill the guilty and not other members of their families. In this and in other respects

Below: King Amaziah of Judah, who was deposed and killed by his son, Uzziah.

Amaziah is generally commended in both Kings and Chronicles for his religious policies, even though idolatrous practices were still allowed to continue in some areas.

Kings briefly describes a victory that Amaziah achieved over the Edomites in the Valley of Salt. Chronicles 25 gives a fuller account of the campaign, describing a census that preceded it, and also a related quarrel with a group of mercenary soldiers. Following the victory over Edom, Amaziah provoked a war with *Joash (2)* of Israel, but was badly defeated. Amaziah himself was held prisoner for a time, Jerusalem was captured, part of the city wall was destroyed and the temple and royal treasury were looted.

Like his father, Amaziah was subsequently deposed and killed after a conspiracy, being succeeded by his son *Uzziah*. The defeat by Israel is explained and the conspiracy justified in Chronicles by the statement that Amaziah brought some Edomite gods back to Jerusalem after his early victory and worshiped them.

Amaziah was also the name of three other personalities in the Old Testament, one of whom was a priest who reported an unfavorable oracle of *Amos* to King *Jeroboam (2)*.

Amon

Amon was the son and successor of *Manasseh (2)* as king of Judah. Amon's mother was Meshullemeth, and he was 22 years old when he came to the throne. His reign was short – lasting only two years – probably dating from 642-640 B.C. He worshiped idols and sacrificed to them. He was killed in a conspiracy of his officers, but the people rebelled against this and set his young son *Josiah* on the throne as his successor.

Amon was also the name of an important god in the Egyptian pantheon, mentioned in a single passage in the Book of Jeremiah. Another **Amon** was an official in Samaria in the service of *Ahab*.

Amos

The Book of Amos, although normally placed third of the prophetic books in Protestant and Roman Catholic bibles, is, in fact, the oldest of the books of the Old Testament completely devoted to the life and preaching of a single

prophet, rather than merely including prophets' activities along with other historical information. Comparatively little is known about Amos as a man, and no information about him appears other than in his own book. Most modern commentators believe that the Book of Amos as it now exists was indeed overwhelmingly the work of a single person, with only a few passages inserted by later editors. The book itself tells us that he lived in the reigns of *Uzziah* of Judah and *Jeroboam (2)* of Israel, and scholars usually believe that the prophecies date from later in their reigns, *c.* 750 B.C.

The opening words of the book explain that Amos lived in Tekoa, which was a village near Bethlehem, and that he was a shepherd. A later passage adds that he also collected fruit from

Above: The stern and uncompromising prophet Amos, as imagined by Gustav Doré.

sycamore trees, but had been called away from his usual occupation and compelled to prophesy by the Lord because of the wickedness of the people of Israel, Judah and the surrounding nations. The only other event from Amos's life that is recorded is that his message of disapproval provoked annoyance in the religious establishment. The priest *Amaziah* of Bethel (who presumably served the idol there) reported Amos to Jeroboam for conspiring against him and, when the king chose to ignore the matter, tried himself to send Amos away to preach in Judah.

Amos's message is a universal one; he condemns the wickedness of

Israel, but also notes and reproves evil conduct in other states. The people of Israel have allowed themselves to be seduced from pious behavior by luxurious living and low moral standards; they oppress the poor and only go through the motions of religious observance: "'I hate, I despise your festivals, and I take no delight in your solemn assemblies.'" Instead, he says "'let justice flow down like waters, and righteousness like an ever-flowing stream.'" Israel's failure to reform will bring the severest divine punishment of disaster, dispossession and exile. The gloomy message is only moderated in the final verses of the book, in which a time when Israel is restored to prosperity is foreseen.

Amram

Amram was descended from *Levi*. His wife was *Jochebed*, who was also his aunt, and their three children were *Miriam, Aaron* and *Moses*. He is said to have died in Egypt at the age of 137. He is listed in genealogies in Exodus 6, Numbers 3 & 26, and I Chronicles 6 & 24.

Another personality of the name **Amram** appears in Ezra 10.

Andronicus

Andronicus was one of the officials of Antiochus, and was appointed by him as his viceroy while he was absent quelling a revolt. The high priest, Onias, had been deposed in favor of Menelaus, who paid Andronicus a bribe in the form of gold vessels taken from the temple, also taking the opportunity to sell some more elsewhere. Onias, who was living in a sanctuary near Antioch, denounced this crime when he heard of it. Andronicus lured him out of the sanctuary and then killed him.

Antiochus returned and, although he is usually described very unfavorably in the Books of Maccabees, he too was outraged, and executed Andronicus in punishment.

Aram

Aram was one of the sons of *Shem*, son of *Noah*. Like the others of his family, he was regarded traditionally as the ancestor of a group of people – in this case the Arameans – who settled in what is now Syria.

Araunah

See *Ornan*.

Arioch

1. Arioch appears in Genesis 14, where he is described as being king of Ellasar, an area probably near the Euphrates which cannot now be definitely identified. He fought in various wars, allied with and against other kings, and in particular in the campaign against Sodom and Gomorrah, in which *Lot* was taken prisoner and later rescued by *Abraham*.

2. Another Arioch was a leading official of *Nebuchadnezzar*, who was ordered by the king to kill all the "wise men" of Babylon for their failure to interpret one of the king's dreams. Arioch's position is given variously in different biblical translations as either chief executioner or captain of the royal bodyguard. The dream in question was eventually interpreted by *Daniel* (Daniel 2).

Left: Aram, the son of Shem, depicted in stained glass in Canterbury Cathedral, *c.* 1178 A.D.

Below: Artaxerxes, son of Xerxes, grants liberty to the Jews, as seen in a Doré woodcut.

Artaxerxes

Artaxerxes was the name of three Persian kings. In the Bible the name appears in several places in the Books of Ezra and Nehemiah, but it is not invariably certain which of the kings is meant by the various references. The name is also used in some translations of the Greek version of Esther, but here it is fairly clear that Xerxes (known usually as *Ahasuerus*) is meant.

The prophet *Nehemiah* was cupbearer to one Artaxerxes (generally believed to be Artaxerxes I Longimanus, who reigned *c.* 464-423 B.C.), and

received permission from him to return to Jerusalem.

The Book of Ezra describes a letter of protest written to Artaxerxes by the Samaritans, warning that the "rebellious" city of Jerusalem was being rebuilt; Artaxerxes then had work halted. Artaxerxes is also said to have permitted *Ezra* and others to go to Jerusalem, and authorized the spending of money from the royal treasury to help him in reviving proper religious services. These incidents may also concern Artaxerxes I, or perhaps Artaxerxes II Mnemon (404-358 B.C.).

Right: A Babylonian terracotta statuette of Astarte (Ishtar), dated *c.* 2000 B.C.

Below: King Asa – a stained-glass window in St. Dyfnog's Church, Llanrhaeadr, North Wales.

Asa

Asa was the third king of Judah after the division of the monarchy between Judah and Israel. He succeeded his father, *Abijah*, and eventually reigned for 41 years – it is believed between 911-870 B.C. He appears extensively in I Kings and II Chronicles, and in both he is praised for his religious zeal. He is also briefly mentioned in I Chronicles and Jeremiah.

Asa is particularly commended in both Kings and Chronicles for removing idols from temples throughout the land. In Kings he is also credited with expelling male prostitutes from the temples, and returning votive gifts made by his father. Chronicles describes repairs to the altar of the Lord and pious oaths and sacrifices. In Chronicles these religious deeds are said to have been inspired in part by the prophet *Azariah*. Both accounts also describe how Asa removed Maacah (who seems to have been his grandmother, although the text is not entirely clear) from her position as queen mother, and destroyed an idol she had made to the goddess *Asherah*.

Asa was also a notable commander. Both Kings and Chronicles describe a victory over King *Baasha* of Israel, achieved by Asa bribing *Ben-hadad (1)*, king of Aram-Damascus, to give up his alliance with Baasha. This success was followed by the destruction of fortifications that Baasha had built, and their replacement by Asa with others protecting Jerusalem from the north. In addition, Chronicles describes a victory achieved with divine help over Zerah the Ethiopian. In this campaign, Asa is said to have had an army of 580,000 men and Zerah one million, however, these figures cannot be regarded as being historically accurate.

Chronicles contrasts this victory, achieved by reliance on the Lord, with the victory over Baasha, achieved with the help of Ben-hadad. The seer Hanani warned Asa that, because of this, the remainder of his reign would be troubled by wars, and was imprisoned by Asa for this unwelcome prediction.

After reigning for 39 years, Asa famously became "diseased in his feet," but because he relied on his doctors and "did not seek the Lord," the disease worsened and he died two years later. Asa was given an elaborate burial in Jerusalem and was succeeded by his son *Jehosaphat*.

Asahel

Asahel was the son of King *David*'s elder sister, Zeruiah, and brother to *Abishai* and *Joab*. Asahel was one of David's picked band of Thirty.

After the death of *Saul*, David's army of Judah under *Joab* fought with an army of Israel led by *Abner*, supporting one of Saul's sons. Abner was forced to retreat and was pursued personally by Asahel, who "was swift of foot as a wild gazelle." Asahel presumably wished to have the honor of capturing or killing the enemy general. Abner was unwilling to fight him, but had to kill him; as a consequence Abner was later murdered by Joab. Asahel was buried in his father's tomb at

Bethlehem. It is interesting that the father of Asahel and his brothers is never named.

The name **Asahel** is also used by three other personalities in the Old Testament.

Asaph

Asaph was one of the chief temple musicians in the time of David. He and others, including *Ethan* and *Heman*, led the music in worship of the Lord in Jerusalem. Asaph was of the tribe of Levi, and in later times a guild of temple singers was named after him. Musical instruments employed included harps, lyres and bronze cymbals.

The name Asaph also appears in the titles of 12 psalms, which may indicate that these were associated with the guild of Asaph, or possibly that they, or at least some of them, were composed by the guild or even Asaph personally.

Asenath

Asenath was the Egyptian wife of *Joseph*, and mother of *Manasseh (1)* and *Ephraim*. She was given in marriage to Joseph by *Pharaoh (2)* after Joseph had gained power and influence at pharaoh's court. She was the daughter of Potiphera, a priest of the god On. (See also *Potiphar.*)

Asher

Asher was the second son of *Zilpah*, who was maid to *Leah, Jacob*'s first wife, who gave her to Jacob as his concubine. Asher took part with his brother and half-brothers in selling *Joseph* into slavery in Egypt, and went with them to buy grain in Egypt in the subsequent famine. Later, Asher's family settled in Egypt at Joseph's suggestion.

Like his brother and half-brothers, Asher gave his name to one of the tribes of Israel.

Asherah

Asherah was one of the leading goddesses in the Phoenician and Canaanite pantheon. In non-biblical sources she is described as being the consort of El, the chief god, and an opponent of *Baal*. Asherah is associated with various fertility cults. In the Old Testament the position of Asherah is less precisely described,

and she is variously associated and confused with Baal and *Astarte*. In the Old Testament texts the word *asherah* often appears, meaning the idol associated with the goddess. The word is usually translated as "sacred poles" or "pillars."

During the reign of *Ahab* his wife *Jezebel* was criticized for killing the true prophets and replacing them with prophets of Baal and Asherah, but these prophets were defeated by *Elijah* with the help of a display of divine power (I Kings 18).

Astarte

Astarte was a Canaanite goddess associated with fertility. Like *Asherah*, references to the goddess in the Bible are often not precise and may denote another goddess, Anath. The name of Astarte is also spelled Ashtoreth and Ashtaroth in various translations of the Old Testament. She may have been the female partner of *Baal* in the forms of the cult adopted by the Israelites at various times.

Athaliah

Athaliah was the daughter of *Ahab* and *Jezebel*, and the wife of *Jehoram (2)*. After his death and the death of their son and his successor, *Ahaziah*, she seized the throne of Judah in her own right. She was the only queen to rule either of the kingdoms of Israel or Judah.

Ahaziah was a casualty of the revolt in which the army commander, *Jehu*, seized the throne of Israel and killed *Jehoram (1)*. Athaliah decided to use the opportunity to eliminate all of his family (even though he was her son), but Jehosheba hid Ahaziah's infant son, *Joash (1)*, from her. Jehosheba (also known as Jehoshabeath) was either Ahaziah's sister (but is not described as being Athaliah's daughter, although she may have been), or Joash's elder sister.

Seven years later, the priest Jehoiada hatched a conspiracy to have Joash anointed as king and Athaliah killed. The account in Chronicles adds to the simpler version included in Kings that Jehoiada was Jehosheba's husband. With the connivance of the Levites and the royal guard, Joash was acclaimed as king in the temple and, when Athaliah arrived to investigate the noise caused by the ceremony, she was dragged outside and killed. Following her death, an altar of *Baal* was destroyed and its priest killed. This, presumably, was the motivation of the revolt from Jehoiada's point of view, but it is not explicitly stated in either of the versions of the story in the Old Testament.

Azariah

See *Abednego* and *Uzziah*.

Azariah is a common name in the Old Testament, appearing more than 20 times. Bearers of the name, in addition to the above, include the high priest, son of *Zadok*, in King *Solomon*'s reign; another official of Solomon's, son of the prophet, *Nathan*; a prophet in the reign of *Asa*; and high priests in the reigns of *Uzziah* and *Hezekiah*. The name Azariah may also have been the personal rather than the throne name of Uzziah. The name was also briefly used by the angel Raphael during his appearance to *Tobit* and his son.

Right: A stela portraying Baal, from Ras-Shamra, Syria.

Baal

The word "Baal" means owner, master or lord, and was a name given to one of the chief Canaanite gods. Like other gods of the ancient world, Baal had various manifestations (hence the frequent Old Testament use of the plural, the Baals), but the most common seems to have been as the storm god. In the Canaanite mythology, Baal and various other gods fought a never-ending battle, each killing the other in turn and being reborn. This process represented the cycle of nature, and worshipers re-enacted aspects of this in various fertility rites associated with the cult.

Right: A medieval depiction of Balaam, his ass, and the angel.

The Israelite people joined in the cult of Baal at various times, and were roundly condemned by the prophets for doing so. Baal appears as early in the Old Testament as the Book of Numbers, and regularly throughout the history of the kingdoms of Judah and Israel. The historical accounts of the kingdoms were largely compiled from a Judahite perspective, which in part explains the standard condemnation of virtually every monarch of the Israelite kingdom for his repetition of the idolatrous practices of *Jeroboam (1)*, the first king of Israel.

The most dramatic episode in the campaign by the prophets to remove the cult of Baal was the confrontation in the reign of *Ahab* between *Elijah* and the prophets of Baal on Mount Carmel, in which Elijah was victorious and the false prophets were executed. Ahab was particularly condemned for supporting *Jezebel* in her efforts to introduce the cult of Baal more widely. In contrast, a few years later, *Jehu* was praised for his efforts to stamp out the cult.

Worship of Baal denied the ultimate power of the Lord to influence such matters as the forces of nature, and devalued religious belief and practice so that they became simply a means of securing natural benefits, without any emphasis on moral values or transcendental matters.

Baal-zebub

Baal-zebub appears in II Kings 1 as the god of the Philistine city of Ekron. King *Ahaziah* sent messengers to enquire of the god whether he would recover from injuries he had recently sustained. *Elijah* met them on their way and sent them back to the king.

The Hebrew name Baal-zebub is best translated as "Lord of the Flies", which seems an unlikely name for a god and is probably a corruption of a name which originally meant lord of the earth, or some similar expression. In the New Testament the name appears as that of a demon whom the Pharisees falsely associated with Christ.

Baanah

See *Rechab*.

Baasha

Baasha was the third king of the separate kingdom of Israel. He is believed to have reigned in the first decades of the ninth century B.C. He came to power after forming a conspiracy against *Nadab* and assassinating him during a siege of the Philistine town of Gibbethon. He then had all of Nadab's family killed, thus fulfilling the prophecy that had been made against *Jeroboam* and his descendants.

For most of his reign Baasha was at war with Judah. He was successful for a time, capturing Ramah and beginning to fortify it to blockade Jerusalem. However, King *Asa* bribed the ruler of Damascus, *Ben-hadad (1)*, to attack Baasha, and this forced him to withdraw.

In religious affairs we are told that Baasha was no better than Jeroboam and his family had been, and he was accordingly cursed by the prophet *Jehu*. Baasha died after a reign of 24 years and was buried at Tirzah. His successor was his son *Elah*.

Balaam

Balaam was a prophet or magician, but was of Mesopotamian rather than Israelite origin. He is portrayed in two distinct lights in different sections of the Book of Numbers, in which he chiefly appears, and which most scholars believe reflect the preservation of different traditions. His origins and genealogy are given consistently: he was Balaam, son of Beor from Pethor in Mesopotamia, and his role in biblical events followed a summons by the Moabite King Balak.

Balak sent to Balaam for help when the Israelites arrived in Moab during the Exodus. The first strand of tradition tells how Balaam sent the first group of Balak's emissaries away because the Lord told him to, and was ready to send a second group away when the Lord instructed him to go with them, but only to do what the Lord told him. Balaam was also warned in the same vein during his journey to Balak, when his donkey refused to go farther, for no apparently good reason. The donkey, however, was able to see an angel blocking the way, and when the angel was revealed to Balaam he was again warned only to say what the Lord told him to.

When Balaam met Balak he said, "'I have come to you now, but do I have the power to say just anything? The word God puts in my mouth that is what I must say.'" Balak took Balaam to a suitable site from which the prophet could curse Israel. Balaam told Balak to build seven altars and make sacrifices on them but, as instructed by the Lord, Balaam then blessed the people of Israel rather than cursing them. This process of altar-building and sacrifice followed by a blessing, not a curse, was repeated twice more, after which Balak lost his temper and told Balaam to return home. The third blessing is interpreted by some as foretelling the coming of the Messiah.

Above: Balaam's sacrifice: in a moment of high drama, Balaam blesses Israel, to the fury of King Balak.

Balaam duly left, but gave a fourth blessing before he departed, foretelling future Israelite victories over their enemies.

This generally favorable account of Balaam is found in Numbers 22-24. Interestingly, a quotation from the last of Balaam's blessings formed part of the first-ever message sent by electric telegraph after its invention in the nineteenth century.

The second strand of accounts of Balaam's role appears briefly in Numbers 31, in Deuteronomy, and in Joshua (and he is mentioned also in Nehemiah and Micah). Balaam is described as having incited the women of Midian to seduce the Israelites from true worship into following the *Baal* of Peor, or alternatively of having fruitlessly tried to curse Israel. For these crimes he was put to death.

Barak

Barak led an Israelite army to victory over the Canaanites in a battle at Mount Tabor. He was summoned by the prophetess *Deborah*, and told to raise an army of 10,000 men from among the tribes of Naphtali (his own tribe) and Zebulun. He said that he would only undertake the task if Deborah accompanied him, which she did. The forces of the Canaanite general, *Sisera*, were powerful, including 900 chariots, but when it came to battle the Lord threw them into a panic, and they fled. Barak pursued Sisera to Elon-bezaanannim only to discover, on his arrival there, that Sisera had already been killed by *Jael*. The story of the battle and pursuit appears in Judges 4, and Judges 5 consists of Deborah's song of rejoicing and praise for the victory, which is said to have secured peace for Israel for 40 years. Judges 5 may, in fact, be an earlier description of the events.

Baruch

Baruch, son of Neriah, was a scribe who assisted the prophet *Jeremiah* and appears with Jeremiah in the Book

Below: Barak and Deborah, by Francesco Solimena, one of the finest decorative artists of the late Baroque period.

of Jeremiah. The deuterocanonical/apocryphal Book of Baruch purports to have been written by Baruch, but few biblical scholars accept that this was the case. Baruch was a contemporary of Jeremiah around the turn of the seventh and sixth centuries B.C., whereas the Book of Baruch seems to have been composed several centuries later. This entry therefore only discusses the references to Baruch in the Book of Jeremiah.

Probably in the winter of 605-4 B.C., Jeremiah summoned Baruch to take down a complete record of all the oracles that Jeremiah had delivered in the course of his career, and told him that, when this was done, he was to go to the temple and read them aloud to the people. (Jeremiah was banned from entering the temple at the time.) The oracles principally foretold the coming destruction of Jerusalem, and were regarded as offensive, if not downright blasphemous, by King Jehoiakim, with whom Jeremiah had already quarreled.

Baruch duly read the oracles out in the temple, once in public and a second time to a group of temple officials. They told Baruch that they would have to report the matter to the king, and advised him that he and Jeremiah should go into hiding. When the oracles were read to the king, he burned the scrolls that they were written on. This, however, only inspired the prophet to dictate the material to Baruch once again, along with additional matter.

At another time Jeremiah called on Baruch to witness a land purchase within the prophet's family. The prophet's willingness to undertake this, despite his belief that the nation of Judah was about to be overrun and devastated, was symbolic of his further, optimistic conviction that a restoration would take place at some future time.

Later, after the fall of Jerusalem, Jeremiah prophesied against the survivors' decision to flee to Egypt following the murder of Gedaliah, the Babylonian governor. This did not please his hearers, and they blamed Baruch for suggesting such an unwelcome response. The move to Egypt took place anyway, and Jeremiah and Baruch were taken there too.

Right: Bathsheba at the Well, a seductive depiction by Peter Paul Rubens.

Baruch is one of the few Old Testament personalities whose name appears in a contemporary non-biblical source, a clay seal bearing his name and dating from the late seventh century having been found.

Barzillai

Barzillai and his companions, Shobi and Machir, brought supplies to *David* and his men when David was retreating in the early stages of his campaign against *Absalom*. When David invited him to come to live at his court after he had defeated Absalom, Barzillai refused on account of his age (he was 80 years old), but sent his son, Chimham, in his place. One of David's last instructions to *Solomon* was to be kind to Barzillai's family.

Basemath

Basemath appears in Genesis as one of the wives of Esau. In Genesis 36 she is said to be the daughter of *Ishmael*, elsewhere described as *Mahalath*, and in Genesis 26 she is described as the daughter of Elon the Hittite, known elsewhere as *Adah*.

A second personality called **Basemath** was one of the daughters of *Solomon*, and married one of his officers, Ahimaaz.

Bathsheba

Bathsheba was the daughter of Eliam, and the wife of one of *David*'s senior officers, *Uriah* the Hittite.

David saw her bathing one day when he was walking on the roof of his

house in Jerusalem, and saw how beautiful she was. Uriah was away with the army at the time, involved in the siege of Rabbah. David found out who Bathsheba was, and had her brought to him; they committed adultery and as a result she became pregnant. David recalled Uriah from the campaign, ostensibly to ask him to report to him, but really so that Uriah could spend time with his wife, and thus the actual paternity of the child would be concealed. Instead Uriah returned to the army without going home, so David ordered *Joab*, the army commander, to send Uriah on a dangerous attack in the hope that he would be killed.

After Uriah's death David married Bathsheba but, as warned by the prophet *Nathan*, their child died. David and Bathsheba's second son was then born, and survived. This child was *Solomon* (II Samuel 11 & 12).

Bathsheba also appears in the early chapters of I Kings, initially being lobbied by *Nathan* to join him in persuading David to name Solomon rather than *Adonijah* as his successor, and later suggesting to Solomon at Adonijah's

request that he (Adonijah) be allowed to take *Abishag* as his wife. Solomon was respectful to his mother, but refused the request and had Adonijah killed.

In a passage in I Chronicles she appears with her name spelt as Bathshua, and this verse also mentions three more of her sons.

Belshazzar

Belshazzar appears in the Book of Daniel as the son of *Nebuchadnezzar* and king of Babylon. The author of the Book of Daniel lived some four hundred years later than the events described, and, in this and other respects, is believed not to have been strictly historically accurate. Babylonian sources identify a Belshazzar who was the son of King Nabonidus but did not himself become king.

The biblical Belshazzar held a feast and used vessels taken by his father from the temple in Jerusalem, from which to serve the wine for his guests. Immediately a hand appeared and began writing on the wall of the royal palace. The king sent for his wise men

Above: John Martin's *Belshazzar's Feast.* Martin specialized in apocalyptic subjects, and contrasts the sumptuousness of the setting with a sense of forboding in a masterly fashion.

to interpret the writing, but they could not. His queen then suggested that *Daniel*, who had interpreted dreams for the king's father, might be able to help. Daniel refused the offered reward for this service, and admonished Belshazzar for his wickedness: "'You have praised the gods of silver and gold, of bronze, iron, wood, and stone, which do not see or hear or know; but the God in whose power is your very breath, and to whom belong all your ways, you have not honored.'" Daniel told the king that the days of his kingdom were numbered, that it had been weighed in the balance and found wanting, and would be given to the Medes and Persians. Later that same night Belshazzar was killed.

Belteshazzar

See *Daniel.*

Benaiah

Benaiah was one of the senior soldiers in the army of *David*. His personal feats included the killing of two Moabite champions and an Egyptian. David made him the commander of his body-guards, the Cherethites and Pelethites. He was loyal to David throughout the king's life, notably during the rebellions of *Absalom* and *Adonijah*. He helped to install *Solomon* as David's successor at David's command.

After David's death Benaiah supported Solomon and personally executed *Adonijah*, Shimei and *Joab* at the new king's order. Solomon appointed him to overall command of the army in succession to the discredited Joab.

Ben-hadad

The Old Testament mentions two or three personalities by the name of Ben-hadad, but does not carefully distinguish between them. All (or both) seem to have been kings of the powerful state of Aram-Damascus, to the north of Israel in the area of modern Syria, during the ninth century B.C. The following descriptions are based on the belief that there were three kings of the name, but some commentators suggest that the first and second of these were, in fact, a single king, reigning from *c*. 880-842 B.C.

1. A King Ben-hadad of Damascus was paid by *Asa* of Judah to attack Israel from the north when Asa was being hard-pressed by the southward moves of King *Baasha*. The ploy was successful, and Baasha was forced to abandon his advance and hurry back north to meet the threat.

2. Ben-hadad was also the name of an adversary of King *Ahab* of Israel. Ahab defeated him in two successive campaigns, the first of these only after Ahab's capital of Samaria was besieged. Ben-hadad and Ahab then made a treaty, in which Ben-hadad promised to return territory previously taken from Israel by his father [*Ben-hadad (1)*], and granted Israel trading rights at Damascus. Ben-hadad was subsequently murdered by *Hazael*, probably one of his officers, who then succeeded him as king. As well as the siege of Samaria mentioned above, which is described in I Kings 20, a siege of Samaria by a Ben-hadad is mentioned in II Kings 6. The king of Israel defending the town is not named, however, and there is no certainty if this is the same or a different incident, and the same or a different Ben-hadad.

3. Ben-hadad III was the son and successor of *Hazael* as king of Aram-Damascus. He was regularly defeated in his battles with King *Joash (2)* of Israel.

Benjamin

Benjamin was the youngest son of *Jacob*, and the second child of *Rachel*, who died giving birth to him. Rachel named him Ben-oni, but his father chose Benjamin as the child's name instead. Benjamin was the only one of his father's children to be born in Canaan; *Joseph* was Benjamin's only full brother.

When Jacob's sons went to Egypt to buy grain during a time of famine, Jacob kept Benjamin, the youngest, at home. When the sons met their half-brother and did not recognize Joseph, he demanded that they return home and bring back Benjamin to prove the truth of the story that they were telling. When they returned, Joseph gave all the brothers a feast, surprising them by correctly seating them according to their ages, and giving Benjamin five times as much food as the rest. Finally Joseph had Benjamin falsely accused of stealing a silver cup and, after *Judah* had spoken up for Benjamin, Joseph revealed his true identity. Benjamin's family accompanied Jacob and the rest of the clan to settle in Egypt subsequently.

Like his brother and half-brothers, Benjamin was regarded as the forefather of the tribe of Israel that bore his name. The tribe of Benjamin was smaller in number than the others, but its members were known for their military prowess.

The name **Benjamin** is also used by three other minor personalities in the Old Testament.

Bezalel

Bezalel was the chief craftsman singled out by the Lord in his instructions to Moses to make the fittings and furniture of the tabernacle. He was a member of the tribe of Judah and the son of Uri, son of Hur. He is described as being a master of various trades, "and I have filled him with divine spirit, with ability, intelligence, and knowledge in every kind of craft, to devise artistic designs, to work in gold, silver, and bronze, in cutting stones for setting, and in carving wood, in every kind of craft."

The principal account of the furnishing of the tabernacle in Exodus 35-39 does not clearly distinguish between the work done personally by Bezalel, or by his chief assistant, *Oholiab*, or by the various other skillful men employed. However, Bezalel is specifically credited with having made the Ark, and in II Chronicles 1 he is said also to have made the bronze altar.

Another personality called **Bezalel** appears in Ezra 10

Bildad

With his friends *Eliphaz* and *Zophar*, Bildad came to see *Job* after he had been afflicted by the Lord. At first Job tolerated his suffering, and they sat silently by him for seven days, but then Job began to curse the Lord and his misfortunes. In turn the three companions remonstrated with him, but failed to win him over. Eventually they gave up and, after Job had repented, they were ordered by the Lord to make a sacrifice to atone for their failure to persuade him.

Bildad's contribution to the debate was firstly to remind Job that "'if you are pure and upright, surely then he [the Lord] will rouse himself for you and restore to you your rightful place'", further commenting that the works of the wicked are transitory at best. Later Bildad described the misery and fear that accompany wickedness, and finally he told Job that all mortals are sinful and subject to the Lord.

Bilhah

Bilhah was given by *Laban* to his daughter, *Rachel*, as her maid at the time of her marriage to *Jacob*. Rachel was childless for some time after the marriage, and asked Jacob to have children by Bilhah instead that she (Rachel) could help to raise. Bilhah subsequently gave birth to two sons, *Dan* and *Naphtali*.

Bilhah later had an illicit affair with *Reuben*, son of *Leah*, the eldest of Jacob's sons.

Boaz

Boaz was a native of Bethlehem, and is one of the chief characters in the Book of Ruth. He visited his workers in his fields one day during the harvest, and there found a young woman, whom he did not know, gleaning behind the harvesters. He asked who she was, and discovered that her name was *Ruth*, and that, although she was a foreigner, she was the widow of a relative of his. Boaz knew of her and of her mother-in-law, *Naomi*, who was also a widow, and had heard how Ruth had helped Naomi. He therefore spoke kindly to her, and told his workers to ensure that she was able to pick up a decent quantity of grain. This special treatment of Ruth continued throughout the harvest.

Below: Boaz meets Ruth in his fields. This meeting would eventually lead to marriage.

Naomi realized that, as a relative, Boaz might wish to perform his family duty and marry Ruth. She therefore had Ruth go to see Boaz again after the threshing of the harvest. Boaz was attracted by Ruth's good behavior, but told her that he could not marry her himself unless a closer relative first declined to do so. The next day he arranged to ask the relative whether he wanted to marry Ruth and, when the relative declined, Boaz married her himself.

They later had a son called Obed, whose son in turn was *Jesse*, the father of *David*.

Cain

Cain was the first-born son of *Adam* and *Eve*. The story of his life and quarrel with his younger brother, *Abel*, appears in Genesis 4. Cain grew crops while his brother became a shepherd. They both prepared an offering to the Lord, and for unexplained reasons Abel's lambs were preferred to Cain's produce; Cain was angry and envious and was warned against sin by the Lord. Cain lured Abel into the field and murdered him. The Lord asked where his brother was, and Cain said that he did not know, for he was not his brother's keeper. The Lord could not be deceived in this way, saying "'Listen; your brother's blood is crying out to me from the ground!'"

The Lord banished Cain to wander in the land of Nod, east of Eden, having first set a mark upon him at Cain's request, so that no one would murder Cain in turn. Cain married and had a son, *Enoch*, and among his descendants were *Jabal, Jubal* and *Tubal-cain*.

The story of Cain and Abel has numerous components. It is said to symbolize the age-old rivalry between nomadic herders and settled pastoralists. Both of these signify comparatively advanced stages of human development. When this rivalry is combined with Cain's fears that he will himself be murdered during his wanderings, and with his success in finding a wife, it is clear that he and his brother cannot literally be understood as being the children of the first human beings.

The theme of sin's attraction and its inevitable punishment by an all-knowing but merciful God is obviously important. The first murder that Cain commits is also a step in the moral decline that will continue until the great punishment of the Flood.

Caleb

Caleb was one of the group of 12 spies, one from each tribe, sent out by *Moses* to spy out the land of Canaan. Caleb was a member of the tribe of Judah. As with many other personalities in the Old Testament, it is not always easy to distinguish in references to Caleb if a single individual (there may possibly have been two of the name) is meant, or a tribal or family group. In various genealogies and lists of landholdings in I Chronicles and elsewhere, Caleb is variously described as being both the son of Jephunneh and of Hezron. Part of the reason for thinking that these Calebs may be a single individual or members of the same family, however, is that they are both described as living in Hebron and in southern Judah.

Certain acts were clearly attributable to an individual called Caleb, however. When the Israelites arrived on the borders of Canaan in the early stages of the Exodus, Moses decided to send spies, each a leading man of his tribe, into the Promised Land; Caleb was chosen from the tribe of Judah. Moses instructed them to discover how fertile the land was, how numerous the people, and how strong their defenses. When the spies returned 40 days later, they reported that the land was rich and fertile, but that the people were very strong and numerous. Most said that the people were too strong to be overcome by the Israelites, but Caleb, supported by *Joshua*, disagreed, saying, "'If the Lord is pleased with us, he will bring us into this land and give it to us, a land that flows with milk and honey. Only, do not rebel against the Lord; and do

Left: Cain slays Abel with the jawbone of an ass, as depicted in a stained-glass window in St. Mary's Church, Addington, Buckinghamshire.

Above: Caleb's Daughter at the Springs, after the seventeenth-century French painter, Poussin. Achsah's dowry included water rights.

not fear the people of the land, for they are no more than bread for us; their protection is removed from them, and the Lord is with us; do not fear them.'"

The people did not want to follow this advice, and this so angered the Lord that He appeared to Moses and threatened to inflict a pestilence on the people, but Moses interceded, and the Lord decided instead that the Israelites should wander in the wilderness for 40 years, and that no adult then living, except Caleb and Joshua, would enter the Promised Land. The Lord also promised Caleb that his descendants would own land in Canaan.

Later Moses was instructed to appoint 12 men to apportion the land of Canaan between the tribes. Caleb was chosen again as the representative of Judah.

After the Israelites had captured the land of Canaan under Joshua's leadership, Caleb reminded him of the Lord's promise, and was allocated the town of Hebron in which to live. Caleb successfully expelled the sons of Anak, the local chiefs, from Hebron. He also attacked nearby Debir, with the help of his nephew, who joined him in return for being allowed to marry Caleb's daughter, Achsah. Achsah persuaded her father to give her various water rights as part of her dowry.

Canaan

Canaan was the grandson of *Noah* and son of *Ham*. The family was cursed by Noah after the episode of Noah's drunkenness. Canaan was also the name of the territory in which the Israelites settled. Canaan's brothers were Cush, Egypt and Put, who were regarded as being the ancestors of the peoples living in Africa (Cush is modern Ethiopia, but a definite identification of Put is more difficult). That the Canaanites were regarded as ethnically related to these groups and, by Noah's curse, to be looked upon as slaves, reflects the Israelite opposition to these, the indigenous peoples of their chosen land.

Chedorlaomer

Chedorlaomer was a king of Elam in the time of *Abraham*. He and a group of allies attacked Sodom and Gomorrah and carried *Lot* off among the prisoners. Abraham followed after him, defeated him in battle, and freed the captives.

Cozbi

Cozbi was the daughter of a Midianite leader called Zur. She and her lover, *Zimri*, were killed by the priest *Phinehas (1)* after the Lord had sent a plague against the people of Israel because the Moabite women had corrupted them and had persuaded them to worship the false god, *Baal.*

Cyrus

The King Cyrus of Persia who appears in the Old Testament is otherwise known as Cyrus II, or Cyrus the Great, who founded the Achaemenid Persian Empire. He succeeded to the throne of the vassal kingdom of Anshan in 559 B.C., soon conquered his supposed overlords, the Medes, and, by the time of his death in 530 or 529, ruled a massive empire spanning Asia Minor.

Little of this appears in the Bible, however. In the Old Testament Cyrus was praised for his generosity toward the Jews. He permitted many of the exiled people of Judah to return home, and encouraged them to rebuild the temple in Jerusalem. He also gave orders that all the items confiscated from the temple by *Nebuchadnezzar* should be returned. References to Cyrus occur chiefly in the Book of Ezra, but he is mentioned in II Chronicles and Isaiah. In Isaiah 44 & 45 Cyrus is described in Messianic terms, and is named as "my shepherd" by the Lord.

The several references to Cyrus in the Book of Daniel are not thought to be historically accurate, in line with much of the material in the book.

Dagon

Dagon was a god worshiped by the Philistines. From non-biblical sources it appears that the cult of the god was widespread, and may have originated in the Euphrates Valley.

Temples of Dagon appear in three episodes in the Old Testament. *Samson* killed himself by pulling down the temple of Dagon at Gaza. The supremacy of the true God was demonstrated in I Samuel 5 when the Ark was captured by the Philistines and placed in the temple of Dagon at Ashdod. The idol of Dagon was first found fallen on its face and then, the next morning, was discovered toppled over and broken. Finally, after *Saul*'s defeat and death, his head was briefly placed in the temple of Dagon.

Below: The magnificent tomb of Cyrus the Great, king of Persia, in Pasargadae, his capital (now in Iran).

Dan

Dan was the fifth son of *Jacob*, and the elder of his sons by *Rachel*'s maid, *Bilhah*. He and his brother and half-brothers were associated together in selling *Joseph* into slavery, and later they were sent to Egypt by Jacob to buy grain, where they met Joseph once more.

Dan is also the name of one of the 12 tribes of Israel which settled principally in the northern parts of the Holy Land.

Daniel

The Book of Daniel begins with a description of how Daniel was deported to Babylon by King *Nebuchadnezzar*, and much of the book then goes on to recount various events that happened to Daniel there under Nebuchadnezzar and his successors. This would place these events in the first half of the sixth century B.C. However, the writer of the book shows no detailed knowledge of the Persian kings but, particularly in the visions of Daniel that are described in the later chapters of the book, does show

knowledge of events that happened much later than the seeming setting of the book. From detailed examination of such matters, scholars generally believe that the book was written in the period 167-64 B.C. and, while it may contain material from much older traditions, it cannot be regarded as an accurate historical source. In certain respects the stories were also clearly intended to be a commentary on events of the time when they were written. Nonetheless, the stories of Daniel are among the best known in the Bible, and should therefore be summarized here.

The account begins by describing how the king had various of the deportees brought to serve in his palace. Daniel, Hananiah, Mishael and Azariah (see *Abednego*), who had been given the Babylonian names Belteshazzar, Shadrach, Mesach and Abednego, were unable to eat the food offered to them because it violated their dietary laws, and so became vegetarians and, to the palace-master's surprise, continued to thrive. This is one of the sections in the book aimed at the readers of its own time when, in fact, dietary observance had

Above: The beautifully drawn Madaba Map, featuring the land of Dan.

Right: Daniel in the lions' den; a detail from an early Christian sarcophagus.

been forbidden by Antiochus Epiphanes.

Next Daniel interpreted a dream of Nebuchadnezzar's when none of the other wise men of the kingdom could do so. The dream concerned a huge, elaborate statue which was broken into tiny bits and carried away by the wind. Daniel told the king that it described how his dynasty would be supplanted eventually by others, but that they would finally be replaced by the kingdom of God, which would supersede all other kingdoms.

Daniel, interestingly, is not mentioned in the next story, in which his companions were thrown into the fiery furnace (again see Abednego), but he reappears to interpret a further dream of the king. Daniel explained that the dream presaged a period of madness from which Nebuchadnezzar would suffer, but that he would be restored to health. This duly transpired and, when he recovered, Nebuchadnezzar began

David

David, son of *Jesse*, was the second king of Israel. He succeeded *Saul*, and is thought to have reigned for some 40 years at the end of the eleventh century into the early part of the tenth century B.C. He and *Moses* are generally regarded as the two most important figures in the Old Testament, central to the creation of the Israelite/Jewish national identity, and to the formation and development of their distinctive religion. However, despite the clear importance of David that emerges from the Bible, no such figure is mentioned at all in any of the non-biblical accounts or archaeological finds from the period that have been discovered so far.

Clearly David does have an enduring significance. Christians will note how the Gospels carefully trace the ancestry of Christ to David. That supposedly derogatory remarks made about David by a senior Israeli politician could lead to a public scandal in Israel while this book was being written, shows that David is not neglected by modern Jews either.

In the Old Testament the main narrative of David's life is found in the Books of Samuel and in I Kings 1 & 2, and in a parallel account in Chronicles, but there are numerous references to him in other books too. The main account of David's life is quite clearly constructed from a variety of ancient sources. Biblical scholars generally agree that Samuel and Kings reached something like their modern form in the period of the Israelites' exile in Babylon in the sixth century B.C. It seems likely, however, that the material now included in these books was composed on a wide variety of dates over the preceding centuries, perhaps going back as far, in some cases, as times closely contemporary with David himself. The Chronicles account is believed to have been compiled somewhat later, and to have drawn on the earlier Samuel/Kings as well as other sources.

Traditionally, David was regarded as the author of the sacred songs collected in the Book of Psalms, 73 of which have his name in their titles. His musicianship is also alluded to in other passages, but there is no direct evidence for his authorship of the psalms, and some of them seem from their language to be from a more modern period. While they shed a great deal of light on the religious beliefs and practices of their author or authors, and of the Israelites as a whole, and also have great spiritual value, they do not tell us anything significant about events in the life of their author(s), whether this was David or not.

At first sight it is hard to comprehend the favorable reputation that David has attained. This, after all, was an adulterer (with *Bathsheba*) and a murderer (of her husband *Uriah*) – matters not lightly forgiven in any society; he lived a violent, and far from blameless, life in other respects; he took service for a time with his people's enemies, the Philistines; he was an extortioner and perhaps again an accomplice to murder (*Nabal* and *Abigail*); he had difficult relations with various members of his family; he was slow to punish crimes committed by his supporters; and he instructed his son and successor, *Solomon*, to take ruthless revenge on various of his adversaries, disregarding previous promises to the contrary.

Despite all this David is lauded as having been the ideal king of Israel. There is no attempt to whitewash his reputation in the Old Testament and make of David some kind of moral exemplar. He lived in violent times, and the Chronicles account has him being denied permission to build the temple because he has had such an excessively violent life, but, within this context, he was the most successful king that the Israelites ever had. Above all, he brought prosperity and unity to the country, enlarged its territory, and subdued its enemies. Amid all this, the picture given of David is of a real human being, with the all too human characteristics of anger, lust and fear, distraught at the death of his rebellious son *Absalom*, unable to punish *Joab* for his murders because of the debt owed for past services, capable of true friendship with *Jonathan* and, most importantly, diverted from his previous upright life by his attraction to Bathsheba.

A completely detailed account of his life would repeat much material included in other entries in this book, so instead a briefer summary is included here. Readers are referred also to the list of related personalities at the end of this article.

David's rise to prominence began with his anointing as Saul's successor by *Samuel*. He was taken up by Saul and his court either because of his musical skills or because he killed *Goliath* (the account is ambiguous). He became the kingdom's leading soldier, provoking the jealousy of the increasingly unstable Saul. He married *Michal*, Saul's daughter, and became fast friends with Jonathan, Saul's son,

Left: Detail of Michaelangelo's famous marble statue, *David*, in the city of Florence. David is portrayed in his youth by the sculptor.

Right: The Triumph of David, splendidly envisaged by French painter Nicolas Poussin.

and, until David's arrival, Saul's leading soldier. Both Jonathan and Michal helped him escape when Saul finally decided to kill him and he was forced to begin a life as a bandit and exile.

In his exile he had help from *Ahimelech* and the priests of Nob, sought refuge with the Philistine King *Achish*, but thought better of it, feigned madness and escaped, before settling for a time in the Adullam area and establishing a bandit gang that would become the core of his later army. From time to time Saul sent expeditions to try to capture him and twice, in the course of these, Saul was left literally at David's mercy, with David declining each time to kill him. During this period David and his followers supported themselves in part by what was clearly extortion. An argument relating to this led to the supposedly natural death of a prosperous farmer, Nabal, after which David married his widow, Abigail. David had at least six wives and numerous concubines in the course of his life.

After being harried for so long, David left the kingdom and took service with Achish, who made David governor of his town of Ziklag. From here David and his men carried out raids against various bands of desert nomads, but told Achish that he was attacking Israel. Achish then wanted David to serve with him in the war against Saul, which had been resumed. The other Philistine kings objected to David, suggesting that he would have divided loyalties, although David was evidently willing to be loyal to them. He left the Philistine army and was very conveniently occupied punishing an Amalekite attack on Ziklag when Saul was defeated and killed. David could thus genuinely claim to have had no part in this, and was deeply upset at the deaths of both Saul and Jonathan.

For a time Saul's ineffectual son *Ishbaal* was maintained as king of Judah by Saul's general, *Abner*. Ishbaal was soon murdered by two of his

Above: David, having seen Bathsheba bathing, summons Uriah; a painting by Marc' Antonio Franciabigio.

Below: David brings the Ark of the Covenant to Jerusalem amid huge rejoicing.

Above: David and Saul, by Ernst Josephson.

Right: The Building of the House of King David, by Francesco Pesellino.

officers, and Abner was killed by Joab, one of David's men. David was now undisputed king. He then came to Jerusalem, which had never yet been held by the Israelites, captured it, and set in train various building works. He also planned to bring the Ark of the Covenant to Jerusalem, which he did, after a mishap on the way. The account in Chronicles describes in considerable detail the organization that he established for the various categories of temple priests, musicians, gatekeepers, and so on. David wished to build a temple in Jerusalem, but later *Nathan* told him that this was not the will of the Lord.

As king, David won further military successes, but in the course of one of these campaigns he fell for Bathsheba, seduced her and made her pregnant, had her husband, Uriah, killed, and married her shortly afterward. Their

Samson's home, but it is not made explicit in the narrative whether she was herself a Philistine or an Israelite. When the Philistine leaders heard that Samson was seeing her, they bribed her to find out the secret of his strength so that they could capture him.

Three times Samson replied to her nagging with spurious tales of methods by which he could be subdued. Finally she pestered him so relentlessly that he told her the truth: that he would be weakened if his hair were cut off. Delilah arranged for a man to do this while Samson was asleep, and he was captured when he awoke.

Dinah

Dinah was the daughter of *Jacob* and his first wife, *Leah*. After Jacob and his family left their father-in-law, *Laban*, they settled initially at Shechem, on land bought from *Hamor*. Hamor's son, also *Shechem*, raped Dinah and fell in love with her. He asked his father to arrange a marriage, to which Dinah's brothers first pretended to agree. However, led by *Simeon* and *Levi*, they then attacked the town, killed both Shechem and Hamor, and took Dinah away.

Doeg

Doeg was an Edomite, and the chief shepherd of *Saul*'s flock. After *David* had quarreled with Saul, Doeg happened to be at Nob, a city of priests, when David came there and was given assistance by the chief priest, *Ahimelech*. He reported this to Saul later, and Saul ordered his men to kill the priests of Nob. They refused, but Doeg took on this task, leading an attack which killed 85 priests, including Ahimelech, and laid waste their town.

Ebiasaph

Ebiasaph was a son of *Korah*, of the Levite tribe. Korah died, swallowed up by the earth, after being one of the leaders of a rebellion against *Moses* (Numbers 26 and other locations), but his sons were spared. Ebiasaph appears in the long genealogies in the early chapters of I Chronicles, where his descendants are described as having the task of "guarding the threshold of the tent, just as their fathers had guarded the entrance to the encampment of the Lord" (N.A.B.).

The name Ebiasaph is also spelled as Abiasaph in Exodus 6.

Edna

Edna was the wife of *Raguel*, and the mother of *Sarah (2)*. She and her husband, who was a kinsman of *Tobit*, lived in the city of Ectabana. They were visited by Tobias, Tobit's son, who was on an errand for his father, but decided also that he wished to marry Sarah. Previous husbands of Sarah had all been killed by a demon, but with the help of the angel, Raphael, Tobias avoided this fate. They parted happily from Edna and Raguel after the wedding, when the couple went to stay with Tobit, but after his death they returned to take care of Edna and her husband.

Eglon

Eglon was a Moabite king in the period of Judges. His story, and that of his adversary, *Ehud*, appears in Judges 3. For a period of 18 years Eglon controlled the area around Jericho. Ehud came to him bringing tribute from the Israelites and then, pretending that he

Below: The illuminated twelfth-century Winchester Bible shows Doeg slaying the priests.

had a secret message to deliver, arranged to speak to the king alone in a room in his palace. Ehud then produced a concealed weapon and stabbed Eglon to death. Eglon was very fat, and the knife went in so deep that it was completely covered by his fat. Ehud locked the door and made his escape successfully, since the king's servants did not wish to disturb Eglon in his chamber. Ehud then led a successful revolt against the Moabites, expelling them from the territory that they had held.

Ehud

In the period of Israelite history described in the Book of Judges, the account relates how the people periodically fell into corrupt practices, encountered misfortunes, and were then redeemed by the appearance of a judge who led them back to correct behavior. Ehud was one such judge. He was a member of the tribe of Benjamin, and in his time much of the land of Benjamin had been ruled for some 18 years by a Moabite king called *Eglon*. Ehud

went to see Eglon, bringing gifts, and then contrived to speak to him alone, on the pretext that he had a secret message. Ehud then produced a concealed dagger, stabbed and killed Eglon, and made his escape. He finally followed up this assassination by leading a successful campaign to expel the Moabites from their captured territory.

Below: A fourteenth-century stained-glass panel in the French church of St. Etienne, Mulhouse, shows Ehud killing the Moabite king, Eglon. Ehud's act led to the expulsion of the Moabites.

Elah

Elah was the son and successor of *Baasha* as king of Israel. His reign was brief – only two years – and ended unfortunately. One of his military commanders, *Zimri*, formed a conspiracy, and assassinated him when he was drunk at a feast. Zimri then killed everyone else in Elah's family, fulfilling the prophecy that had been made against Baasha for his idolatrous practices.

The name **Elah** is also used by four other personalities in the Old Testament, including the father of Hoshea.

Eleazar

Eleazar was one of the sons of *Aaron*, and his successor as high priest. Eleazar was the father of *Phinehas (1)*.

Moses was instructed to make elaborate sacred vestments for Aaron and his sons, and that Aaron's were to be passed on to his sons at his death. Eleazar's older brothers, *Nadab* and *Abihu*, were killed by the Lord for failing to observe the correct ritual, and Eleazar, his father, and his younger brother, *Ithamar*, were forbidden to mourn for them.

Eleazar and Ithamar were both already priests while their father was alive, and Eleazar was particularly responsible for the care of the various items in the sanctuary. Eleazar was instructed by Moses to make a covering for the altar out of the bronze censers that had formerly belonged to the accomplices of *Korah*, after they had been killed to end their rebellion.

When Aaron died on Mount Hor, Moses took his vestments and put them on Eleazar, appointing him as his father's successor.

After the plague had been inflicted on the Israelites in Moab, Moses and Eleazar were instructed to take a census. Once the armies had been victorious over the five kings of Midian, Moses and Eleazar also joined in issuing instructions on how to apportion booty in war, and on the rules for purification and cleanliness, both of booty, and of soldiers who had killed an enemy soldier in battle. Eleazar, along with *Joshua*, was also appointed by Moses as one of those who was to divide the Promised Land between the tribes once it had been conquered. How they carried out this duty is explained at various points in the Book of Joshua. Eleazar otherwise appears principally in Numbers.

Eleazar was buried at Gibeah by his son, Phinehas.

Eleazar was the name of several other personalities in the Old Testament. One of these was a prominent warrior in *David*'s army. Others appear in Ezra and in Nehemiah. Two more appear in the deuterocanonical/apocryphal Books of Maccabees. Of these, one was a brother of *Judas*, killed in battle when an elephant fell on him, while the other was an elderly scribe who was tortured to death after he refused to eat pork.

Eli

Eli was a high priest in Shiloh. A man named *Elkanah* and his wife, *Hannah*, were accustomed to offer sacrifices regularly at the temple. One day Eli saw Hannah at the temple, and thought at first that she was drunk, because she was moving her lips seemingly without saying anything. In fact, she was praying that she would have a son, and promised that she would dedicate such a child to the Lord's service. Eli gave her his good wishes and in due course the child, *Samuel*, was born, and was brought to Eli to work as his servant.

Eli had two sons, *Hophni* and *Phinehas (2)*, who were also priests, but were thoroughly immoral, especially in misusing the materials brought for sacrifice. Eli admonished them for their behavior, but they paid no attention to him and carried on as before. Eli was warned by another unnamed prophet that, because of his sons' sins, his family would be punished by the Lord, and that Hophni and Phinehas would both die on the same day.

While the boy Samuel was serving Eli, he had a vision of the Lord in which he was told of the punishment soon to come to Eli and his family. When Samuel heard the voice of the Lord calling him in the middle of the night, he at first assumed that it was Eli, and went to see what he wanted. When this had happened three times, Eli realized that the Lord was speaking to Samuel, and told him to return to his bed and reply to the Lord on the next occasion. Eli therefore knew that Samuel had had a vision, and accordingly asked him in the morning what it had contained. Samuel did not want to give him the bad news but, when he did, Eli accepted it as the Lord's will.

There followed two battles between the Israelites and the Philistines, in both of which the Philistines were victorious. In the second battle, the Ark of the Covenant was captured, and both of Eli's sons were killed. When Eli heard the news he fell off his chair, broke his neck, and died.

Eliakim

See *Jehoiakim*.

Eliakim was also the name of one of the senior officials of *Hezekiah*, involved in negotiations on his master's behalf with the Assyrians, and praised for his conduct by *Isaiah*.

Eliezer

Eliezer was the younger son of *Moses* and *Zipporah*. The name is also used by nine other minor personalities in the Old Testament, including *Abraham*'s steward.

Elihu

Elihu was one of the four who argued with *Job* after he complained of his afflictions. Elihu allowed Job's three friends, *Bildad, Eliphaz* and *Zophar*, to speak first because they were older than him but, angry at their failure, he then took over. Elihu's message emphasizes the power of the Lord and the impossibility of men understanding His works: "'God thunders wondrously with his voice; he does great things that we cannot comprehend.'" Job's misery was ended after Elihu had spoken and he repented.

Elijah

Elijah is one of the most vividly described personalities appearing in the Old Testament. He was a prophet in the reigns of kings *Ahab, Ahaziah (1)* and *Jehoram (1)* of Israel. Unusually for such an important personage, we are given no information about his genealogy, and his home village or district of Tishbe is otherwise unknown,

Top right: Rebecca and Eliezer, by Cabarel. This particular Eliezer was Abraham's steward, and was searching for a wife for Isaac when he met Rebecca by a well.

Right: Elijah and the Prophets of Baal – a sketch by Philips de Koninck.

Above: Elijah Fed by the Ravens, a painting by Washington Allston.

Left: Elijah rebukes King Ahab; a nineteenth-century stained-glass window in Lincoln Cathedral.

apart from its general location in Gilead, east of the Jordan. Some scholars believe that a separate collection of stories of Elijah may once have existed, and would have given more details of his antecedents. This idea suggests that selections from this collection were made by the writer or writers who compiled the account we now have in Kings. Elijah chiefly appears in I Kings 17-19 & 21, and II Kings 1 & 2.

Elijah first appears following the marriage of Ahab and *Jezebel*, and the increase at her urging of the worship of *Baal* and other false gods. Elijah foretold a long period of drought as punishment for this. Elijah himself was told by the Lord to go and live in the Wadi Cherith, where he could drink from the wadi and would be fed by ravens.

When the wadi dried up in due course, Elijah was sent to live at Zarephath near Sidon, where he found lodging with a poor widow. She had little food, but Elijah promised her that it would be miraculously renewed and would suffice. Later her son became ill and seemed to stop breathing. The widow complained to Elijah, "'What have you against me, O man of God? You have come to me to bring my sin to remembrance, and to cause the death of my son!'" However, Elijah went to the boy, prayed for assistance, and the boy was revived.

After three years of drought, the Lord told Elijah to go to see King Ahab once again. Elijah arranged the meeting through the king's servant, *Obadiah (1)*. When Elijah met the king, Ahab accused him of being the "'troubler of Israel'", but Elijah replied that the king and his family were the cause of the problems, "'because you have forsaken the commandments of the Lord and followed the Baals.'" Elijah then challenged the king to arrange a contest of faith between him and the 450 prophets of Baal, to establish who was following the true God.

The contest was held at Mount Carmel. The prophets of Baal were unable to call down fire on the altar that they had built for the sacrificed bull, no matter how much they chanted, danced or made themselves bleed. Elijah built an altar of 12 stones, one for each tribe of Israel, and then even had the watchers soak the wood from which he built the fire round the altar. He prayed to the Lord, and the whole offering and the altar were burned away. The people recognized the work of the true God, and helped Elijah put the prophets of Baal to death. This outcome so angered Jezebel that Elijah had to go into hiding once again.

Elijah left his servant behind at Beersheba and, alone and depressed, set off into the wilderness. On his first night he lay down and asked God to be allowed to die, but an angel appeared to him twice, making him eat the food and drink the water that had miraculously appeared. Elijah then traveled on for 40 days and nights until he reached Horeb (also known as Mount Sinai, where Moses had received the law). There Elijah also had an encounter with the Lord. A great wind, an earthquake and a fire occurred, but the Lord's appearance was not in any of these, rather in the silence that followed, famously translated in the Authorized Version as a "still small voice." Elijah was told to return and appoint *Hazael* as king of Damascus, *Jehu* as king of Israel, and to establish *Elisha* as his own successor as prophet. On the journey back he duly met Elisha, who was plowing, and Elisha followed him from then on.

Elijah had a further confrontation with Ahab over the matter of *Naboth*'s vineyard. After Jezebel had contrived the judicial murder of Naboth, Ahab took possession of the vineyard he had coveted. The Lord told Elijah to go to Ahab and curse him for his wickedness, but when Ahab repented, the Lord told Elijah that he would defer the punishment on the family until the time of Ahab's son.

After Ahab's death in battle, he was succeeded by his son, Ahaziah (1). Ahaziah hurt himself in a fall and sent his servants to ask the prophets of Baal if he would recover from his injuries. Elijah met them on their way, and sent them back to the king, saying that, because he had chosen to make his enquiries of Baal, the Lord had decided that he would not, in fact, recover. Ahaziah twice sent parties of soldiers to arrest Elijah for this unwelcome message, but each time they were consumed in a divine fire when they tried to execute their orders. The third time Elijah went with the soldiers and personally repeated the message to the king, who duly died.

Finally Elijah was taken up to heaven in a whirlwind. Elijah tried to persuade Elisha not to follow him during this episode, but Elisha insisted, and witnessed the final event. In their last conversation Elisha asked Elijah to be allowed to "'inherit a double share of your spirit.'" After Elijah had gone, Elisha picked up his mantle, and his role as Elijah's successor was confirmed to others when he struck the waters of the Jordan with the mantle, as Elijah had earlier done, and parted them in the same way so that he could cross.

Elijah has come to have an important role in Jewish traditions, with his return being expected as a forerunner to the Messiah. Elijah is specifically described in this way in the Book of Malachi. Customs observed during the Passover and at the circumcision of young boys allude to the hope that Elijah may return. Elijah is also mentioned several times in the Gospels and other New Testament books.

The name **Elijah** was borne by three other personalities.

Below: Elijah restores the widow's son to life; after a painting by Benjamin West.

Eliphaz

With his friends *Bildad* and *Zophar*, Eliphaz argued with *Job* when he cursed the Lord for his afflictions. Like his friends and companions, Eliphaz reminded Job of the mercy and compassion of the Lord, and the justice of divine punishment for sinfulness. In particular he criticized Job's arrogance in claiming a "monopoly of wisdom" (N.J.B.). "'What do you know that we do not know? What do you understand that is not clear to us? . . . Are the consolations of God too small for you, or the word that deals gently with you?'"

All the arguments failed to convince Job, and the three were later instructed by the Lord to offer a sacrifice to atone for this failure.

Another **Eliphaz**, the eldest son of *Esau*, appears in Genesis.

Elisha

The prophet Elisha was the successor of *Elijah* as the principal prophet in Israel. His career overlapped with the reigns of Kings *Jehoram (1), Jehu, Jehoahaz (1)*, and *Joash (2)* of Israel. Elisha was also involved, although less extensively, with kings *Jehosaphat, Jehoram (2)*, and *Ahaziah (2)* of Judah. Elisha's father was Shaphat, and they were natives of Abel-meholah.

Elisha is first mentioned in I Kings 19, during the solitary journey of Elijah to Mount Horeb during which the Lord gave Elijah three instructions: he was to anoint *Hazael* as king of Aram (Syria), Jehu as king of Israel, and choose Elisha as his successor. In the event, it was to be Elisha rather than Elijah who carried out the first two commissions.

Above: Johann Friedrich Overbeck's interpretation of Elijah being carried up to heaven.

Elijah immediately traveled to Abel-meholah, where he found Elisha at work plowing. Elijah placed his mantle symbolically around Elisha's shoulders, and Elisha ran after him and promised to follow him. Elisha killed two of his plow oxen and cooked them, using his plowing equipment as fuel for the fire, to make a meal for his neighbors, and then began life as Elijah's servant.

Nothing is related of Elisha's life as Elijah's servant until shortly before Elijah's death. Elijah tried to leave Elisha behind on what both realized was to be Elijah's final journey, but Elisha refused to be left. Elisha asked Elijah to be given "a double share of your

spirit," and Elijah told him that this would be granted if Elisha was able to see Elijah being taken away. Elisha indeed saw Elijah being transported into heaven in a whirlwind. He tore his clothes in mourning, picked up Elijah's mantle, and used it miraculously to cross the Jordan without getting wet. This was seen by another group of prophets, and they acclaimed Elisha as Elijah's successor.

His first public confirmation of his role came when he purified the unsatisfactory water supply of the city of Jericho. There then followed the rather disturbing incident in which, teased by a group of small boys because of his baldness, Elisha cursed them, so that 42 of them were mauled by bears.

Elisha was then asked by Jehoram of Israel to help him during a campaign that he and Jehosaphat were conducting against the Moabites. Elisha was with the army, which had become stranded in the desert, short of water. He correctly foretold that a nearby wadi would become filled by water overnight, but only after protesting to Jehoram that "'were it not that I have regard for King Jehosaphat of Judah, I would give you neither a look nor a glance.'" (King Jehoram was a noted idolater).

II Kings 4, 5, and the first part of chapter 6, also relate a series of miracles that Elisha performed for individuals in what might be called his "private capacity." Two of these, the repeated replenishment of a jar of oil,

Above: Elisha receives the mantle of Elijah – an illustration from the Winchester Bible.

Below: The Miracles of Elisha; a Stothard watercolor from the Painted Chamber.

and the resurrection of a dead child, are identical with miracles performed by Elijah. Additionally, in the case of the child, he was conceived after Elisha had blessed a previous childless marriage. Later, while the child was dead, Elisha's servant, Gehazi, tried to turn away the boy's mother when she sought help and then, sent ahead by Elisha, failed in a first attempt to revive him. Elisha also made unpleasant and possibly poisonous food wholesome for a group of prophets, and multiplied 20 loaves into sufficient food for 100 people. *Naaman*, a commander in the Syrian army, was miraculously cured of leprosy. Elisha refused payment for this but, when Gehazi tricked Naaman into giving him some money, supposedly for needy prophets, Elisha knew without being told, and Gehazi accordingly contracted Naaman's malady. Finally, Elisha made an iron ax head, lost in the River Jordan, float to the surface to be found.

Elisha also performed miracles in support of Israel's armies in their wars with Aram-Damascus. On a number of occasions he forewarned the Israelites of the movements of Aramean raiding parties. When the king of Aram realized what was happening and sent a force to capture Elisha, Elisha prayed to the Lord for them to be made blind, and then led them into the Israelite capital of Samaria, where they were at the Israelites' mercy. Their sight was then restored and, at Elisha's request, they were allowed to return home unharmed, an experience which deterred them from repeating their raids for some time.

Later, during a full-scale siege of Samaria by the Arameans, food ran very short, and the king blamed Elisha for Israel's misfortune and sent men to kill him. Elisha foretold, however, that the siege would be lifted by the next day, and that ample food would then become available. This came to pass when the Arameans were thrown into a panic by the Lord and fled, leaving all their supplies behind.

Elisha then visited Damascus and was consulted by *Ben-hadad (2)* as to whether he would recover from an illness. Ben-hadad sent Hazael, one of his officers, to see Elisha for this purpose, and Elisha told Hazael that the Lord had chosen him as the next king. When Hazael returned to see Benhadad, he murdered him. Later still, Elisha fulfilled the final part of the instruction given to Elijah, when he ordered one of his followers to go and visit Jehu and anoint him as king of Israel. Jehu then began his rebellion and killed Jehoram (1) and his ally, Ahaziah (2).

Elisha's last prophecy was given when he was on his deathbed. Joash (2) came to visit him and was deeply upset at the prophet's obviously imminent demise. Elisha ordered him to fire an arrow out the window and then strike the ground with other arrows. Joash did so three times, and then stopped. Elisha was angry, and said that he should have repeated the process five or six times, and that accordingly the victories over Aram represented by the action would not be wholly decisive.

After Elisha's death there occurred a further miracle associated with him. A funeral service was interrupted by an armed raid, and the mourners hurriedly threw the body into Elisha's grave. As soon as it touched Elisha's bones, the body came back to life.

Elkanah

Elkanah was the father of the prophet *Samuel*. He had two wives, Peninnah, who had several children, and *Hannah*, whom he loved dearly although she had none. Hannah was upset that she could not have children, even though Elkanah tried to console her by reminding her of their love for each other. Elkanah and his family made regular sacrifices at the temple at Shiloh, and on one occasion when they were there Hannah made a special prayer asking the Lord to give her a child. The Lord answered her prayer, and she and Elkanah had a son called Samuel, whom they dedicated to service in the temple with the priest *Eli*. They later had other children too.

Elkanah was also the name of a commander in the army of *Ahaz*.

Enoch

1. Enoch was the son of *Cain*, and is named in a genealogy in Genesis 4. Cain named the first city after his son.

2. A second Enoch is named in Genesis 5 as being a descendant of *Seth*, third son of *Adam* and *Eve*. He was the father of *Methuselah*.

In the Old Testament, Enoch is mentioned only in this passage in Genesis,

Above: Enoch, as shown in a twelfth-century stained-glass window in Canterbury Cathedral.

and in a genealogy at the beginning of I Chronicles. He appears also in Jewish traditions, and in Ethiopic and Slavonic Books of Enoch. Excerpts related to the Ethiopic Enoch have also been found among the Dead Sea Scrolls. In these sources Enoch is portrayed as being a chosen one, or as an archangel.

Enoch also appears in the New Testament in Hebrews, in a passage praising the faithful: "By faith Enoch was taken so that he did not experience death . . . For it was attested before he was taken away that 'he had pleased God.'"

Ephraim

Ephraim was the younger son of *Joseph*, born in Egypt to Joseph's Egyptian wife, *Asenath*. Genesis 48 records how Joseph brought Ephraim and his elder brother, *Manasseh (1)*, to see their grandfather, *Jacob*, near the end of his life. Jacob's eyesight was failing, and when he gave the brothers his blessing he laid his right hand on Ephraim, the younger of the two. Joseph was angry at this at first, thinking that his father had made a mistake, but Jacob said that it was no mistake, and that Ephraim's descendants would be the greater people.

Like their uncles – Joseph's half-brothers and brother – Ephraim and Manasseh came to be regarded as the forefathers of tribes of Israel, although, as with their uncles, their inclusion in the various listings of the tribes is not consistent throughout the Old Testament.

The situation of a younger son inheriting more than the elder was a common theme in the family, Joseph, Jacob and *Isaac*, among Ephraim's immediate forebears, all having followed this pattern. The story of Jacob's blessing may reflect the later power of the tribe of Ephraim, rather than being an authentic event that occurred in the family history.

Esar-haddon

Esarhaddon (as his name is more commonly spelled outside the Bible) was one of the sons and the successor of *Sennacherib* as king of Assyria, and reigned from 681-668 B.C.

II Kings and Isaiah describe Sennacherib's assassination by two of his sons before Esarhaddon acceded to the throne. Assyrian records confirm that Esarhaddon indeed had to suppress a rebellion by his brothers to make good his claim to the crown.

A verse in Ezra suggests that Esarhaddon allowed some of the Israelites who had been exiled by *Sargon* and Sennacherib to return, and Assyrian sources note that *Manasseh (2)*, king of Judah, paid him tribute.

Left: A basalt stela from Sam'al, dated 671 B.C., telling the story of Esarhaddon's victory over Pharoah Tirhakah (or Taharka) of Egypt. Following this, the Assyrians occupied much of Egypt for a number of years.

Esau

Esau was the elder twin son of *Isaac* and *Rebekah*, and the brother of *Jacob*. Rebekah had a difficult pregnancy, and was told by the Lord during it that she was carrying twins who would be the forefathers of separate and quarreling nations, with the older eventually serving the younger. Esau was born first, and was covered in red hair at his birth. He grew up to be a skilled hunter and outdoor man, and was his father's favorite, while Jacob was quieter and favored by their mother. However, both Isaac and Rebekah were disappointed when Esau married, at the age of 40, a number of Canaanite or Hittite women. These are given various names at different points in Genesis: *Judith* and *Basemath*, or *Adah* and *Oholibamah*.

On one occasion Esau returned from the countryside exhausted, and asked Jacob, who was cooking at the time, for some food. Jacob replied that he would sell it to Esau in return for Esau's birthright as the elder son. Esau was so weak from hunger that he accepted, and is condemned by the author of Genesis for thus despising his birthright.

Later, when Isaac was old and his sight was failing, he asked Esau to hunt for game to make a special meal of the type that Isaac particularly liked, saying that in return Esau would receive his father's blessing. Rebekah overheard this, and had Jacob bring two choice kids from the flock so that she could prepare a suitable meal for him to present to his father instead of Esau. She gave Jacob some of Esau's clothes and put skins on his neck and hands so that he should have the feeling and appearance of his brother to the partially-sighted Isaac. The deception was a success, and Isaac gave Jacob the blessing intended for Esau, appointing him particularly as lord over his brothers.

Esau then returned from his hunting trip, and the deception was revealed. Isaac was unable to revoke his blessing of Jacob, but gave Esau a blessing also. He did not foretell the wealth offered to Jacob, but instead said, "'By your sword you shall live, and you shall serve your brother; but when you break loose, you shall break his yoke from your neck.'"

Esau was understandably angry at all that had been done to him, and decided that he would kill Jacob as soon as Isaac had died. Rebekah heard of this, and arranged that Jacob should be sent away to stay with kinfolk, on the pretext that he, too, would otherwise be likely to find a Canaanite wife. Esau now realized how much his marriages had displeased his parents, and accordingly found another wife – this time from within his own people – marrying *Ishmael*'s daughter, who is variously named *Mahalath* and Basemath.

Esau and his brother did not meet for many years thereafter. Esau settled in the land of Seir and prospered in the meantime. When Jacob decided to return to Canaan, he worried that Esau might still be harboring a grudge against him, and took elaborate precautions to placate his brother. He need not have worried, for Esau received him kindly, only reluctantly being persuaded to accept the presents that Jacob offered. Esau wanted to spend time with his brother, but Jacob avoided this and went his separate way.

Both brothers were present at the burial of Isaac.

Esau was regarded by the Israelites as being the forefather of the Edomites. The conflict of the brothers clearly reflects in part the changing relationship between the two peoples. The Genesis text, however, does seem to depict elements of real personalities rather than entirely symbolic ones, and to the detached observer Esau's conduct might readily seem to be more pleasant and virtuous than that of his brother.

Below: George Frederick Watts's depiction of Esau meeting Jacob.

Esther

Esther and her adoptive father and natural uncle, *Mordecai*, are the central characters of the Book of Esther. The Book of Esther exists in both a Hebrew and a Greek text. The Greek text is rather longer, with some additional passages and other differences. The additional passages in the Greek are regarded as deuterocanonical/apocryphal, but the overall sequence of events is similar in the two versions.

After King *Ahasuerus* of Persia had quarreled with his wife Vashti and divorced her, he ordered beautiful young women from throughout his realm to be brought to his harem as possible replacements for the queen. Esther was one of those chosen in this way and, after she had been given elaborate beauty treatments, was taken to the king, who fell in love with her and made her his queen.

Esther was a Jew (her Jewish name was Hadassah), and had been brought up by her uncle Mordecai after her parents had died. Mordecai had told her not to reveal that she was a Jew when she entered the royal harem.

Mordecai was a loyal royal official, but he quarreled with *Haman*, the king's chief minister. Haman extended his hostility to Mordecai to a hatred of all Jews, and contrived to have the king issue a decree ordering that all Jews were to be killed. Mordecai managed to send a message to Esther telling her what was planned, and she agreed to visit the king specially to try to avert the slaughter. Such a visit to the king without being summoned could be punished by death, but Esther agreed to take that risk.

At this point in events the Greek text includes a long prayer to the Lord by Esther for His aid, and graphically describes her fear when she went to see the king. On this visit she was successful in reminding the king how favorably he looked upon her. That night the king could not sleep (because of the Lord's intervention, in the Greek text), and reviewed some old royal records, which included an account of how Mordecai had previously foiled an assassination plot but had gone unrewarded. In the morning Haman was shocked when the king accordingly

Above: Esther before Ahasuerus, by Tintoretto, the sixteenth-century Venetian painter.

told him to give Mordecai high honors. It is worth noting that the Hebrew text of Esther contains no explicit mention of God at any point in the book, nor does the eventual success of Mordecai and Esther depend in any way in the Hebrew version on divine intervention or assistance.

Later, at dinner, Esther told the king how Haman had plotted against the Jews, which made the king very angry. The king misinterpreted an attempt by Haman to beg Esther for mercy as an assault upon her, and ordered his execution. Esther was given all his family's property, and the king issued a second decree, allowing the Jews to arm themselves and destroy their enemies, which they did successfully.

Mordecai was appointed as the king's chief minister in Haman's place. He and Esther sent instructions to the whole Jewish community instituting the Feast of Purim in remembrance of the deliverance. This feast remains an important one in the modern Jewish religious calendar.

There is some uncertainty as to how far the Book of Esther depicts historical characters. Non-biblical records pertaining to the Persian Empire are extensive and, other than of the king himself, contain no mention of the people or events described in the book. Some scholars also suggest that the Feast of Purim may originate with some form of Mesopotamian spring festival, and that the events narrated in Esther were composed later to give the festival an appropriate origin. One piece of evidence in favor of this is that the names Esther and Mordecai seem to be linguistically related to the Mesopotamian deities Ishtar and Marduk.

Ethan

Ethan, son of Mahol, appears in I Kings 4 as one of several, presumably very wise, men, whose wisdom was nonetheless exceeded by that of *Solomon*.

A second **Ethan**, son of Kushaiah, was one of the three musicians put in charge of performing services before the tabernacle by *David*. As well as singing, their duties included the sounding of bronze cymbals. Other instruments mentioned include harps and lyres (I Chronicles 6 & 15).

Two other personalities of the name **Ethan** appear in genealogies elsewhere in I Chronicles.

Eve

Eve was the first woman, wife and companion of *Adam*, and mother of *Cain, Abel* and *Seth*.

When she was first created (but not named), using one of the first man's ribs as related in Genesis 2, she was described as being a partner and helper, and was clearly given an equal status. She was then tempted by the serpent, ate the forbidden fruit, and

Below: A view of the interior of the monument known as the tomb of Esther and Mordecai at Hamadan, now part of modern-day Iran.

gave the man some also. For disobeying His command, the Lord punished them both. The woman was to suffer pain in childbirth, to desire her husband physically, but to be ruled by him. This secondary status was confirmed subsequently when the man named her Eve, since the naming of animals had previously been symbolic of the man's special status over them.

Later Jewish and Christian tradition confirms a negative view of Eve and, by extension, of women as a whole. In Old Testament times there is no doubt of the inferior social and legal position in which women were placed. Numerous legal provisions make clear the lesser value placed on women's lives and rights. In the New Testament, in Timothy and Corinthians for example, woman's creation subsequent to man, her susceptibility to temptation from the serpent, followed by her persuasion of Adam to join her in her sin, are all mentioned in support of male superiority. This division is not, in fact, supported by a careful reading of the material in Genesis. The creation of the woman is seen rather to make an equal partnership of "one flesh," and after the forbidden fruit is eaten, the man and woman are together, hide from the Lord together, and are both punished.

Left: A detail from an early Christian sarcophagus showing Adam and Eve. As in most artistic depictions, the couple are nude, indicating their halcyon life before the Fall.

Above and below: Adam and Eve as portrayed by Hugo van der Goes (above), and Hieronymous Bosch (below; detail from the *Garden of Earthly Delights*).

Ezekiel

The prophecies of Ezekiel make up the Book of Ezekiel. In addition, Ezekiel is mentioned briefly in the deuterocanonical/apocryphal Book of Sirach, and in the apocryphal IV Book of Maccabees. In the Book of Ezekiel itself, the use of personal names is sparing, and the prophet's name only appears twice. Instead, when he receives the word of the Lord, he is addressed as "mortal" (in the N.R.S.V.), which often appears in other translations as "son of man."

Bearing this in mind, it will be no surprise that, in common with the other later prophets, few personal details of the life of Ezekiel are given or emerge. He was the son of Buzi, and became a priest. His prophetic career is described as beginning in 593 B.C. (many of the prophecies recorded are dated), and it continued until at least 571. No information is given of his death, although later Jewish tradition suggests that he was killed in exile in Babylon by one of his countrymen because of his preaching against idolatry. He had been deported to Babylon

following *Nebuchadnezzar*'s attack on Jerusalem in 597, and lived in Babylon at a place called Tel-abib, near the River Chebar. He had been married, but his wife died in Jerusalem shortly before the Babylonian attack. The Lord instructed him at that time to mourn her only briefly and privately, which he did, even though he had loved her. At points in the course of his career Ezekiel is described as being unable to speak, but it is not clear whether this means a temporary personal disability, or lack of divine inspiration, or a prohibition placed by the authorities on his public preaching and oratory.

Many different theories have been advanced as to the date when the Book of Ezekiel was composed, and of the extent to which it was the work of the prophet himself. A majority of modern writers believe that the book was indeed principally the work of the prophet, recorded around the time and under the situation in which he lived, but that it has been subject to some editing and emendation in later years.

The prophetic content of the book can be divided into four separate parts.

The first section, roughly Chapters 1-24, is a series of oracles relating the repeated wickedness of the Israelites and the doom that this has brought upon them. The second section extends this condemnation to various foreign nations, Tyre and Egypt being prominent among them. The third section discusses the restoration and deliverance that is to come, and the conclusion gives detailed instructions for rebuilding the temple, and for the ritual of worship that is take place in the new Israel.

The all-encompassing power of the Lord is stressed throughout, not only over Israel, but over all nations. But the individual must take full responsibility for his own actions: "A child shall not suffer for the iniquity of a parent, nor a parent suffer for the iniquity of a child; the righteousness of the righteous shall be his own, and the wickedness of the wicked shall be his own."

Below: Ezekiel, as seen in a stained-glass window in Lyons Cathedral.

Right: Ezra the scribe, from an early manuscript.

The imagery in the visions of Ezekiel is vivid and bizarre, beginning with the description of the chariot of the Lord in the first chapter. Ezekiel himself is also often instructed to take unusual symbolic actions: lying on first one side then the other for a prescribed period, or making a miniature map of Jerusalem, or shaving his head and casting some of his hair to the winds.

Below: A seventh-century mosaic of the angel Gabriel at the church of Panagia Angeloktistos at Kiti, Cyprus.

Ezra

Ezra was a priest or scribe living with the exiled Jewish community in Babylon, who was authorized by the Persian emperor *Artaxerxes* to return to Jerusalem. The dating of Ezra's life and works is difficult. Artaxerxes was one of two Persian emperors of that name: Artaxerxes I (reigned 464-423 B.C.) and Artaxerxes II (404-358). Ezra is said to have returned to Jerusalem in the monarch's seventh year, but some scholars suggest that a word may be missing from the text, and that the correct reading should be the thirty-seventh year (of Artaxerxes I, i.e., 428). There are problems with both dates in the reign of the first Artaxerxes, related to conditions in the Persian Empire of the time, and also because they would suggest an overlap between the work of Ezra and *Nehemiah* which is not clearly mentioned in the Bible. For these reasons, many biblical scholars prefer a date of 398 for Ezra's return to Jerusalem, but most remain in favor of the traditional date of 458.

Whatever the speculation about exactly when he lived, Ezra appears in the Books of Ezra and Nehemiah. These books were once regarded as being a single entity, and have only been divided in the present way since the third century A.D. Modern opinion is that this "single" book was composed, at the same time as Chronicles, in the fourth century B.C.

Ezra was sent to Jerusalem by the king to ensure that the correct Israelite religious practices were being followed there, and was given money to pay for sacrifices and other items for the temple. It was generally Persian policy to support the native religions of the lands that they governed. Ezra was instructed to teach the Law, appoint judges, and punish wrongdoers. The royal officials were told to help him with money as he needed it, and not to require priests and other servants in the temple to pay any taxes.

Ezra was also accompanied by a number of his co-religionists, but he was disappointed to find, when he reviewed his party, that no Levites were with them at first, so he sent for some from the shrine at Casiphia.

When they reached Jerusalem, Ezra was shocked to discover that many of the people had married foreign women. He called a great assembly, gathered in the pouring rain, and instructed the people to put away all their non-Jewish wives, a process that took over two months to complete because so many divorces were involved.

Ezra also gathered another assembly to read to the people the complete book of the Law that he had brought with him from Babylon. This had a profound emotional effect on the congregation, who realized the errors that they had fallen into. They then revived the correct celebration of the festival of tabernacles. Ezra finally led the congregation in a prayer confessing the sins of Israel.

Ezra also appears in the apocryphal Books of Esdras, Esdras being a Greek form of the name Ezra.

Gabriel

Gabriel is the name of an angel who appeared twice to *Daniel*. In Daniel 8 he helped interpret Daniel's vision of the ram and goat, and in Daniel 9 commented on the captivity that had been foretold by *Jeremiah*.

Gad

1. Gad was the elder son of *Zilpah*. Zilpah was maid to *Leah, Jacob's* first wife, who gave her to Jacob as his concubine. Gad took part with his brother and half-brothers in selling *Joseph* into slavery in Egypt, and went with them to buy grain in Egypt during the subsequent famine. Later Gad's family settled in Egypt.

Like his brother and half-brothers, Gad gave his name to one of the tribes of Israel.

2. Gad was a prophet who assisted *David*. He appears in two parts of David's story. After David had fled from *Saul*, Gad warned him not to remain in hiding in the cave of Adullam, but to go into the land of Judah. Later Gad appears in both versions of the story of David's census and the purchase of the threshing floor of *Ornan*. Gad first presented David with the choice of famine, devastation, or plague as punishment for calling the census, and then later passed on the Lord's command to make an altar on the threshing floor.

Gad is also named in I Chronicles 29 as one of the authors that the Chronicler has drawn on for his account.

Gedaliah

Gedaliah was appointed as governor of Judah by the Babylonians after the capture of Jerusalem in 587 B.C. His father was Ahikam, a court official.

Some of the army and its generals had not surrendered to the conquerors; these leaders came to visit Gedaliah at Mizpah, and were urged by him to cooperate. Not all chose to do so, and Gedaliah was assassinated shortly afterward by *Ishmael (2)*.

Gedaliah is also the name of four other personalities in the Old Testament. One of these was a temple musician in the time of David.

Gershom

Gershom was the name of three personalities who appear in the Old Testament. The first was the eldest son of *Levi*; the second was the eldest son of *Moses*, on whom his mother performed an emergency circumcision; the third was a companion of *Ezra* in the return from Babylonian exile.

Gideon

Gideon, son of *Joash*, was a military leader of the Israelites in the period of the judges. His exploits are described in Judges 6-9. His career began at a time when the Israelites were suffering greatly from attacks by the Midianites. One day, when Gideon was threshing some grain, an angel came to him, and commissioned him to take the lead in the fight, confirming the truth of the vision by burning up a sacrifice that Gideon laid out.

Below: Gideon reduces the strength of his army by testing the alertness of his men.

Gideon's first task was to break down an altar of *Baal* that was nearby, and use the sacred pole that went with it as the wood for a sacrifice. Gideon and his servants did this by night, and were defended against his angry neighbors by his father, Joash, who said that if Baal was a real god he could take action himself. This led to Gideon being given the alternative name Jerubbaal, which meant "Let Baal contend against him." Gideon's selection was then further confirmed by two miraculous signs involving a woolen fleece.

Gideon mobilized a large force to fight against the Midianites but, when they were assembled, decided to reduce the strength of his army to a more manageable number. The spiritual reason given is that the Lord wished to demonstrate clearly that the coming victory was achieved by His intervention rather than by the Israelites themselves alone. Gideon first sent home any of his men who were afraid, and then most of the remainder who did not stay fully alert when going to drink at a pool. This left him with 300 men opposed to the large Midianite army.

Gideon and his servant Purah made a personal reconnaissance of the Midianite camp, and were reassured to hear a conversation in which one Midianite described a dream which a second interpreted as foretelling an Israelite victory. The victory was achieved when Gideon's force moved up that night, surrounded the Midianite camp, and threw it into a panic with the loud noise of trumpets and the war cry "A sword for the Lord and for Gideon!" The Midianites were so frightened that they fought among themselves as they fled. Gideon arranged to make their defeat even more decisive by having the men of the tribe of Ephraim, who had not so far fought in the campaign, block the fords across the Jordan to prevent the Midianite retreat.

Gideon himself next followed up his success by pursuing those Midianites who had managed to get across the Jordan, deep into the lands to the east. He asked for help, but was refused by the people of the towns of Succoth and Penuel. Angrily he continued on his way, and completed the rout of the Midianite force, capturing and later executing two of their kings. On the way back he carried out reprisals against the two towns.

For all this good work Gideon was offered the kingship for himself and his family by the people of Israel, but he refused, saying, "'I will not rule over you, and my son will not rule over you; the Lord will rule over you.'"

Eventually Gideon had 70 sons by his various wives and concubines, and died "at a good old age." After his death, however, the people returned to evil ways, and Gideon's son *Abimelech* committed terrible crimes.

One curiosity of the description of the career of Gideon is that it provides the first clear mention in the Old Testament of camels being domesticated for the use of man.

Gog

Gog appears in Ezekiel 38 & 39, where he is described as being the ruler of the land of Magog (but see also *Magog*). The precise location of Magog is not known, but Gog is described as being the leader of a coalition of northern invaders of Israel, summoned by the Lord to attack Israel, only to be defeated by divine intervention as a means of the Lord demonstrating his greatness and holiness.

Left: Gideon and the Fleece, a painting from the Avignon School.

Right: A statue of Gog at the Guildhall in the City of London.

N. de Clerck ex.

1600

Above: David and Goliath, a depiction after William Blake. David was the only one brave enough to take up the giant's challenge.

Left: David holds aloft the head of Goliath, cut off with the giant's own sword. Exact details as to Goliath's size vary, but according to one account he was six cubits and a span in height – nearly 13 feet tall.

Goliath

Goliath was the giant Philistine killed by *David*. Their encounter appears in I Samuel 17. *Saul's* army and the Philistine army had gathered at Socoh, and each day Goliath paraded in the valley between the two camps, challenging any Israelite who dared to single combat. As well as being a giant of a man (the ancient Hebrew and Greek texts of the Old Testament give different measurements), he was also well armed and armored. David was not originally serving with the army, but arrived bringing provisions for his three eldest brothers, who were. He decided to take up Goliath's challenge, but was unable to manage Saul's armor, which Saul offered to lend him. Instead he went against Goliath armed only with a stick, five smooth stones, and his sling. He hit Goliath on the forehead with one of the sling stones, and then cut off the giant's head with his own sword.

In II Samuel 21 Goliath is killed by another warrior called Elhanan of Bethlehem, and this conflicting tradition is reconciled by the later I Chronicles 20, which credits Elhanan with killing Goliath's brother, Lahmi. II Samuel 21 also includes the passage in which *Abishai* saved David by killing the giant Ishbibenob. It seems likely that various traditions have become intermixed in all this, and that the traditional story of David and Goliath may not be entirely reliable.

JOHNSTON PUBLIC LIBRARY
JOHNSTON, IOWA 50131

Above: The Italian sculptor Donatello's statue of the prophet Habakkuk.

Gomer

Gomer was the wife of the prophet *Hosea*. She bore Hosea three children, but was unfaithful. Biblical scholars debate whether Gomer should be regarded as being a real person, perhaps a temple prostitute whom Hosea loved not wisely but too well, or whether their relationship is wholly allegorical. The Book of Hosea draws parallels between the prophet's love for his unfaithful and unworthy wife and God's love for Israel.

Gomer was also the name of the eldest son of *Japheth*, son of *Noah*.

Habakkuk

In common with other books of the "minor prophets," the Book of Habakkuk gives no personal details whatsoever of the prophet who is stated to have delivered the oracle that it contains. Modern biblical scholars generally believe that the book was written originally *c.* 605-600 B.C., after the Babylonians, led by Nebuchadrezzar (see *Nebuchadnezzar*), had defeated the Egyptians at Carchemish in 605, and as they were establishing their domination across the Near East.

In the first section of the book, Habakkuk complains that the Lord is allowing the evil of his times to go unpunished: "'why do you look on the treacherous, and are silent when the wicked swallow those more righteous than they?'" The divine reply is that punishment in the shape of the Babylonians is on its way. Habakkuk is also concerned that such a punishment will only replace one wicked form of rule with another, but God's answer is that, "'there is still a vision for the appointed time; it speaks of the end and does not lie. If it seems to tarry, wait for it; it will surely come, it will not delay.'" In the meantime, "'the righteous live by their faith.'"

The middle section of the book is a series of curses or "woe oracles," predicting appropriate punishments for oppressors, and the final part is a hymn of praise to the Lord. The prophet's final conclusion is that, although his material circumstances remain adverse, "'I will rejoice in the Lord; I will exult in the God of my salvation.'"

Habakkuk also appears in the deuterocanonical portion of the Book of Daniel known as Bel and the Dragon, a much later composition than the Book of Habakkuk, in which, assisted by an angel, he helped *Daniel* by bringing him food on one of the occasions when Daniel was in the lions' den.

Hagar

Hagar was a slave-girl of *Sarah (1)*, and became the concubine of Sarah's husband, *Abraham*. Sarah could not have children, and suggested to Abraham that he should father a child with Hagar. Sarah then became jealous, which led to two similar episodes. The first occurred before the birth of Hagar's son, *Ishmael (1)*, and the second when Abraham and Sarah themselves had a son, *Isaac*. On both occasions Hagar was sent into the wilderness, and the angel of the Lord appeared to her and promised that her son should have many descendants. On the second occasion, Hagar had abandoned Ishmael to die of thirst when she had the vision, and in it she was also shown where there was a well. After Ishmael had grown up, Hagar found him a wife in Egypt.

Hagar appears in Genesis 16 and 21.

Below: The angel saves Hagar and Ishmael.

Haggai

The minor prophet Haggai appears principally in the short book of the Old Testament bearing his name. He is also mentioned briefly in the Book of Ezra, where his prophetic work is associated with that of *Zechariah* too. No personal details of the prophet appear at all, but the events recorded by the Book of Haggai all take place within a few months during the second year of the reign of *Darius*, which can be precisely dated to 520 B.C.

After the Jewish community had been re-established in Jerusalem from 537 B.C., with the start of the return from exile in Babylon, some attempts to rebuild the temple had been made, but had come to nothing. The career of Haggai began with his attempt to put pressure on *Zerubbabel*, the governor of Judah, and Joshua (also known as *Jeshua*), the high priest, to resume work on the temple. Haggai told them that the poor harvests and other problems of the community had been caused by the failure to build the temple: "'You have looked for much, and, lo, it came to little; and when you brought it home, I blew it away. Why? says the Lord of hosts. Because my house lies in ruins, while all of you hurry off to your own houses. Therefore the heavens above you have withheld the dew, and the earth has withheld its produce.'"

Inspired by this message, the community joined together to carry out the work. Haggai then reassured the people that the Lord was with them, and that the restored temple would be the scene of his universal reign in due course; this despite the comparative poverty of the new building as against the original Temple of Solomon.

There then follows an obscure ruling on cleanliness and uncleanliness relating first to consecrated meat, and then to dead bodies. This may be a comment in some way on the rejection of offers from the Samaritan sect to participate in the rebuilding. Finally, the prophet reassured Zerubbabel that he and his line were favored, and that they would endure through the coming upheavals leading to the establishment of the divine kingdom.

Right: A woodcut of 1546 shows Noah being discovered in a drunken stupor by Ham and his brothers. Noah cursed Ham's descendants for this.

Ham

Ham was the second son of *Noah*, and was saved with the rest of the family in the ark. Later, when Noah was lying drunk and naked in his tent, Ham saw this and told his two brothers, *Shem* and *Japheth*. They covered their father up, and when he awoke he cursed all Ham's descendants. Whether the offense was simply one of disrespect, or whether "looking on his father's nakedness" implies some form of sexual act, is not known.

Ham is then described as being the ancestor of the peoples of Arabia and Africa, who were to be subject to the descendants of Shem. This passage was often subsequently used in support of racist views, justifying the enslavement of people of African origin.

Haman

Haman was, for a time, the chief minister in the court of the Persian king, ·*Ahasuerus*. The Book of Esther tells how he was promoted to this post despite the loyalty that another official, *Mordecai*, had demonstrated when he foiled an assassination plot. Haman was angered when Mordecai refused to bow before him as everyone else had to do. Mordecai refused to do this because he was a Jew. Haman's anger then was transferred toward the Jewish people as a whole, and he persuaded the king to order the complete

extermination of the Jews because their different customs supposedly denied them the right to be tolerated.

Mordecai's adopted daughter, *Esther*, had become queen, and Mordecai arranged for her to persuade the king to change his mind. She invited the king and Haman to join her in a banquet, after which the king remembered the service that Mordecai had done, and tricked Haman into honoring him. At another banquet the following day, Esther told the king what Haman planned for the Jews. The king was so angry that he went outside for a short while, and when he returned he saw Haman beside the queen, begging for his life, but the king thought he was assaulting her, and had him executed.

Hamor

Hamor was the ruler of the city of Shechem (probably modern Nablus) in the time of *Jacob*. His son, also *Shechem*, raped *Dinah*, Jacob's daughter, and wanted his father to arrange for him to marry her. Dinah's brothers at first went along with the proposal, but then *Simeon* and *Levi* attacked the town, killed both Hamor and Shechem, and carried their sister away.

Hananiah

Hananiah was a prophet in the time of *Zedekiah* and *Jeremiah*, with whom he quarreled. His encounter with Jeremiah is described in Jeremiah 28. Hananiah was from Gibeon, and his father's name was Azzur.

Jeremiah had predicted to Zedekiah, and various other kings with whom Zedekiah was forming an alliance, that any rebellion against *Nebuchadnezzar* would be defeated. Jeremiah had taken to wearing a yoke around his neck to symbolize the subjection that the Israelite people would have to continue to bear. Hananiah then appeared and contradicted this prediction, saying that within two years all the holy items taken from the temple would be returned, and with them would come back from exile all those taken away to Babylon. When Jeremiah argued wih him, Hananiah took Jeremiah's yoke and broke it. Jeremiah did not at first know how to answer this, but returned some time later to predict that Hananiah would shortly die because of his rebellion against the Lord. Hananiah died later the same year.

Hananiah is a fairly common name in the Old Testament, being borne by 14 other personalities. One of these was the companion of *Daniel*, better known by the Babylonian form of his name, Shadrach (but see *Abednego*).

Hannah

Hannah was one of the two wives of *Elkanah*, and the mother of the prophet *Samuel*. For much of her marriage Hannah was unable to have children and this distressed her, especially because she was taunted for this by Elkanah's other wife, Peninnah. Elkanah tried to console her by reminding her of their love for each other, but she continued to wish for a child.

The family made regular sacrifices at the temple at Shiloh, and Hannah prayed there that she should have a son, and promised that, if she did, the boy would be dedicated to the Lord's service. The high priest, *Eli*, saw her praying, and at first thought that she was drunk, since her lips were moving without sound coming out. She explained what she was doing, and Eli added his blessing to her prayer.

In due course she and Elkanah had a son, whom they named Samuel, and gave him into the Lord's service as Eli's helper. Each year, as the boy grew up, she visited him in the temple, bringing him new clothes, as well as making her annual sacrifice. She and Elkanah had three other sons and two daughters after Samuel.

Hazael

Hazael was a king of Aram-Damascus who fought, usually successfully, against Israel and Judah during the reigns of *Jehoram (1)* and *Ahaziah (2)*, and later also of *Jehu*. Hazael was sent by his predecessor, *Ben-hadad (2)*, to visit the prophet *Elisha* when Ben-hadad was ill, so that the prophet could be asked whether the king would recover. Elisha told Hazael that the king would certainly recover and would certainly die. When Hazael returned he murdered Ben-hadad by placing a wet cloth across his face, and took the throne. Elisha had foretold that Hazael would do great evil to the people of Israel, and Aram-Damascus seems indeed to have been the dominant power in the area around this period toward the end of the ninth century B.C., to the detriment of Israel.

Heman

Heman, son of Mahol, appears in I Kings 4 as one of several, apparently very wise, men, whose great wisdom was still exceeded by that of *Solomon*.

A second **Heman**, son of *Joel* and grandson of *Samuel*, was one of the three chief musicians appointed to lead services by *David*. It is interesting that the same duplication of names between a wise man and a leading temple musician also occurs with *Ethan*.

Hezekiah

Hezekiah was the son and successor of *Ahaz* as king of Judah. His reign is difficult to date precisely, in part because of contradictions in the text of II Kings – probably *c.* 716-687 B.C., but possibly 726-698. His mother was Abi or Abijah.

Hezekiah was, first of all, a righteous king. II Kings 18 gives a brief account of the religious reforms that he undertook to restore the correct worship of the Lord and remove idolatry from throughout Judah. II Chronicles also describes this, but in far greater detail, mentioning a rigorous cleansing of the temple, extensive sacrifices, destruction of idols, and an unusually well-attended celebration of the Passover.

This last is especially interesting, in that Hezekiah is said to have invited worshipers from throughout both his own kingdom and the former kingdom of Israel, by then under Assyrian control, to come to Jerusalem. Some of the Israelites came, but many scornfully refused. So many did attend that the rituals could not be properly observed, and Hezekiah asked the Lord for forgiveness for this laxity, which was granted.

After the death of *Sargon*, Hezekiah joined in a rebellion against his successor, *Sennacherib*. Chronicles describes how, when Judah was threatened by Sennacherib's army, Hezekiah set to work to improve the organization and equipment of his own forces, and also added to the fortifications of Jerusalem. In particular, he improved the water supply to the city to enable it to hold out better against attack. The so-called Hezekiah's Tunnel, which directs a spring from outside the old walls of the city to a point inside, can still be seen.

When Sennacherib attacked, however, Hezekiah had little alternative but to surrender and to pay him a huge

Below: Isaiah cures King Hezekiah's boils with a fig poultice.

ransom. The Assyrian account describes how Hezekiah was imprisoned for a time "like a bird in a cage." An Assyrian force also came to Jerusalem and demanded the surrender of the city. After asking *Isaiah*'s advice, Hezekiah maintained his defiance and the Assyrians left, after being punished by heavy casualties inflicted by an angel.

At some point in his reign Hezekiah became very ill (his ailment is described as a boil, ulcer, or inflammation in various translations). With divine approval, Isaiah applied a fig poultice, and the injury was cured.

A section of the sayings collected in the Book of Proverbs is described as being "other proverbs of Solomon that the officials of King Hezekiah of Judah copied."

Hiram

Hiram was king of Tyre in the time of *David* and *Solomon*. He had good relations with both, sending cedar wood and skilled workers to help David in building work, and giving more extensive help to Solomon in the building of the temple. As well as payment in wheat and olive oil, Solomon ceded to him some territory in return for his assistance. He also co-operated with Solomon in maritime trading ventures in the Red Sea.

Hiram was also the name of a skilled worker in bronze sent by King Hiram to work on Solomon's temple. Hiram the king's name is alternatively spelled as Huram, and the metal worker's is sometimes spelled Huram-abi.

Hobab

See *Jethro*.

Hophni

Hophni was one of the immoral sons of the high priest, *Eli*. He and his brother, *Phinehas (2)*, were priests in the sanctuary, but they were accustomed to abuse the rites of sacrifice and to seduce women at the temple. After a defeat for the Israelites during a campaign against the Philistines, Hophni and his brother brought the sacred Ark from the sanctuary to the army, in an attempt to restore the army's morale. This failed, however, and a second defeat followed, in which the Ark was captured, and Hophni and his brother

killed. Eli had already been warned in a prophecy, and in the appearance of the Lord to Samuel that his two sons would die on the same day for their immorality.

Hosea

The Book of Hosea tells very little of the personal life of the prophet of the same name, other than of his difficult marriage to the adulterous *Gomer*. He gave unusual names to her three children, which imply that he did not believe that he was their father. Hosea seems to have been from the northern kingdom of Israel rather than Judah, and may have lived around 750 B.C., or perhaps a little later. The only other personal detail given is that his father's name was Beeri.

The surviving texts of the Book of Hosea are described by biblical scholars as being among the most difficult to understand clearly and translate accurately. Scholars have also debated how much of the book can be attributed to the teaching of Hosea himself, or at least to his near contemporaries, and how much may be the product of later writers.

The first section of the book contains these brief biographical details and, more importantly, compares the difficult relationship between Hosea and his wife with the Lord's attitude towards his people of Israel. Just as Hosea cannot bring himself to part

Above: A dramatic engraving of the prophet Hosea, surrounded by episodes of his life.

finally from his wife, so the Lord will eventually forgive the sins of Israel: "'The Lord said to me [Hosea] again, "Go, love a woman who has a lover and is an adulteress, just as the Lord loves the people of Israel, though they turn to other gods and love raisin cakes."'"

One of the principal complaints that Hosea makes throughout the book is of the people's idolatry, and their readiness to worship *Baal* and other false gods. The rebukes for this and other immoralities are generally accompanied by warnings of the punishment to come: "they sow the wind, and they shall reap the whirlwind." Drunkenness and lechery are among the vices castigated, and also criticized are attempts by the kingdom of Israel to seek the help of foreign alliances, rather than relying on the Lord.

Finally, forgiveness is offered: "'I will heal their disloyalty; I will love them freely, for my anger has turned from them.'"

Hoshea

Hoshea, son of *Elah*, was the last king of Israel before the kingdom finally fell to the Assyrians. He reigned *c.* 732-23 B.C. Hoshea clearly represented the pro-Assyrian party within the elite of Israel, as *Menahem* and *Pekahiah*

among his predecessors also had, but his immediate predecessor, *Pekah*, had not. Hoshea paid tribute to Assyria from what remained of the kingdom of Israel after the victories of *Tiglath-pileser*. However, after Shalmaneser came to the Assyrian throne, Hoshea tried to arrange an alliance with the Egyptians. Shalmaneser invaded, and quickly captured (and presumably executed) Hoshea. After further fighting, Israel was completely conquered by 721 B.C., and the leading inhabitants were deported to Assyria.

According to Numbers 13, **Hoshea** was also the original name of *Joshua*, which was changed to Joshua by *Moses* himself.

Hushai

Hushai figures importantly in the story of *David* and *Absalom*. Hushai is described as being David's friend (capitalized as Friend in some translations), which may signify a particularly important royal adviser. When Absalom openly rebelled and David immediately left Jerusalem, Hushai tried to join David, symbolizing his distress by tearing his coat and putting earth on his head. David instead asked him to go back to Jerusalem and spy on Absalom, and in particular to counteract what would be likely to be the wise advice of his former counselor, *Ahithophel*, who had genuinely defected. This Hushai successfully did, inducing Absalom to delay his pursuit of his father. David's armies in due course won a decisive battle, and Absalom was killed.

Immanuel

Immanuel, according to Isaiah 7, was the symbolic name, meaning "God is with us," to be given to a child of the house of *David*, who would know how to choose good and refuse evil. It is not clear whether this prophecy referred only to the immediate situation of the royal family and the imminent birth of *Hezekiah*, or if it is also a more general prophecy relating to the coming of the Messiah.

Left: A Doré woodcut shows Jacob receiving Isaac's blessing in place of Esau. This deception raised Jacob's status over Esau.

Right: Together the half-brothers Isaac and Ishmael bury their father, Abraham, in the family tomb.

Isaac

Isaac was the second son of *Abraham*, but the first child of Abraham and his wife, *Sarah*. In turn, *Isaac*'s wife was *Rebekah*, and their twin sons, *Esau* and *Jacob*. Isaac appears in most instances as a supporting character in the lives of his father and sons; most events attributed to his life are told rather more from their points of view.

When he was a baby, Isaac's mother had his half-brother, *Ishmael*, and Ishmael's mother, *Hagar*, expelled from the household to protect Isaac's rights of inheritance. Later, when Isaac was still young, the Lord tested Abraham by having him prepare a sacrifice in which Isaac was to be the victim, only to have Abraham substitute a goat at the last stages.

Abraham later sent his servant to find a wife for Isaac among his kin in Syria. Rebekah, daughter of Abraham's nephew, was brought back and married Isaac. Like his father and mother, Isaac later briefly passed off his wife as his sister, also deceiving a King *Abimelech*. Isaac, again like his father, was involved in a dispute with Abimelech over water rights and wells in the area of Beersheba. It seems likely that the stories of the wife/sister and the wells in Abraham's and Isaac's lives have become confused over time before being recorded by the various biblical sources.

Finally, when he was an old man and nearly blind, Isaac was deceived by Rebekah and his younger son, Jacob. Feeling that his death was near, Isaac sent Esau to hunt for game for him, but Rebekah prepared food and had Jacob disguise himself and serve it to his father. Isaac then blessed Jacob and appointed him as chief of the family. When Esau returned, and the deception was discovered, Isaac refused to retract his blessing. Jacob and Esau were estranged thereafter. However,

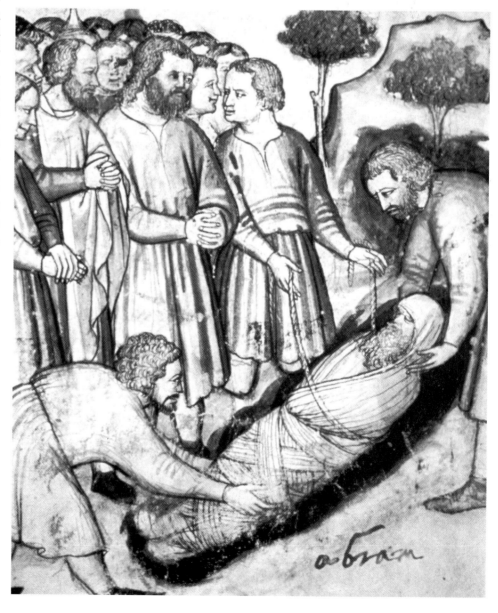

a later passage describes Isaac's death at the age of 180 and his burial, by his twin sons, in the Cave of Machpelah, alongside his father and mother.

Isaiah

The prophet Isaiah was perhaps the greatest of the Hebrew prophets. The opening words of the Book of Isaiah tell us that Isaiah was the son of Amoz, and that his visions came to him in Judah and Jerusalem in the reigns of *Uzziah, Jotham, Ahaz* and *Hezekiah.* This means that his prophetic career embraced almost the whole of the second half of the eighth century B.C. One of his visions appeared to him in the year of Uzziah's death (probably 742), and he was certainly active at the time of the Assyrian advance on Jerusalem in 701. He was married and had at least two sons, who were given symbolic names related to aspects of his preaching.

Isaiah appears almost exclusively in the Book of Isaiah. The discussion of

Below: A detail from Michaelangelo's painting of Isaiah in the Sistine Chapel.

aspects of his relationship with Hezekiah in II Kings 19 & 20 are virtually identical to Isaiah 37 & 38, and the material in Isaiah may have been copied from Kings at an early date. Neither Isaiah nor Kings gives much additional information about events in Isaiah's life beyond what is noted in the paragraph above.

Many of Isaiah's oracles are introduced as "concerning Judah and Jerusalem," and from his fairly close connections with Hezekiah in particular, it has been suggested that he came from a well-to-do or noble family. The vision of 642 B.C. seems to have been his calling to his vocation, and apart from this his participation in four other incidents is recorded.

He advised Ahaz not to be afraid when *Pekah* of Israel allied with Aram-Damascus to attack Judah, foretelling that both Israel and Aram would fall to the real danger, the Assyrians. Later, in the reign of Hezekiah, he criticized the king for his contacts with an envoy from Babylon. This visit may have been part of the creation of the alliance that led to the rebellion against the Assyrians and eventually the attack on Jerusalem in 701. When the Assyrians summoned the city to surrender, Hezekiah was worried, and sent a delegation to consult Isaiah. Isaiah replied that there was no need for concern, and that the Assyrians would leave. When they did not immediately do so, Isaiah sent the king a longer message to the same effect, giving the Lord's verdict on *Sennacherib*, the Assyrian king: "'Because you have raged against me and your arrogance has come to my ears, I will put my hook in your nose and my bit in your mouth; I will turn you back on the way by which you came.'" Finally, when Hezekiah was ill, Isaiah predicted that he would die, and then passed on the Lord's changed decision to grant him a further 15 years of life. To confirm this, Isaiah applied a poultice of figs to the boil that had been troubling Hezekiah, and he was cured.

These incidents form only a small part of the Book of Isaiah, which is one of the best-loved and most influential books of the Old Testament. Isaiah includes extensive Messianic predictions that have helped bring it to the center of the development of both Christian and Jewish religious thinking. In addition to this, the language and imagery of the book is vivid and arresting, providing many familiar expressions to religious teaching and to other aspects of modern life. One of many possible examples of this is the part of Chapter 2 v.4 that is inscribed near the entrance to the United Nations' building in New York: "they shall beat their swords into plowshares, and their spears into pruning hooks; nation shall not lift up sword against nation, neither shall they learn war any more."

It is now generally agreed by biblical scholars that Chapters 40-66 of Isaiah do not in some senses "belong" with the remainder of the text of the book, largely because of the way in which they comment on much later events than the eighth century B.C., when the prophet lived. They are believed to have a different authorship from the earlier chapters, and accordingly their content is not discussed further here (see "*Second Isaiah*"). The earlier sections of Isaiah are also believed to have been the work of a number of hands, making up a collection of discourses attributed to the prophet but not directly recorded by him; however, they do combine in a coherent religious message of lasting importance that has the authentic ring of a single personality.

Texts of the Book of Isaiah were among the items discovered as part of the "Dead Sea Scrolls" at Qumran. The material found from Isaiah was the most complete of any of the books of the Old Testament. Modern translations have made a number of small amendments to their interpretation of Isaiah in the light of material from Qumran, but the traditional Hebrew text, dating in its oldest-surviving edition to the tenth century A.D., is virtually identical to the far older Qumran version. However, it should be noted that material from other Old Testament books is not as similar in the Qumran and the received texts.

The first chapters of Isaiah concentrate on repeated condemnations of the wickedness of Jerusalem and its rulers. There is, however, the promise of a better future to come in the time of the Messiah: "For a child has been born for us, a son given to us; authority rests upon his shoulders; and he is named Wonderful Counselor, Mighty God, Everlasting Father, Prince of Peace. His authority shall grow continually, and there shall be endless peace for the throne of David and his kingdom. He will establish it and uphold it with justice and righteousness from this time onward and forevermore." This golden age shall see a transformation of the condition of the people: "with righteousness he shall judge the poor, and decide with equity for the meek of the earth; . . . with the breath of his lips he shall kill the wicked." It shall be a time of peace: "The wolf shall live with the lamb, the leopard shall lie down with the kid."

Oracles against other nations follow, and Israel is warned not to rely on their support, but to depend on the Lord: "Alas for those . . . who trust in chariots because they are many and in horsemen because they are very strong, but do not look to the Holy One of Israel or consult the Lord!"

Ishbaal

Ishbaal, also known as Ishbosheth, was the fourth son of *Saul*. He was 40 years old at the time of his father's death, and survived him by two years. Aided by *Abner*, and seemingly largely at his instigation, Ishbaal established a kingdom around Mahanaim across the Jordan. His decline began when he quarreled with Abner over Abner's association with *Rizpah*, who had been one of Saul's concubines. Abner decided after this to transfer his loyalty to *David*, but was killed shortly afterward by *Joab*. The defection and death of Abner left Ishbaal frightened, and his cause defeated. Two of his soldiers, Rechab and Baanah (see *Rechab*), decided to murder him. They cut off his head and brought it to David, presumably expecting a reward, but David put them to death and had Ishbaal's head properly buried.

The name Ishbaal means "man of Baal," and the alternative form Ishbosheth, "man of shame," arises because of an unwillingness on the part of later scribes to write the name of the Cannaanite deity.

Ishbosheth

See *Ishbaal*.

Ishmael

1. Ishmael was the eldest son of *Abraham* by *Hagar*, slave-girl to Abraham's wife *Sarah*. It was an accepted custom of contemporary communities that a man who could not have children with his wife could try to have them with a concubine, but in such cases the rights of the woman and the child were supposed to be protected. Sarah had been jealous when Hagar first associated with Abraham, and forced Hagar to flee into the desert. Hagar returned to give birth to Ishmael, after an angel of the Lord appeared to her and promised that she would have many descendants through her son. Ishmael was to be, the angel prophesied, "'a wild ass of a man, with his hand against everyone, and everyone's hand against him; and he shall live at odds with all his kin.'"

When Ishmael was 13 years old, he was circumcised with the rest of the household, in confirmation of Abraham's covenant with the Lord.

After *Isaac* was born, Sarah again became jealous, and wished to favor her son over Ishmael; she persuaded Abraham to send Hagar and Ishmael away once more. Wandering without water in the desert, Hagar briefly abandoned the boy to die, but was shown a well by the Lord, who also confirmed Ishmael's destiny as the founder of a great nation.

Ishmael grew up to become an expert archer, and lived in the area of Sinai known as Paran. He married an Egyptian woman, and had 12 sons before his death, aged 137.

In both Jewish and Muslim tradition, Ishmael is regarded as being the forefather of the Arabs. In the Koran no name is given to the son to be sacrificed by Abraham when he is tested by the Lord. Muslims generally believe that this was Ishmael, rather than Isaac. There is also a legend that Ishmael and his mother are buried at Mecca.

2. After Jerusalem had been captured by *Nebuchadnezzar,* and *Gedaliah* had been appointed as governor, Ishmael and his supporters were one of a number of armed groups and leaders still at large who had not surrendered to the Babylonians. They came to visit Gedaliah at Mizpah, and he assured them that the Babylonians would treat them well. Ishmael clearly did not believe this, because he returned to Gedaliah later with ten supporters, and assassinated him, followed by others who arrived at Mizpah the following day.

Right: Jacob's Dream, by Domenico Feti. In this dream the Lord promised Jacob that he would be the father of a large and successful nation.

He then carried off as captives all the people of the town. The captives were released by other soldiers under *Johanan,* but Ishmael escaped.

The name **Ishmael** is borne by three other minor personalities in the Old Testament.

Israel

See *Jacob*.

Issachar

Issachar was the fifth son of *Jacob* and *Leah*, his first wife, and the ninth of Jacob's sons to be born. Like his brothers and half-brothers, he participated in the selling into slavery of *Joseph*, the subsequent purchase of grain from Egypt during the famine, and joined the family in settling in Egypt thereafter.

Also like his brothers and half-brothers, one of the tribes of Israel is named after him.

Ithamar

Ithamar was the youngest son of *Aaron*. He and his brother, *Eleazar*, were spared when their other brothers, *Nadab* and *Abihu*, were killed. Ithamar's personal priestly duties included supervising the transport and construction of the tabernacle. He was regarded as being the forefather of a priestly clan.

Above: Jacob wrestles the angel, by Doré.

Jabal

Jabal is found in Genesis 4, a descendant of *Cain*, and is described as the "ancestor of those who live in tents and have livestock." Either he or *Abel* may be regarded as the first nomadic herdsman.

Jacob

Jacob was the younger twin son of *Isaac* and *Rebekah*, and the brother of *Esau*. Rebekah had a difficult pregnancy, and was told by the Lord that she was carrying twins who would be the forefathers of separate and quarreling nations, with the older eventually serving the younger. Esau was born

first, and grew up to be a skilled hunter and outdoor man, and his father's favorite. Jacob emerged from the womb clutching his brother's heel, grew up to be quieter, and was favored over Esau by their mother.

On one occasion Esau returned from the countryside exhausted, and asked Jacob, who was cooking at the time, for some food. Jacob decided to take advantage of the situation, and replied that he would sell it to Esau in return for Esau's birthright as the elder son. Esau was so tired that he accepted.

Later, when Isaac was old and his sight was failing, he asked Esau to hunt for game to make a special meal of a type that Isaac particularly liked, saying that in return Esau would receive his father's blessing. Rebekah overheard this, and had Jacob bring two choice kids from the flock so that she could prepare a suitable meal for him to present to his father, forestalling Esau. Jacob pointed out that his father might touch him and detect the imposture, since he had a smooth skin and his brother was very hairy. Rebekah told him not to worry, and gave him some of Esau's clothes and put skins on his neck and hands so that he should have the feeling and appearance of his brother to the partially-sighted Isaac. The deception was a success, and Isaac gave Jacob the blessing intended for Esau, appointing him particularly as lord over his brothers, and foretelling that he would prosper. Esau then returned from his hunting trip and the deception was revealed, but Isaac would not revoke his blessing.

Esau was understandably angry at all that had been done to him, and determined that he would kill Jacob as soon as Isaac had died. Rebekah heard of this, and decided that Jacob should flee to live with her brother *Laban* until Esau's anger had passed. She persuaded Isaac that Jacob should go to her kinfolk, on the pretext that he would otherwise be likely to find a Canaanite wife.

One night on his journey, Jacob had a dream as he slept, in which the Lord promised him that he would be the founder of a numerous and successful people. When he awoke he set up a pillar of stones, including the stone that had been his pillow, to mark the spot. He named the place Bethel and said, "'This is none other than the house of God, and this is the gate of heaven.'"

Jacob next arrived to live with his uncle, Laban, and his family, and looked for a wife. He met and fell in love with *Rachel*, Laban's younger daughter, who was more attractive than her elder sister, *Leah*. Jacob worked for Laban for seven years in order to marry Rachel, but Laban substituted Leah for her sister on their wedding night, because he said it was improper for the younger sister to be married first. (The bride would have been veiled during the wedding ceremony and the consummation of the marriage, so Jacob would not have realized the deception.) Jacob was angry, but agreed to marry both sisters in return for another seven years of work.

Jacob loved Rachel and did not love Leah. Because Leah was not loved, the Lord granted her children, and she hoped that this would change Jacob's views about her, especially since Rachel at first did not have any children. Leah had four sons. Because she evidently could not have children, Rachel gave Jacob her maid, *Bilhah*, as his concubine. Bilhah and Jacob had two sons. Next Leah gave Jacob her maid, *Zilpah*, as a concubine and she, too, had two sons. Then Leah herself had two more sons and a daughter, *Dinah*. Eventually Rachel had a child of her own, *Joseph*.

When the 14 years of service that Jacob had promised in return for his wives had passed, Jacob continued to work for Laban. The agreed payment for this was that he was to be given all the dark and speckled sheep and goats in the flock. Laban tried to cheat him, but Jacob was more clever and gained large herds of his own, although Laban also prospered. Nonetheless, resentment arose between the two.

After a further six years of work on these terms, Jacob decided to move back to his homeland. Rachel and Leah both went with him, agreeing that their father had acted badly. Rachel also stole the images which represented Laban's household gods. Possession of these indicated the family headship, and they should therefore have been left with Laban for him to pass to his sons. When Laban caught up with Jacob and his wives, Jacob offered to have the thief of the gods executed, if they could be found. Rachel had not told Jacob what she had done, and successfully concealed the images when her father searched for them.

Jacob and Laban agreed to part in peace, and sealed the covenant that they had made by building a pillar of stones to mark the boundary between their territories. Jacob agreed not to ill-treat either of his wives, or take any new wives, and also made a sacrifice to mark the agreement.

Journeying on, Jacob made elaborate preparations to meet Esau once again, fearful that he would still be angry. He sent servants ahead with presents for his brother, and followed behind with his immediate family. One night he sent them ahead across a ford

Left: Jacob and Rachel, by Raphael. Jacob fell in love with Rachel on first sight, and in the end had to work for Laban for 14 years to marry her.

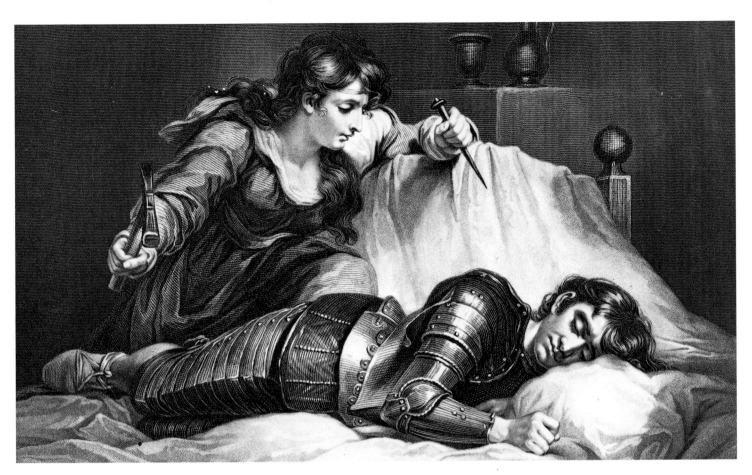

in a river. Throughout that night Jacob wrestled with an unnamed and mysterious man. Neither had the better of the wrestling match, but at the end of it the man dislocated Jacob's hip. Jacob still refused to let him go, unless he was given a blessing; the man said that Jacob was to change his name to Israel, and gave the blessing. The meaning of this incident is very obscure: the mysterious wrestler is clearly some type of divine being, and the episode may represent in some way Jacob's assertion of his right to cross the river border and enter into the land of Canaan.

The reunion with Esau proved to be amicable, despite all Jacob's fears. Esau invited Jacob to travel with him, but Jacob made an excuse and went his own way to Shechem, where he settled. There then followed the rape of Dinah and the revenge of the family, led by her brothers, *Simeon* and *Levi*.

Following this, Jacob was fearful of reprisals, and set the family on the move once again. He first had them bury all the images of gods, and set off from Shechem for Bethel, where he planned to build an altar. In the course of this work the Lord appeared again to Jacob, confirmed his position as father of the nation, and repeated the change of his name to Israel.

Shortly afterward in the family's travels, Rachel gave birth to a second son, whom she called Ben-oni. Rachel died immediately after the birth, and Jacob changed the child's name to *Benjamin*. Jacob buried her, and erected a monument over her grave. Jacob then went to visit his father, Isaac, who died, aged 180. Both Jacob and his brother were present at the burial of Isaac, according to Genesis 35, although it is possible that this information comes from a later insertion to the main sections of their stories.

After this point Jacob effectively becomes a minor character in the stories of Joseph and his brothers. Jacob sent Joseph to see his brothers on the occasion when they sold him into slavery, and was distraught when the brothers returned with their tale of Joseph's death. Many years later, during the famine that Joseph had foretold from pharaoh's dream [*Pharaoh (2)*], Jacob sent his sons, except Benjamin, the youngest, to Egypt to buy grain. This brought about their reunion with Joseph, and eventually the removal of the whole family to live in Egypt, confirmed to Jacob as the correct course when, at Beer-sheba, he had a further vision of the Lord.

Jacob was joyfully reunited with Joseph, and lived in Egypt for 17 years.

Above: Jael Smote the Nail into his Temples, by James Northcote. Thus Sisera died at the hand of a Kenite woman.

When he felt his death drawing near, he summoned Joseph and Joseph's two sons, blessed them, and then blessed in turn each of his own sons before he died, aged 147. Jacob had asked his sons to bury him in the family's tomb in the Cave of Machpelah. Jacob's body was therefore embalmed and taken to Machpelah by all the brothers, with an elaborate escort provided by pharaoh.

Jael

After the victory of *Barak* over *Sisera* recounted in Judges 4, Sisera fled from the battlefield and tried to take refuge with Heber, a Kenite, and his wife, Jael. Jael invited him into their tent, telling him not to be afraid. She gave him milk when he asked for something to drink but, when he fell asleep, killed him by driving a tent peg through his head. She showed the body to the victorious general, Barak, who arrived shortly afterward. In the prophetess *Deborah*'s celebration of the victory in Judges 5, Jael is described as being "of tent-dwelling women most blessed."

Japheth

Japheth was the third son of *Noah*, and was saved with the rest of the family in the ark. He and his eldest brother, *Shem*, covered up their father in the episode of Noah's drunkenness. In the table of nations Japheth was traditionally regarded by the Israelites as being the ancestor of the Indo-European peoples of the regions of the Black Sea and Greek Islands.

Jeduthun

Jeduthun was one of the leaders of the temple musicians in the time of *David*. The "sons of Jeduthun" became one of the temple choirs, and the name appears in the title of several of the psalms, suggesting that these were normally sung by that choir.

Jehoahaz

1. Jehoahaz succeeded his father, *Jehu*, as king of Israel, and reigned for 17 years at the end of the ninth century B.C. He appears principally in II Kings 13. Like his predecessors and successors on the throne of Israel, he is ritually castigated for following the

Left: A sixteenth-century stained-glass window at St. Neot, showing Noah and his family building the ark.

Below: The Captivity of Jehoiachin, King of Israel – from Stothard's watercolors from the Painted Chamber at Westminster.

sins (idolatry) of *Jeroboam (1)*, and this is said to be the reason for Israel's continued misfortune.

During Jehoahaz's reign, this misfortune manifested itself as continuing defeats inflicted by King *Hazael* of Aram-Damascus and his son and successor *Ben-hadad (3)*. However, Jehoahaz continued to call on the Lord for assistance. This was forthcoming, and Israel did not fall completely under Hazael's domination, although Jehoahaz's army was reduced to a strength of 50 horsemen, 10 chariots, and 10,000 infantrymen. The biblical text says that "the Lord gave Israel a savior," which has since been interpreted to mean that the Aramean forces were drawn off by attacks from the Assyrians from farther north and east.

2. A second Jehoahaz was briefly king of Judah in 609 B.C. He succeeded his father, *Josiah*. Pharaoh *Neco* of Egypt first imprisoned him, then deposed him, and finally deported him to Egypt, where he died. In Jeremiah 22 he is called by the name Shallum.

Jehoahaz is also a spelling of the name otherwise given as *Ahaz*.

Jehoash

See *Joash*.

Jehoiachin

Jehoiachin was the son of *Jehoiakim* and Nehushta, and succeeded his father as king of Judah, reigning for

three months in 598-597 B.C. Jehoiakim had begun a rebellion against *Nebuchadnezzar*, but had died before Nebuchadnezzar arrived with his army to put it down. Jehoiachin surrendered immediately and he, along with many of the people of Judah and treasure from the temple, was taken off to Babylon. *Zedekiah* was installed as the new king.

Jehoiachin never returned to Jerusalem, but is said to have been well treated, at least in the later part of his exile, being released from prison and dining with one of Nebuchadnezzar's successors. Babylonian records include an account of Jehoiachin receiving food from the royal kitchen in the reign of Nebuchadnezzar.

Jehoiakim

Jehoiakim was the brother and successor of *Jehoahaz (2)*. His original name was Eliakim, but he was given the new name by Pharaoh *Neco*, who deposed Jehoahaz and replaced him with Jehoiakim. Jehoiakim's father was *Josiah*, and his mother was Zebidah.

For the first part of his reign, Jehoiakim paid tribute to Neco, raising taxes to do so. Next, presumably following the important victory of *Nebuchadnezzar* over the Egyptians at Carchemish in 605 B.C., II Kings 24 tells that Jehoiakim "became his servant for three years." He then rebelled against Nebuchadnezzar, and had to fight off attacks from a number of desert peoples allied to the Babylonians, before dying in

598, just before Nebuchadnezzar arrived with his army to subdue him. His son and successor *Jehoiachin* had to surrender.

Jehoiakim was also an adversary of the prophet *Jeremiah*. He was criticized for building himself "a spacious house," while practising "oppression and violence." Jeremiah foretold that, "'With the burial of a donkey he shall be buried – dragged off and thrown out beyond the gates of Jerusalem.'" Some historians suggest that Jehoiakim was indeed assassinated.

Jehoiakim was particularly annoyed by the gloomy predictions for the kingdom's future that were central to Jeremiah's preaching. At the beginning of his reign Jeremiah was not punished for one such episode, but another prophet, *Uriah*, was chased to Egypt by the king's men, brought back, and executed. In Jehoiakim's fourth year, Jeremiah arranged for *Baruch* to read a record of his preaching in the temple. When this came to the notice of the temple officials they advised Jeremiah and Baruch both to hide from the king. The scrolls were read to the king, who burned them as soon as he had heard their contents. Jehoiakim then tried unsuccessfully to arrest Jeremiah and Baruch, but they eluded him.

Jehoram

1. Jehoram was the brother and successor of *Ahaziah (1)* as king of Israel. Their father was *Ahab*, and their mother was *Jezebel*. Jehoram called on *Jehosaphat* of Israel to help him in a campaign against King *Mesha* of Moab, who rebelled some time shortly after the death of Ahab. Their army got into trouble on the way to attack Mesha, but they were helped by the prophet *Elisha*. Elisha warned Jehoram that he was only helping the army because Jehosaphat was present, and foretold that the much-needed water would be available the next day. After that the campaign went well, until they came to attack the final Moabite stronghold, where they were defeated.

Several incidents described in II Kings 5, 6 & 7 involve an unnamed king of Israel, the prophet Elisha, and the people of Aram-Damascus. These incidents are more fully discussed in the entry for Elisha, but the king may have been Jehoram.

Jehoram was wounded near Ramoth-gilead in a further campaign

against *Hazael* of Damascus, and went to Jezreel to recover. One of Jehoram's officers, *Jehu*, inspired by being anointed by a representative of Elisha, staged a rebellion against Jehoram. When Jehu arrived at Jezreel Jehoram asked him if all was well, but Jehu replied, "'What peace can there be, so long as the many whoredoms and sorceries of your mother Jezebel continue?'" Jehu then killed Jehoram and his ally King *Ahaziah (2)* of Judah, throwing Jehoram's body onto the ground that had formerly been *Naboth*'s vineyard, and then going on to kill Jezebel too. This fulfilled the oracle that *Elijah* had delivered because of Ahab's and Jezebel's guilt in the murder of Naboth.

2. Jehoram, king of Judah was the eldest son and successor of *Jehosaphat*, and reigned *c.* 850-843 B.C., beginning his reign when he was 32 years old. His wife was *Athaliah*, daughter of *Ahab* and *Jezebel*. The accounts of his reign in both Kings and Chronicles are influenced by his marriage, and through it his association with the wickedness of the family of *Omri* and of Jezebel.

Although the kingship was reserved for Jehoram, Jehosaphat gave important gifts to his other sons. When Jehoram became king, however, he had

Below: Jehosaphat, as seen a stained-glass window at St. Dyfnog's Church at Llanrhaeadr in North Wales, dated 1533.

his brothers and a number of other officials put to death. He is also said to have built illicit shrines, and to have allowed idolatrous practices. II Chronicles 21, in which these allegations are found, also adds that he received a letter from the prophet *Elisha* condemning all this, and foretelling a painful death for Jehoram. Some scholars regard this letter as a later addition by the compiler of the Chronicles account and not genuine.

Early in his reign, the territory of Edom to the south of the Judahite heartland revolted, and Jehoram was defeated in battle. Edom, and the outlet to the trade of the Red Sea that it permitted, was never entirely recovered by Judah after this defeat. The Chronicles account also includes attacks by the Philistines and others on Judah, in which Jehoram's wives and sons were killed, apart from his youngest son, named as Jehoahaz in this passage of the Old Testament, but usually known as *Ahaziah (2)*.

Following this, Jehoram duly suffered from the bowel disease that had been predicted, and died in pain two years later, according to the Chronicler, to no one's regret.

The name **Jehoram** is also spelled as Joram in some translations, and was used by three other personalities in the Old Testament.

Jehosaphat

Jehosaphat was the son and successor of *Asa* as king of Judah. He was the fourth king after the split between Judah and Israel, and his mother's name was Azubah, daughter of Shilhi. He was aged 35 when he came to the throne, and reigned for 25 years, approximately 874-850 B.C.

Jehosaphat is generally commended for his religious and social conduct. Like most of his near contemporaries, his life is covered in both Kings and Chronicles. Kings tells us that he followed the policies of his father in religious matters, especially in expelling male prostitutes from the temple, but did not destroy all the shrines of other gods. II Chronicles repeats this praise but, in separate passages, says both that he did (Ch. 17 & 19) and did not (Ch. 20) remove the "high places and sacred poles". Chronicles also describes how he first sent priests out to travel the country to teach the people the Law, and later how he went on such journeys personally, as well as appointing judges and priests specifically instructed as to the fairness with which they should proceed.

Jehosaphat also participated in various military campaigns. Both Kings and Chronicles describe one of these, to recapture Ramoth-gilead from Aram-Damascus, in some detail. Although Jehosaphat's ally in this venture, *Ahab*, king of Israel, is more harshly described in the Old Testament, the reality seems to have been that he was the senior partner in the alliance, drawing on the success of his father, *Omri*, in strengthening Israel. Jehosaphat's son, *Jehoram (2)*, was married to Ahab's daughter, *Athaliah*. The preliminaries for the campaign also led to an encounter with the prophet *Micaiah*.

When Ahab summoned Jehosaphat to join him on the campaign, Jehosaphat asked to be reassured that the venture had divine approval. Four hundred prophets were assembled, and all advised that the attack would succeed. Jehosaphat was not reassured, however, and asked for further confirmation. Ahab agreed to consult Micaiah, although he hated the prophet and had always had unwelcome predictions from him in the past. Micaiah first gave a favorable response but, when challenged to speak candidly, foretold a terrible defeat for Ahab. Micaiah explained that the prophecies from the other seers had been inspired by a lying spirit sent by the Lord to tempt Ahab into disaster.

Despite this information, Ahab and Jehosaphat went on their campaign but, when it came to battle, Ahab took the precaution of fighting in disguise. Despite this, Ahab was fatally wounded by a stray arrow and died at the end of the day. Jehosaphat retreated home safely.

Only one other event is recorded in both Kings and Chronicles: that Jehosaphat tried to build a fleet, probably on the Aqaba arm of the Red Sea, but that the ships were wrecked. Kings adds that *Ahaziah (1)*, Ahab's eldest son and successor, tried to persuade Jehosaphat to make a second attempt at this project, but Chronicles states that the failure of the only attempt was a divine punishment for doing it in association with Ahaziah.

Kings alone describes another campaign undertaken in alliance with Israel: *Jehoram (1)*, brother and successor of Ahaziah, summoned Jehosaphat to join him in attacking King *Mesha* of Moab. Jehosaphat persuaded his allies to consult the prophet *Elisha*, who was involved in a miracle to bring water to the thirsty army. The battles went very well until Mesha, attacked in his last stronghold, publicly sacrificed his eldest son, which so daunted the army of Israel that they retreated, presumably taking Jehosaphat with them.

Chronicles also describes a further campaign. In it, Jehosaphat was frightened by the approach of an allied force of Moabites, Ammonites and Edomites, gathered his people in the temple to pray for assistance and, heartened by a prophecy, marched out to fight, only to discover that the attackers had quarreled among themselves, and were all dead.

When Jehosaphat died he was succeeded by his eldest son, Jehoram (2).

Jehosaphat is also the name of three other personalities in the Old Testament. Two of these were court officials in the time of *David* and *Solomon*.

Jehu

Jehu was king of Israel from c. 843-816 B.C. His father was Nimshi. Jehu was the leading soldier in the army of *Jehoram (1)*. Jehoram was wounded in a campaign against Aram-Damascus in battle near Ramoth-gilead, and had to return to Jezreel to recuperate. The army remained in the field and, while they were there, *Elisha* sent a young (unnamed) prophet to visit Jehu and anoint him as king of Israel. This convinced Jehu and the other officers of the army of his right to take the throne.

Jehu set off immediately for Jezreel. He was seen coming and recognized by the furious way in which he drove his chariot. Jehoram sent out messengers to meet him to discover what news he brought. Jehu did not give them any reply so that, when the king himself came out, he was taken unawares when Jehu first condemned the king's mother, *Jezebel*, for her wickedness, and then attacked. Jehoram was quickly killed, and his body was left on the former vineyard of *Naboth*. Jehoram's ally, *Ahaziah (2)* of Judah, died shortly afterward, possibly at the hands of Jehu (although the accounts of his death in Kings and Chronicles differ). Jehu followed up this killing immediately by seeking out

Jezebel and having her killed too.

Jehu then wrote to the leading men of Samaria, telling them to select a king from among the surviving descendants of *Ahab*, who could contest the throne with him. Completely cowed by Jehu's killing of the two kings, they instead submitted themselves to his will. He then told them to put all 70 members of Ahab's family to death, which they did. Jehu also killed various of Jehoram's priests and other friends and servants, and also some members of Ahaziah's family. The killings that Jehu authorized mainly pass without comment in II Kings, where they are principally discussed, but they are briefly mentioned and criticized in Hosea 1.

Having consolidated his authority, Jehu then set about ending the worship of *Baal*, which had been the reason why he had first been named to *Elijah* as a future king and then anointed by Elisha's representative. He had all the priests and adherents of Baal assembled in Samaria, on the pretext that he wished to offer a special sacrifice. Once they were all there, he attacked them with his soldiers, killed them, and demolished the temple. However, although we are told that the Lord commended Jehu for this, we are also told that he did not entirely give up idolatrous practices, maintaining the golden calves at Bethel and Dan.

Having discussed religious matters at some length, the remainder of Jehu's 28-year reign is dismissed in some three verses in II Kings 10, and seems to have consisted of a gradual series of defeats at the hands of *Hazael* of Aram-Damascus.

Assyrian records of this period refer to a king of Israel who was a son of *Omri*, and he is depicted on the so-called "Black Obelisk" as paying tribute to Shalmaneser III. This king is usually believed to have been Jehu, although, if it was, the Assyrians were evidently not aware of his ancestry.

Jehu was also the name of the prophet who foretold the doom of King *Baasha* and his family, and was later involved in both praising King *Jehosaphat* for his religious conduct, and criticizing him for his alliance with *Ahab*. The name **Jehu** was also borne by three others in the Old Testament.

Jephthah

Jephthah was one of the judges of Israel who provided military leadership in the period before the establishment of the monarchy. He appears in Judges 11 & 12. He was the bastard son of a prostitute, and had been expelled from the community of Gilead by his half-brothers, in case he tried to claim rights of inheritance. Jephthah became a bandit chieftain, and it was presumably his success in this vocation which inspired the elders of Gilead, where he had been born, to ask him to return and lead the fight against the Ammonites. Jephthah agreed, on condition that he became chieftain of Gilead.

When this was accepted, he first tried to negotiate a peace with the Ammonites, pointing out that the

Below: Jephthah's Daughter, by Herbert Gandy. This painting depicts the tragic moment when Jephthah's daughter rushes to meet him, not knowing that he has sworn to sacrifice whoever meets him first in return for victory.

Right: The sacrifice of Jephthah's daughter.

Israelites had long had legal possession of the disputed territory. Diplomacy came to nothing and, before he went off to war, he made a vow to sacrifice whoever he first met coming out of his house on his return if he was victorious. The victory was duly gained, but on his return Jephthah met his daughter. She agreed with him that he must fulfill his vow, and he did so.

Later Jephthah successfully led the people of Gilead in a feud against the tribe of Ephraim. Jephthah first defeated them in battle, and then cut off their retreat at the fords over the Jordan, killing many more. He judged Israel in all for a period of six years until his death.

Jeremiah

The prophet Jeremiah appears throughout the Book of Jeremiah, which is, in fact, the longest in the Bible. The arrangement of the text of the book is not orderly – the various passages that are readily dated are not in chronological sequence, for example – and the Hebrew text, which Old Testaments in English normally follow, is substantially longer than the ancient Greek version, and has its material in a different order. Therefore, although the book contains a good deal of biographical information about the prophet, it is far from easy to organize this into a coherent account.

The opening verses of the Book of Jeremiah describe him as being the son of Hilkiah, from Anathoth (a town of the Levites), and say that his vocation began in the thirteenth year of King *Josiah* (probably 627 B.C.). His career spanned the period from then until the fall of Jerusalem in 587, and extended briefly after that. The period saw the demise of the Assyrian Empire and its supersession by the Babylonians. For Jerusalem and Judah, it was a time for being a minor player on the edges of a great power struggle, which finally swallowed them up.

It has been suggested as an alternative that 627 B.C. was the date of Jeremiah's birth, since the episodes in his career that are dated do not begin until 609, and because the Book of Jeremiah

Left: Jeremiah consults the angel as to whether or not to leave Judah.

Right: The image of the prophet Jeremiah, carved in stone in the abbey church at Moissac.

does not mention the undoubtedly important religious reforms that Josiah undertook from 621. Other personal details are that he did not marry, because of what he expected would happen to any children that he might have. He would not join in any celebrations nor mourn for anyone, because mourning and rejoicing would alike come to an end.

Josiah was killed in battle in 609 and *Jehoiakim* was installed in his place by Josiah's conqueror, Pharaoh *Neco*. Jeremiah and *Jehoiakim* were bitterly hostile to one another. At the beginning of Jehoiakim's reign, the Lord instructed Jeremiah to preach publicly in the court of the temple of the need for repentance to forestall the disaster to come. This brought an official enquiry and calls for his execution. At another time he was flogged and placed in the stocks overnight.

His clearest provocation against the king came in 605, when he instructed the scribe, *Baruch*, to write down, at his dictation, a complete account of the prophecies he had delivered to that point in his career and, when this was done, to go to the temple and read them out. When the contents of this message became known to the temple officials, they warned Baruch and Jeremiah to go into hiding from the king. The king burned the scrolls from which Baruch read and tried, unsuccessfully, to arrest Jeremiah and his scribe. Jeremiah promptly replaced the burned material with a repeated dictation to Baruch. It has been speculated that a copy of this account may have been one of the sources for the present text of the Book of Jeremiah.

Jeremiah also criticized the king for his lavish life-style and his oppression of the weak, and foretold a degrading end, "the burial of a donkey".

Following the accession of *Zedekiah*, Jeremiah continued his gloomy predictions of imminent disaster. Zedekiah consulted him on a number of occasions. He rebuked the king for inconsistent and unfair policy with regard to slaves, but most of the oracles related to the overall political situation. Jeremiah took almost a pacifist line, advising the king not to rebel against the Babylonians, and saying that, if he followed this course, he would be spared, but if he did not, he would be killed and Jerusalem destroyed. Zedekiah seems to have believed Jeremiah on some occasions, but was unable to impose this policy on his supporters and the people.

During a break in the final siege, Jeremiah tried to leave the city temporarily and was arrested and imprisoned for desertion. Zedekiah had him moved to a more comfortable confinement. He was again imprisoned because of the discouraging effect that his preaching was having, and this time was left to die in the bottom of an empty water cistern; Zedekiah had him released. Jeremiah told the king that even then it was not too late to surrender to the Babylonians. The king was too afraid to do so, but, worried that Jeremiah was right, forbade him to tell anyone else of their discussion.

When the city was captured, Jeremiah was well treated. The new Babylonian governor, *Gedaliah*, was murdered shortly afterward, and Jeremiah was consulted by some of the people as to whether they should stay in Judah or flee to Egypt. He told them they should stay, but they refused to accept the advice and took Jeremiah and Baruch with them to Egypt.

In addition to the various incidents described above, the book also has a selection of passages that seem to represent Jeremiah's personal reflections on his life and calling, and say much about his personality and his real doubts and difficulties. In these passages he questions why divine justice is so severe. He wonders why he is punished and let down, when he has followed his call so carefully: "'I did not sit in the company of merrymakers, nor did I rejoice; under the weight of your hand I sat alone, for you had filled me with indignation. Why is my pain unceasing, my wound incurable, refusing to be healed? Truly, you are to me like a deceitful brook, like waters that fail.'" He preaches disaster throughout his career, but complains that this was not what he wanted to occur. At times he wishes he could keep quiet, but he is compelled to speak out: "If I say 'I will not mention him, or speak any more in his name,' then within me there is something like a burning fire shut up in my bones; I am weary with holding it in, and I cannot." He rails against false prophets, but clearly understands the difficulty for the layman in distinguishing between true and false prophecy. At times, too, he despairs that his work and preaching have been fruitless.

Finally, it should be stressed that his prophecies were not exclusively concerned with the destruction of Jerusalem to come, but also look beyond that to a restoration of the exiled people to their homes and a resumption of true worship in the temple. This is to be symbolized by the "new covenant" with the "house of Israel" described in Chapter 31, when the Lord tells Jeremiah, "'I will forgive their iniquity, and remember their sin no more.'"

Jeroboam

1. Jeroboam was the first king of Israel after the split of the united kingdom of *David* and *Solomon* into the two polities of Israel and Judah. He reigned for 22 years in the final decades of the tenth century B.C. His parents were Nebat and Zeruah.

Jeroboam had charge of the labor force from his tribal area under Solomon, but quarreled with the king and had to go into exile in Egypt. Before he went, he had an encounter with the prophet, Ahijah, who tore his coat into 12 pieces, and symbolically gave ten to Jeroboam to signify his future control over ten of the tribes of Israel.

When Solomon died, his son, *Rehoboam*, would normally have succeeded him but, at the assembly convened to confirm this, Rehoboam refused requests to reduce the already heavy tax burdens imposed by his father, and instead threatened to increase them. This led the northern tribes to secede, and they appointed Jeroboam as king.

Jeroboam was concerned that continued visits by his people to the temple at Jerusalem (which remained held by Judah) might dilute their loyalty to his kingdom. He therefore established new sanctuaries at Bethel and Dan, but set up golden calves in them as objects of worship. He also appointed priests who were not Levites. Divine disapproval of this was made clear by a miracle which destroyed one of Jeroboam's altars and temporarily crippled him when he threatened a man of God who denounced him.

Jeroboam continued his sins, and some time later one of his sons, *Abijah*, became ill. Jeroboam sent his wife in disguise to visit the prophet Ahijah to find out what would happen to the child. Ahijah recognized her, and told her to tell her husband that the Lord had decided "to bring evil upon the house of Jeroboam", with many of the family dying unpleasant deaths. The

Above: Jeroboam and the people rebel against Rehoboam.

child, too, was shortly to die and would be much mourned.

Throughout his reign Israel and Judah were often at war. After his death his son *Nadab* succeeded him.

2. Jeroboam was the name of the son and successor of *Joash (2)* as king of Israel, who reigned *c.* 786-745 B.C. His long reign was a time of prosperity and expansion for his kingdom, but is dismissed comparatively briefly in the Old Testament accounts. He seems to have restored the northern boundaries of the kingdom to something close to what they had been in the time of *David*, and to have won victories over Damascus. He is routinely castigated for permitting idolatrous practices in the manner of his predecessors, and was criticized in an oracle delivered by the prophet *Amos*.

Jeshua

Jeshua, son of Jozadak, was the high priest in Jerusalem in the time of *Zerubbabel*. The name Jeshua appears in several places in the Books of Ezra and Nehemiah in the lists of those who returned from the Babylonian exile. It is not always clear how many of these mentions signify this single character, and how many are of others of the same name. Jeshua was certainly involved in the rebuilding first of the altar, and then of the temple itself, and seems also to have been associated with the preaching of *Ezra*.

Jeshua also features in the Book of Zechariah in two of the visions of *Zechariah*. In the first he appears initially with the Lord and Satan in mourning clothes, but is given fine vestments by an angel. This symbolizes the rehabilitation of the priesthood from its criticized position of earlier times to its due post of leadership in the community, provided always that the priests obeyed the Lord. The second passage describes the crowning of the "Branch," with Jeshua's name inserted as the recipient, when most biblical scholars believe that the original text would have had Zerubbabel being crowned. This may have happened because members of the priesthood later became the sole leaders of the community rather than being allied with the monarch.

The name is translated with the spelling Joshua throughout the Books

Left: A stained-glass window at Canterbury Cathedral tracing the Tree of Jesse. A favorite medieval device, this genealogical tree traces the generations of family members from Jesse to Christ.

of Haggai and Zechariah.

The name **Jeshua** is also used by minor personalities who appear in Chronicles as priests in the reigns of *David* and *Hezekiah*.

Jesse

Jesse was the father of *David*, and was a native of Bethlehem. After he had quarreled with *Saul*, the prophet *Samuel* was told by the Lord to visit Jesse in Bethlehem to anoint one of Jesse's sons as the king in succession to Saul. According to this passage, which appears in I Samuel 16, David was the youngest of Jesse's eight sons (of whom only three others are named), but a genealogy in I Chronicles describes Jesse as having seven sons (all named), with David again being the youngest. During his visit to the family the prophet examined and rejected all David's elder brothers and finally anointed David. The passage in Chronicles also names two daughters of Jesse, *Abigail* and Zeruiah.

Saul had become troubled by an evil spirit, and his servants suggested that he might be soothed if someone played the lyre to him during his difficult times. Saul agreed to this, and accepted a further suggestion from his servants that David was suitably skillful. Jesse sent him off to Saul, and David became popular and the king's armor-bearer.

Later, Saul's army was gathered to fight the Philistines, and was being menaced by the giant *Goliath*. Three of David's elder brothers were serving with the army, and Jesse sent David to them with food and to get news of how they were. This set in train the events which led to David killing Goliath.

Later still, when David had been outlawed following his quarrel with Saul, he sent Jesse and his mother to live in Moab for safety. Presumably there they would have joined the family of Jesse's grandmother, *Ruth*.

Jesus, son of Sirach

Jesus, son of Sirach, was the original

author of the deuterocanonical/apocryphal Book of Sirach, also known by its Latin title Ecclesiasticus (not to be confused with Ecclesiastes). The book was for many centuries known only in a Greek manuscript, but since the last years of the nineteenth century other manuscripts in Hebrew have been discovered, first in Cairo, and later among the Dead Sea Scrolls, which now cover about two-thirds of the book, and have largely confirmed the authenticity of the Greek text.

The preamble to the main text in Greek states that the book was written by Jesus, the translator's grandfather. The unnamed grandson came to Egypt in the thirty-eighth year of a King Euergetes, otherwise known as Ptolemy VII, and hence in 132 B.C. This would presumably place the writing of the book around 180 B.C., and this is consistent with internal details in the text also. The Book of Sirach is therefore one of the few in the Old Testament whose author is definitely known.

Jesus, son of Sirach, by his own account, was from Jerusalem, but had also traveled widely. In his book he praised people who devote themselves to the study of the divine law, and this seems to have been his own profession. He says that he composed his book ''for all who seek instruction,'' and his final advice to his readers is: ''Do your work in good time, and in his own time God will give you your reward.''

The book itself, one of the longest in the Bible, is a collection of what is usually called ''wisdom literature.'' It has many similarities to Proverbs, and is a varied collection of short sayings and discussions on a wide variety of topics of interest to the Jewish people. Many of the nuggets of which it is composed are short poems. Many of these praise the Lord and His wisdom, others discuss such virtues as charity and humility, and vices like pride and anger. There are extensive sections of the book on various aspects of the correct ordering of society, including substantial discussion of the subservient role he believed that women should have, as well as material advising respect for parents, generosity to the poor, and many other matters.

Jethro

Jethro was the father-in-law of *Moses*. His name is also variously given as *Reuel* and Hobab at different points in Exodus, Numbers and Judges. Alternatively, Hobab is described at one point as being the son of Reuel. It is not possible now to separate and clarify these different strands of the tradition.

Whatever the personality's name, his story is fairly clear. He is described as being a priest of the Midianites or Kenites. Moses first met his future wife and father-in-law when he fled from Egypt after he had killed an Egyptian for beating a Jew. Moses helped Jethro's daughters to water their sheep, was introduced to Jethro, and married one of the daughters, *Zipporah*. Moses lived with the family, working as a shepherd, and had a son, *Gershom*.

Moses decided to return to Egypt after seeing the vision of the burning bush. He next met Jethro during the Exodus, when Jethro came to the Israelites' camp, bringing with him Zipporah and Moses's two sons. (The birth of the second son, *Eliezer*, is not mentioned in the account.) Jethro was pleased to be reunited with Moses, and commented, '''Now I know that the Lord is greater than all gods because he delivered the people from the Egyptians.''' Jethro confirmed this opinion by offering sacrifices.

The next day Moses was giving judgment in various disputes, and Jethro advised him to lessen his workload by appointing junior judges to hear the less difficult cases. Moses took this advice.

Numbers 10 describes how Hobab was asked to guide the Israelite people in the wilderness. Here Hobab is described specifically as being Reuel's son but, as mentioned above, these two personalities cannot definitely be distinguished from each other or from Jethro.

Jezebel

Jezebel was the wife of King *Ahab* of Israel, and the daughter of Ethbaal, a Phoenician prince. She was a strong adherent of the cult of *Baal*, and tried to have all the true prophets in Israel killed and replaced with prophets of Baal. She kept 450 prophets of Baal in her household, as well as other religious attendants.

The prophet *Elijah* challenged Ahab to allow a contest of faith between himself and the 450. They were unable to bring fire to an offering when Elijah could. Elijah was therefore able to have them killed by the people. This made Jezebel furious, and Elijah again had to go into exile.

Later, Ahab began to covet a vineyard belonging to a man called *Naboth*, and was upset when Naboth refused to sell it. Jezebel sent forged instructions from the king arranging for Naboth to be falsely accused of blasphemy and judicially murdered.

Below: A fifteenth-century Flemish tapestry showing the death of Jezebel.

Ahab was thus able to take over the murdered man's property. For this crime the Lord instructed Elijah to curse Ahab and Jezebel, which he did, saying, "'The dogs shall eat Jezebel within the bounds of Jezreel.'"

In due course, when *Jehu* usurped the throne from *Jehoram (1)*, Ahab's second son, Jezebel met her death in a manner consistent with the curse. Jehu arrived at Jezreel where she was living, and had her thrown out of a high window to her death. Later he decided that, since she was a royal personage, she should have a decent burial. However, when he sent his servants to find her body, they could only find parts of it, indicating that the rest had indeed been eaten.

Below: Stothard's watercolors from the Painted Chamber at Westminster include the story of Joab and Abner.

Joab

Joab was *David*'s principal general. They were probably of a similar age, although David was Joab's uncle. Joab's mother, Zeruiah, was David's eldest sister, and her other sons, Joab's brothers, *Abishai* and *Asahel*, also figure importantly in the story.

Joab's role in David's entourage before David became king is not specifically mentioned anywhere in the Old Testament, but it seems certain that he accompanied David during his time as an outlaw. After the death of *Saul*, Joab became commander-in-chief, and led David's army into a battle with the supporters of *Ishbaal*, led by *Abner*. Abner killed Asahel in the aftermath of an inconclusive engagement. Later, after Abner had quarreled with Ishbaal, he tried to go over to David, but Joab accused him of treachery,

used a pretext to summon him to a private meeting, and killed him. David criticized Joab for this killing, but did not take any action over it.

Assisted by his brother, Abishai, Joab was successful in a campaign against an allied force of Arameans and Ammonites. Next David sent Joab and the army to besiege the Ammonite capital, Rabbah. While this campaign was going on, David fell in love with *Bathsheba*, wife of *Uriah*, and when she became pregnant, had Joab assist him in contriving Uriah's death.

Later, when *Absalom* was in exile following his revenge on Amnon for the rape of *Tamar (2)*, Joab managed to effect a reconciliation between the king and his son by arranging for a woman to consult David regarding a similar legal matter. Although Absalom returned, his conflict with David flared up again later into open

rebellion. Joab was one of the commanders who remained loyal to David. In the course of the decisive battle, Joab heard that Absalom was trapped with his hair caught in a tree, went to him and ruthlessly killed him, despite orders from David that Absalom should be spared.

David was distraught when he heard the news of Absalom's death. Joab reprimanded him for this, saying that David should be more grateful for the loyal service of his troops, and should thank them for it. David, however, decided to appoint Amasa as commander-in-chief in Joab's place, even though Amasa had supported Absalom. Joab took the earliest opportunity of a meeting with Amasa to kill him, and took over responsibility for the campaign against *Sheba*, son of Bichri, on which Amasa had been sent, bringing it to a successful conclusion.

In David's old age Joab finally abandoned his support and transferred his allegiance to *Adonijah*, but David's party were successful in establishing *Solomon*'s right to the throne, and Adonijah's claim collapsed. David's deathbed instruction to Solomon included an order to have Joab killed because of his murder of Abner and Amasa. Joab tried to take sanctuary in the temple, but *Benaiah* killed him on Solomon's orders.

Joash

1. When Joash was a baby, his father, *Ahaziah (2)*, was killed by *Jehu* in Jehu's revolt against *Jehoram (1)*. Joash's grandmother, *Athaliah*, decided to take the opportunity to wipe out the rest of the family and seize the throne of Judah for herself. Joash was the only male member of the family to escape, being hidden by his aunt (or sister), Jehosheba, and the priest Jehoiada.

When he was seven years old, Jehoiada arranged for him to be anointed in the temple, protected by the royal guards and the Levites. When Athaliah heard the noise of the ceremony she went to investigate, was killed, and Joash became king.

Joash reigned for a total of 40 years, being guided throughout the earlier years by Jehoiada. Joash became concerned that the temple was not being properly repaired, and set up a system for passing the taxes raised for the temple direct to the workmen who carried out the maintenance. After Jehoiada's death, however, he became lax in his religious policies, and idolatrous practices were renewed. Joash had Jehoiada's son, *Zechariah*, who was also a priest, executed when he complained about this.

In punishment for this crime, Joash was attacked and defeated by *Hazael* of Aram-Damascus and, according to Kings, had to buy off the attack by giving the attackers valuable items from the temple. According to Chronicles, Joash was also wounded in the campaign. Whether this was the case or not, both accounts describe a conspiracy against him by two of his leading officials, who killed him and set his son *Amaziah* on the throne.

2. The second Joash was the son of *Jehoahaz (1)*, and succeeded his father as king of Israel, reigning *c.* 800-785 B.C. During his father's reign, Israel had lost territory to the advances of *Hazael* of Aram-Damascus. Joash continued the struggle with Hazael's son and successor, *Ben-hadad (3)*.

Shortly before the prophet *Elisha* died, Joash came to visit him. Elisha told Joash to take a bow and shoot an arrow out of the window. Elisha then told him that the arrow was symbolic of victory over Aram, and that Joash should strike the ground with the other arrows that he had. Joash did this three times, which angered Elisha because, he said, the action should have been repeated five or six times. As a consequence, Elisha predicted, and it transpired, that Joash would win three battles but would not triumph overall. By his victories he regained some of the territory his father had lost.

Joash's contemporary as king of Judah for much of his reign was *Amaziah*. After Amaziah had been successful in a battle against the Edomites to the south, he provoked a quarrel with Israel to the north. Joash tried to avoid conflict, but when it developed he defeated Amaziah's army at Bethshemesh, captured Amaziah, advanced to Jerusalem, destroyed part of the city wall, and took away gold and silver from the temple, and other treasure.

Joash was also the name of *Gideon*'s father, who refused to kill his son when Gideon destroyed an altar that Joash had made to *Baal*. **Joash** is the name of several other people in the Old Testament too. The name Joash is sometimes spelled as Jehoash.

Job

The Book of Job is one of the masterpieces of ancient literature, and Job himself is its central character. It is not known when the Book was written (it may have been in the fifth or fourth century B.C., but earlier or later dates are possible), but it is generally believed to have been developed from an older folk tale concerning a pious and rich individual who was tested with misfortunes by the Lord and eventually proved worthy. The Book consists of brief introductory and concluding sections in prose, and a long central section in verse, discussing the role of suffering in the human condition and its place in the divinely-ordained system.

At the outset Job is described as being "blameless and upright" and rich. The Lord pointed out these qualities to Satan, who replied that it is easy for one as well-off as Job to remain righteous. Satan was therefore allowed to make Job suffer, by inflicting misfortunes on his family and his possessions. At first Job was patient and accepted this: "the Lord gave and the Lord has taken away; blessed be the name of the Lord." Satan then suggested that Job would not remain virtuous if he was afflicted personally. Job was given a dreadful skin disease, but he still accepted his situation, rebuking his wife for her failure to do so too.

Job was then joined by three friends, *Eliphaz, Bildad* and *Zophar*, who were shocked by his appearance. After they had sat by him for seven days, Job broke down and railed against his misfortune, cursing the day of his birth. At this point a poetic debate between Job and his friends began. Job's constant cry to his friends and to the Lord throughout was "'make me understand how I have gone wrong.'" Or again he said, "'If I sin, what do I do to you, you watcher of humanity? Why have you made me your target? Why have I become a burden to you? Why do you not pardon my transgression and take away my iniquity?'" In his despair, he accused the Lord of mocking the innocent and making no distinction between the blameless and the wicked, and then he turned on his friends, calling them "miserable comforters".

The friends in turn reminded Job of the mercy of the Lord, and suggested that his punishment must be deserved

Above: Job and his Friends – a fresco by Giotto at the Campo Santo in Pisa.

because of some wickedness, but he denied this steadfastly. Eventually the three gave up the argument and were replaced by *Elihu*, who told Job that humans cannot expect to comprehend the reasons for all that the Lord does, and reminded him that the Lord may use trouble to test his people.

Finally, the Lord answered Job, speaking "out of a whirlwind", listing His heavenly powers and questioning Job's presumption in doubting these. Job realized his fault, repented, and was rewarded, "and the Lord gave Job twice as much as he had before."

Jochebed

Jochebed was the wife of *Amram* and the mother of *Miriam, Aaron* and *Moses*. Like her husband, she was of Levite descent and, according to a genealogy in Exodus 6, she was her husband's aunt. After *Pharaoh (3)* had ordered that all male Israelite children were to be thrown into the Nile, Jochebed gave birth to a baby boy. She hid him in a waterproofed basket among the reeds on the river bank while his unnamed sister (presumably Miriam) watched from nearby. Pharaoh's daughter found the baby, and his quick-thinking sister arranged with her that Jochebed would act as his wet nurse. When the boy was older, Jochebed returned him to pharaoh's daughter, and she named him Moses.

Joel

The Old Testament gives no personal information about the prophet Joel, other than that the name of his father was Pethuel (and nothing beyond the name is known of Pethuel). From detailed examination of the text, most students of the Bible suggest that the book dates from around 400 B.C. The text of the book falls into two distinct sections, and some believe that these are the work of different authors, others that it was principally by a single author – presumably Joel, who is only mentioned in the first verse.

The first section describes an invasion of Judah and Jerusalem by a plague of locusts, which brings great devastation and confirms the need for repentance, fasting, and prayer. The description of the locusts might very well be based on actual experience of such an invasion, and might not simply be a metaphorical device. The second section of the book is an apocalyptic vision, describing how Israel will be restored: "I will pour out my spirit on all flesh; your sons and your daughters shall prophesy, your old men shall dream dreams, and your young men shall see visions." All the other nations will be brought to the "valley of Jehosaphat", and there judged and punished for their wickedness, and for their oppression of the Israelites.

Joel is also a fairly common name elsewhere in the Old Testament, borne by one of the corrupt sons of *Samuel*, and by 12 other personalities.

Johanan

Johanan was an army commander in the period immediately after the capture of Jerusalem by *Nebuchadnezzar*. He was one of a number of leaders who had not yet surrendered to the Babylonians who went to see *Gedaliah*, the governor appointed by the conquerors, to be told that they could expect good treatment.

Johanan warned Gedaliah not to trust *Ishmael (2)*, but despite this warning Ishmael killed the governor shortly afterward. Johanan and his forces pursued Ishmael and freed the captives that he had carried away. However, Johanan and his companions worried that the sequence of events would anger the Babylonians, and decided that they should go to Egypt. They consulted the prophet *Jeremiah* for advice, and he warned against leaving Judah, but they decided to ignore this and went anyway, taking Jeremiah with them.

The name **Johanan** is borne by several other minor personalities in the Old Testament, two of them being soldiers in the time of *Saul* and *David*.

Jonah

The story of Jonah and the whale is in some respects one of the best known of the Old Testament. A prophet Jonah is mentioned in a single verse in II Kings, but nothing more is mentioned about him outside the Book of Jonah itself. Biblical scholars do not agree about when the Book of Jonah was written, but generally believe that it does not represent the biography of a single individual, but should rather be read as a parable commenting on the nature of divine forgiveness and repentance.

The story relates how the Lord called on Jonah to "'Go at once to Nineveh, that great city, and cry out against it: for their wickedness has come up before me.'" Jonah tried to avoid the task by running away on a ship bound from Joppa (modern Jaffa) to Tarshish (possibly in Spain). The ship was caught in a storm and, partly at his own suggestion, the crew threw Jonah overboard to try to appease the Lord and calm the storm. This was successful, but at the same time the Lord sent a large fish to swallow Jonah. It is worth noting that the biblical texts are quite clear on the description of a large or great fish, and not a whale, as in the popular version of the event.

After spending three days and nights inside the belly of the fish,

Below: Jonah is flung to the whale by the crew of the ship in an attempt to appease the Lord and thus halt the storm.

Jonah was vomited up onto dry land, but not before he had confirmed in prayer his recognition of divine power. He was then sent again to Nineveh, and preached so successfully against the wickedness there that the king and all his people repented, causing the Lord to change his mind and decide not to punish the city. Jonah was angry, and decided to sit where he could see the city and what would become of it. The Lord first gave him the shade of a bush to protect him from the sun and hot wind, and then destroyed the bush, leaving Jonah exposed to great discomfort. The Lord then explained that just as Jonah was concerned at the loss of the bush, then He was concerned not to destroy the city without very good cause.

One theme that scholars have noted in the story of Jonah is that foreigners as well as the people of Israel can expect to benefit from the forgiveness of the Lord. As well as this, it can be interpreted as a call for true repentance within Israel itself since, if even the wicked city of Nineveh can be forgiven, so too can Israel for her sins.

Jonathan

Jonathan was the eldest of *Saul*'s four sons by his wife, Ahinoam. When Saul became king, Jonathan was quickly established as one of the leading soldiers in his army, winning a victory over the Philistines at Geba. The Philistines retaliated with an advance toward Michmash, and Saul and Jonathan were only able to oppose them with a small force. The Israelites were in a dangerous situation until Jonathan, assisted only by his young armor-bearer, made a personal sortie against the enemy. They came upon a small group of Philistines and killed about 20 of them. This minor attack nonetheless threw the whole Philistine army into a panic. Saul, who had not known of Jonathan's decision to attack, decided after some delay to follow it up, and the Philistines were routed.

In the pursuit Jonathan happened to find some honey and ate a little of it, not knowing that his father had made a vow that no one in the army would eat that day. At the end of the day Saul consulted a priest for an oracle to decide whether the pursuit should be continued into the night. No answer was given, and so Saul realized that some sin must have been committed. Saul discovered by drawing lots that Jonathan was responsible, and was ready to execute him when he was stopped by an outcry from the people in Jonathan's favor.

When *David* came to see Saul after the death of *Goliath*, Jonathan immediately gave him presents and became his close friend. Saul, however, quickly became jealous of David because of David's growing popularity from his repeated military successes against the Philistines. Saul feared that David might supplant him, and tried both directly to kill him and indirectly to contrive his death. Jonathan tried to persuade his father not to do this.

Eventually David had to go into hiding, but he and Jonathan made a further attempt to effect a reconciliation with Saul. They planned this in a secret meeting in a field, and arranged a code of signals by which Jonathan would communicate to David how he had got on. Jonathan spoke to Saul at a feast, but Saul became very angry and even tried to kill Jonathan. Jonathan went back to meet David, and the two parted sadly. Later, during David's time as an outlaw, the two had a further secret meeting, at which Jonathan promised David that David would succeed Saul, and that Jonathan would support him in this.

Jonathan was with Saul at his final battle at Mount Gilboa at which Jonathan and two of his brothers died with their father. The Philistines took all their bodies, mutilated them and put them on display, but men from Jabesh, the scene of Saul's first victory, came by night and removed the bodies for proper burial.

Jonathan was also the name of a number of other personalities in the Old Testament, including at least one member of David's family and several of David's supporters.

Jonathan the Maccabee

Jonathan was the youngest son of *Mattathias*, and took over the leadership of the Maccabean revolt after the death of his brother, *Judas*. By skillful diplomacy over a number of years, exploiting the divisions between rival Seleucid kings, Jonathan regained control of Jerusalem and became recognized as the high priest. Jonathan even negotiated a renewed alliance with Rome. Eventually, however, he was captured and later executed by Trypho, one of the contenders for the Seleucid throne. His brother, *Simon*, succeeded him as the Jewish leader.

Below: Jonathan takes his leave of David; a woodcut by Georg Wigand of Leipzig, published in 1869. David and Jonathan were firm friends, despite the hostility of Saul.

reprimanded him for this, but did not forget the incident.

Later Joseph was sent to join his brothers when they were away from home with the flocks. They plotted to kill him, except for *Reuben*, who suggested putting him in a pit rather than hurting him directly. Reuben planned to release Joseph later and return him safely to Jacob. *Judah* also suggested selling Joseph into slavery rather than hurting him, and this duly occurred. Reuben was distressed at what had happened, but all the brothers agreed to conceal it from their father, tearing Joseph's coat and covering it in goat's blood to make it look like he had been killed by a wild animal. Joseph was in the meantime taken away and sold as a slave in Egypt.

In Egypt Joseph became the property of *Potiphar*, commander of the royal guard. Joseph did well in Potiphar's service, and became the head of his household. Joseph also matured to become good-looking, and Potiphar's wife became attracted to him. When Joseph refused her advances, she told Potiphar that Joseph had tried to seduce her.

Potiphar had Joseph thrown into prison where again his talents were recognized, and he was soon helping the governor. Some time later two important members of the royal court were also imprisoned because they had offended pharaoh [*Pharaoh (2)*]. They had dreams, which Joseph correctly interpreted as presaging execution for one, and a pardon for the other. The cupbearer, who was the one released and restored to his position, promised to remember Joseph, but forgot to do anything about him for the next two years.

Left: King Joram [also known as Jehoram (I)].

Below: Joseph's brothers show his blood-stained coat to Jacob; from the Golden Haggaddah.

Joram

Joram is an alternative spelling of *Jehoram*, used for both important personalities of that name.

Joseph

Joseph was the elder son of *Jacob* and *Rachel*, Jacob's second and favorite wife. Joseph was born after his father had already had ten sons, by *Leah*, his other wife, and by his two concubines. Later a full brother to Joseph, *Benjamin*, was born, but Rachel died in childbirth.

As a youth Joseph helped his half-brothers with the family's flocks, but told tales about them to Jacob. Jacob loved Joseph more than his other children "because he was the son of his old age", and accordingly gave him a present of a valuable and distinctive robe. (This was the "coat of many colors" which appears in older translations, now thought to be not strictly correct in this wording.) Joseph annoyed his half-brothers still further by telling them of two dreams he had had which clearly seemed to predict that he would later dominate them. Jacob

Above: Joseph is cast into the pit; a miniature from the Golden Haggadah, a medieval Jewish manuscript.

At that time pharaoh had two disquieting dreams, of seven fat cows being eaten by seven thin ones, and of seven thin and diseased ears of corn eating seven plump ones. All his magicians and wise men were unable to interpret these. The cupbearer then remembered Joseph's talents in this respect, and Joseph was brought from prison and shaved and cleaned up before being taken to pharaoh. Joseph told him that the dreams were identical in significance, foretelling seven years of plenty ahead, to be followed by seven years of famine. Joseph advised pharaoh to put someone in charge of storing surplus food in the good years, to cope with the famine to come. Pharaoh gave Joseph the job, appointing him as chief minister throughout Egypt. Pharaoh gave Joseph an Egyptian name, Zaphenath-paneah, and arranged a marriage for him to *Asenath*, daughter of Potiphera, a priest of On. They had two sons, *Manasseh* and *Ephraim*.

Joseph duly set in train measures to store stocks of food in the good years. When the famine came, it affected the whole region, and not just Egypt. Jacob and his family needed grain, and he sent Joseph's ten half-brothers to Egypt to try to buy some, keeping Benjamin at home. When they arrived they had to come to Joseph to make the purchase. He was now so grand that they did not recognize him, but he knew them. He initially treated them harshly, accusing them of being spies, so that they would tell him more about how the family was getting on in their attempts to establish their bona-fide background.

To test their story of an aged father and a younger brother left at home, Joseph told them that he would sell them the grain, but one of them would have to remain behind until the rest returned bringing their younger brother. Reuben told his brothers that these problems were a punishment for their treatment of Joseph. He spoke in the brothers' own language (the negotiation for the corn was being conducted through interpreters), not realizing that Joseph could hear and understand what he was saying. Joseph was touched by what Reuben had said.

Joseph duly selected *Simeon* to remain behind, and added a further test for the remaining brothers by giving orders to his assistants secretly to place the brothers' grain money back in the sacks with the grain they were to receive. They did not discover this until they had returned home to Jacob. At first he forbade them to return with Benjamin, saying that he had first lost Joseph and now Simeon, and that he could not bear to lose a third son. Reuben and then Judah tried to persuade Jacob to change his mind, which he eventually did when supplies had again run short. Jacob gave them presents to take to the Egyptian official, as well as the money that had been returned and more.

When they got back to Egypt, Joseph invited them to dine with him, astonishing them when he had them served in the correct order of their birth, and also ensuring that Benjamin was given far better food. Joseph was only able to control his emotions by leaving the room for a time at the start of the meal.

As a final test, when the brothers were ready to leave, Joseph again ordered his steward to put all the brothers' money in the grain sacks and to put his silver divining cup in Benjamin's sack. After they had left, Joseph sent his steward after them to accuse them of theft. They denied this, of course, but the cup was found as soon as a search was made. They were brought back to Joseph, and Judah made an eloquent plea to be punished instead of Benjamin: "'please let your servant remain as a slave to my lord in place of the boy; and let the boy go back with his brothers. For how can I go back to my father if the boy is not with me? I fear to see the suffering that would come upon my father.'"

At this point Joseph broke down and revealed his identity. The brothers were at first worried that he might seek revenge, but Joseph reassured them that he accepted that he had been brought to Egypt by God to preserve life, and that he did not attach any blame to them. Joseph told the brothers to go home and bring their father back with them to live in Egypt. This invitation was confirmed by pharaoh.

Jacob was overjoyed when he heard that Joseph was still alive, and set out to bring the whole family to Egypt. They were happily reunited. Joseph recommended to pharaoh that the family be allowed to settle in the Goshen area, and pharaoh put them in charge of the royal cattle.

The famine continued, with Joseph first selling grain to the people as long as they had money, then bartering it for their livestock, and finally exchanging it for title to their land. Only the priests and the temple lands stood outside this process, by which pharaoh became the owner of all land in the country. Joseph allowed the people to keep possession of their land, giving them seed also, in return for which they were to pay a tax of a fifth of all their produce to pharaoh.

Jacob and all the brothers lived in Egypt for 17 years, but when Jacob felt his death approaching, he first summoned Joseph, Ephraim and Manasseh to him for a blessing. Joseph was annoyed and tried to correct his father when Jacob put his right hand on Ephraim, the younger of the two. Jacob told him that this was not an accident, and that Ephraim's descendants would be more numerous and important. Jacob then blessed all Joseph's brothers in turn and, before he died, instructed them to bury him in the family tomb at Machpelah. Joseph arranged for the body to be embalmed, and then asked pharaoh, and was granted, a lavish escort for the long and elaborate funeral journey.

When the funeral was over, Joseph and his brothers returned to Egypt and the brothers again became concerned that he still bore a grudge over what had once been done to him. They therefore told Joseph that Jacob had asked them to ask him for forgiveness. Joseph's reply was kind and reassuring: "'Do not be afraid! Am I in the place of God? Even though you intended to do harm to me, God intended it for good, in order to preserve a numerous people, as he is doing today.'"

The whole family continued to live in Egypt, until Joseph's death at the age of 110 and beyond. Before he died, Joseph had them promise that when the time came to return to the land promised to Abraham, that they would take his bones with them. In due course Joseph's bones were taken from Egypt during the Exodus and buried at Shechem.

The tribes of Israel took their names from those of Joseph and his brother and half-brothers. The list of names is not consistent in the various places in the Old Testament in which it occurs. In some places Joseph is described as a single tribe, while in others Ephraim and Manasseh are each individual tribes, while in yet others the tribe of Benjamin forms part of the house of Joseph. The "Joseph tribes" were those which later mainly composed the kingdom of Israel, as distinct from Judah.

The story of Joseph seems to have been compiled from a number of different traditions – the slight confusion as to whether he was sold into slavery by his brothers, or taken away by the slavers without their knowledge, is one example of this. It is likely that much of the story is a pious fiction embodying many such strands of tradition. The Egyptian names found in the story, for example, are more characteristic of roughly the tenth century B.C. rather than the much earlier period in which a historical Joseph would have lived. The message of the story seems to be strongly to urge reconciliation between the tribes of Israel rather than continuing their all too common quarrels.

The name **Joseph** is also borne by three other minor personalities in the Old Testament.

Joshua

Joshua was the successor of *Moses* to the leadership of the Israelite people, and was responsible for taking them across the Jordan to settle finally in the Promised Land. He is the leading character described in the Book of Joshua, but also played a prominent role during the Exodus, as described in Exodus, Deuteronomy, and Numbers. His father was Nun, and he came from the tribe of Ephraim.

Joshua first came to prominence shortly after the Israelites had left Egypt. In the desert they were attacked at Rephidim by the Amalekites, and Moses ordered Joshua to recruit men to fight the battle, which he won. It was, however, crucial to this success that Moses, who was watching, kept his arms raised in the air throughout, which he was assisted in doing by *Aaron* and Hur. Joshua is also mentioned in association with Moses immediately before and after Moses was given the Ten Commandments on Mount Sinai.

When the Israelites first arrived in the land of Canaan, Joshua was one of the 12 scouts sent ahead to survey the land and assess the defensive strength of its inhabitants. Joshua and *Caleb* were the only ones of the 12 who were not daunted by the powerful natives. As a punishment for the timidity of the others, who showed a lack of trust in the divine providence, the Lord condemned the Israelites to a further 40 years of wandering in the wilderness. Of the Israelites living at the time of the first arrival at Canaan, only Joshua and Caleb were to survive to enter the Promised Land. Before the entry to the Promised Land could take place, Moses formally passed over the leadership of the people to Joshua.

Joshua's first objective in his invasion was to capture Jericho. His spies were helped in their initial foray by *Rahab*, a prostitute in the town. The people crossed the Jordan as the advance began, aided by a miraculous stopping of the waters. A memorial to the crossing was set up, and Joshua also had all the men circumcised, since this important custom had been in abeyance in the years in the desert. The Passover was celebrated, and the Israelites found that the supply of manna that had sustained them throughout their wanderings now ceased, since they could begin to live off the produce of Canaan.

The Lord then gave Joshua precise instructions on how to capture Jericho. The army marched around the town each day for six days, with the Ark carried in their midst and priests blowing horns. On the seventh day they marched round seven times, and on a signal the whole force shouted out. This brought the city walls tumbling down. Everyone in the city was killed in the assault that followed, except Rahab and her family.

Next to be attacked was the town of Ai. The first attempt was repulsed because, as Joshua discovered, someone had illicitly kept loot from Jericho.

Joshua found out that a certain *Achan* was the guilty party, and he was executed. Joshua planned his next attack on Ai carefully. He induced the people of the town to advance against a part of his force, pretended to retreat, and trapped them with the remainder of his army. Joshua celebrated the victory by building an altar and offering sacrifice strictly according to the prescribed ritual.

The Gibeonites next made a treaty with Joshua, tricking him into deciding not to attack them, but were condemned to become "hewers of wood and drawers of water for all the congregation." The king of Jerusalem formed an alliance to attack the Gibeonites for giving in to the Israelites, but

Joshua led a force to protect them and won another decisive victory, aided by a great hail storm inflicted by the Lord. The king and his allies were all killed. A series of further victories is then recounted, culminating in a triumph over King Jabin of Hazor. Finally, after other battles, "the land had rest from war."

The next task was to divide the conquered land between the various tribes of Israel. Much of the second half of the Book of Joshua is a detailed listing of how this was done. Joshua had the leading role in making the allotment at the Lord's command, but was assisted by the priest *Eleazar*, Aaron's son.

When Joshua had grown old, he spoke to the elders of the people,

reminding them how they had only achieved their victories and gained their land with the assistance of the Lord. He warned them to continue to obey the law, and in particular to avoid intermarrying with the native Canaanites, and certainly not to worship their gods.

Joshua died at the age of 110, and was buried on his own portion of the allotted land at Timnath-serah in the territory of the tribe of Ephraim, to which he belonged.

Another **Joshua**, a priest in the Books of Haggai and Zechariah, is otherwise known as *Jeshua* in Ezra and Nehemiah.

Josiah

Josiah was the son and successor of *Amon* as king of Judah. His mother was Adaiah. Almost alone of the kings who ruled Israel and Judah, the picture given of Josiah is wholly favorable. He is commended in the brief mention of him in Jeremiah as being fair and just. In the fuller, broadly similar, accounts given in II Kings 22-23 and II Chronicles 34-35 he is also praised: "Before him there was no king like him, who turned to the Lord with all his heart, with all his soul, with all his might, according to all the law of Moses; nor did any like him arise after him."

Josiah was eight years old when he succeeded to the throne after the assassination of his father. He reigned from 640-609 B.C. He is principally remembered for various religious reforms undertaken during his reign. Chronicles places the early development of his religious zeal to the eighth year, when he "began to seek the God of his ancestor", while in the twelfth year "he began to purge Judah and Jerusalem of the high places, the sacred poles, and the carved and the cast images." Both Chronicles and Kings are agreed, however, that the reforms saw their full development from the eighteenth year of his reign.

In that year he seems to have had a program of repair work for the temple set in motion, and sent one of his court officials, Shaphan, to the temple to take charge of payments for the work. While Shaphan was there, the high priest, Hilkiah, drew to his attention an

Left: Joshua commands the sun to stand still during battle with the king of Jerusalem and his allies. This ruse won him more time.

Above: A woodcut of 1495 shows the walls of Jericho tumbling down.

Below: The young King Josiah.

ancient book of the Law that had been found, presumably in the course of the repairs. When this was brought to the king he was distraught to discover how far the religious practices of his time had diverged from what had previously been laid down. Josiah sent to enquire of the prophetess Huldah what the outcome of this would be. She told him that the Lord would punish Judah, but only after his death.

Josiah therefore set in train a comprehensive cleansing of all the evil practices that had grown up throughout the land. All pagan altars and images were removed from the temple in Jerusalem and were burned outside the city. The false priests were all killed, and the house of the male temple prostitutes destroyed. He then repeated the process in a comprehensive trip around the country, visiting Bethel, Beer-sheba, Geba, and other heathen shrines, and defiling or destroying them all. When this was done he celebrated the Passover according to the strict dictates of the Law, ensuring that each group of the Levites fulfilled its proper role.

Modern commentaries suggest that the Law book found in the temple may have been an early version of what is now the Book of Deuteronomy, and it has also been suggested that sections of the Books of Joshua and Kings may have first been composed at this time to support Josiah's religious reforms.

Political conditions of the time may also have contributed to Josiah's work. The Assyrian Empire that had been dominant in the region for many years was in decline, and Josiah's religious changes would scarcely have been possible if Assyrian control was still strong. However, Josiah fell foul of precisely these political developments. The Egyptians under *Neco* tried to assert their power in the region as Assyria crumbled, and Josiah was killed in an encounter with Neco in 609. The account in Kings does not say how Josiah died, and some historians suggest that he may have been assassinated, but Chronicles describes in detail his death in a battle at Megiddo.

Jotham

Jotham was the eleventh king of Judah after the split between Judah and Israel. He is first mentioned as acting as regent for his father, *Uzziah*, when Uzziah was suffering from leprosy in his final years. Jotham reigned in his own right *c*. 742-736 B.C. He is mentioned mainly in II Kings 15 and II Chronicles 27.

He is described as doing what was right in the sight of the Lord personally, but not being zealous enough to correct corrupt practices among the ordinary people. Little else is said about his reign, apart from his building of the upper gate of the temple, and his conduct of a successful military campaign against the Ammonites.

A second **Jotham** was the youngest son of *Gideon*, who escaped the massacre of his brothers by *Abimelech*, and prophesied Abimelech's eventual downfall.

Jubal

Jubal appears in Genesis 4 as the "ancestor of all those who play the lyre and pipe." Like his brother, *Jabal*, and his cousin, *Tubal-cain*, he was descended from *Cain*.

Judah

Judah was the fourth son of *Jacob* and *Leah*, his first wife. Judah persuaded his brothers and half-brothers to sell *Joseph* into slavery, rather than kill him, after they had become jealous of the favorable treatment that Joseph

Left: King Jotham of Judah.

received from their father.

Judah married a Canaanite woman, and they had three sons, Er, *Onan*, and Shelah. Er and Onan were married successively to *Tamar (1)* who, according to the legal custom of the time, should also have been married after their deaths to Shelah. Judah did not make arrangements for this and, in order to have the children to which she was entitled, Tamar disguised herself as a prostitute and solicited Judah. When her consequent pregnancy became known, Judah was angry with his daughter-in-law but, when he was revealed as the father, Judah accepted that she was right, and acknowledged the twin children, *Perez* and *Zerah*.

Later, Judah and his brothers and half-brothers went to buy grain from Egypt during a famine, meeting Joseph once again. After *Benjamin* had been falsely accused of stealing a silver cup, Judah offered to take his punishment for him so as not to break their father Jacob's heart. This act convinced Joseph of the reformed characters of his half-brothers, and he revealed his true identity. Judah and his descendants were with the family when they returned to join Joseph in

Egypt. The tribe of Israel named Judah traced its name and descent from him, as the other tribes did from his brothers and half-brothers.

Several other personalities of the name **Judah** are found in the Books of Ezra and Nehemiah.

Judas the Maccabee

Judas was the son of *Mattathias*, and became the principal leader of the early stages of the Maccabean revolt. He appears in the deuterocanonical/apocryphal First and Second Books of Maccabees. (The books known as Third and Fourth Maccabees are not considered to be canonical in the Protestant, Roman Catholic, or Jewish faiths, and are not discussed here or in the other entries on Judas's family.)

The revolt began when Mattathias killed a government official and, when he died the next year, Judas became the military leader of what was at first a guerrilla band. In his first important victory he defeated and killed Appolonius, governor of the province of Samaria, and then beat a larger army under Seron. Following another success, the Maccabeans were able to enter Jerusalem, where they rededicated and purified the temple. This time of great celebration is still remembered in the feast of Hanukkah.

Various campaigns followed over the ensuing years, with Judas being forced to leave Jerusalem, but his army still remaining very much in being. He won another important victory in 161 B.C. over a general called Nicanor, but was killed in a defeat at Elasa the next year. The revolt did not end, for he was succeeded by his brothers *Simon* and *Jonathan*. His epitaph was "How is the mighty fallen, the savior of Israel!"

Judith

1. Judith was one of the Hittite wives of *Esau*, whom he married to the anger of his parents, *Isaac* and *Rebekah*. Judith's father was Beeri. The naming of Esau's wives is not consistent in the various parts of Genesis in which they appear. (See the entry on *Esau*.)

2. Judith is the heroine of the deuterocanonical/apocryphal book of the same name. The Book of Judith is believed to have been written near the end of the second century B.C., and the events it supposedly describes are set in the time of *Nebuchadnezzar*, more than 400 years before. The historical details, and many of the geographical ones, given in the book do not correspond with what is known from other sources, and the book is generally regarded as effectively a historical novel, with moral and instructional content.

The Book of Judith tells how Judea was attacked by an Assyrian army under a general called Holofernes. The city of Bethulia was besieged and nearly starved into surrender. Judith, a pious widow living in the city, set about ingratiating herself with the would-be conquerors. Holofernes lusted after her, and Judith arranged to be alone with him. He had become drunk at a feast and, taking advantage of this, she used his sword to cut off his head, which she and her servant then smuggled out of the enemy camp. The next morning, when the Judeans made a show of mounting a sortie against the besiegers, soldiers went to Holofernes's tent to wake him, found his headless body, and set in train a panic that routed the Assyrian army.

Right: Korah and his accomplices come to a violent end; an engraving by Doré.

Below: Judith with the Head of Holofernes, by Lucas Cranach.

Kish

Kish was the father of King *Saul*. He was of the tribe of *Benjamin*, and was rich. According to one of the variant accounts in I Samuel, Saul first came to prominence when he went to meet *Samuel* to ask for advice during a long search for strayed donkeys belonging to his father.

Korah

Korah was the leader of a rebellion against *Moses* and *Aaron*, complaining about their rule. Korah and his accomplices were swallowed up by the earth and consumed in fire. The leadership of Moses and Aaron was also miraculously confirmed when a cut branch marked with Aaron's name began to sprout buds (Numbers 16 & 17).

Laban

Laban was the brother of *Rebekah*, and father-in-law of *Jacob*. He first appears in Genesis 24, where he took part in the negotiation with *Abraham*'s servant over the prospective marriage of Rebekah and *Isaac*. He lived in Paddan-aram in Mesopotamia, some distance away from Isaac and Rebekah.

After Rebekah and Jacob had angered *Esau* by fooling Isaac into giving Jacob his blessing, Rebekah sent Jacob to live with Laban for safety, also hoping that Jacob would find a wife there among his kinfolk. On his arrival Jacob met *Rachel*, Laban's daughter, and helped her to water her father's sheep. She told her father of Jacob's arrival, and Laban made him welcome.

Jacob fell in love with Rachel and

made a deal with Laban that he would work for him for seven years in return for being allowed to marry her. When the time for the wedding came, however, Laban substituted his elder daughter, *Leah*, at night after the wedding feast. Jacob slept with her, and did not discover the change until the morning. Jacob protested to Laban, but Laban told him it was wrong that the younger sister should be married first. They agreed that Jacob should also marry Rachel in return for another seven years' service to Laban.

After some years, and the birth of various children to Jacob and his wives and concubines, Jacob told Laban that he wished to leave his service, but Laban replied that instead he should name a fair wage for himself. Jacob said that he should receive all the black and spotted sheep and goats out of Laban's flocks as his share of their growing prosperity. Laban agreed to this, but tried to hide the appropriate animals from Jacob. However, Jacob was too clever for him and contrived,

miraculously, that the best of the flock should come to him.

This process eventually brought hostility toward Jacob from Laban's sons, and Jacob decided to return to his homeland. Laban was away shearing his sheep when Jacob left without warning, and Rachel also stole her father's household gods. Laban set off after them when he heard of this three days later, but the Lord warned him in a dream that he should not harm Jacob. When he caught up with Jacob he asked for an explanation for the secret departure, not even giving Laban time to say goodbye to his daughters and grandchildren, and in particular for an explanation for the theft of the gods. Jacob said that he was afraid that Laban might prevent his daughters leaving, and absolutely denied stealing the gods, since he did not know that Rachel had done this.

Laban was allowed to search for the gods, but did not find them because Rachel had them hidden. Jacob criticized Laban for his lack of gratitude for

Above: The Reconciliation of Jacob and Laban, by Johann Wolfgang Baumgartner.

his long service, and the two agreed to make a covenant of peace. Laban had Jacob promise not to ill-treat his wives and not to marry again, and they also set up a cairn of stones to mark a boundary which neither would pass. The following morning Laban blessed Leah, Rachel, and his grandchildren, and returned home.

Aspects of the story of Laban and Jacob conform to the customs prevailing in northern Mesopotamia around the time when they are believed to have lived, or at least the time from which their stories may originate. Excavations in the 1920s at the ancient city of Nuzi, near modern Kirkuk in Iraq, found numerous stone tablets delineating aspects of the law and customs of the Hurrian people prominent in the area in the middle of the second millennium B.C. The importance of a deathbed blessing such as Jacob received, employment contracts similar to Jacob's with Laban, servants taking the place of a wife who could not have children, and the passing on of family gods from father to daughters in certain circumstances but not in others (as with Laban and Rachel), all figure in these finds.

Leah

Leah was the elder daughter of *Laban*, and the first wife of *Jacob*. When Jacob arrived to live with Laban and his family and look for a wife, he met and fell in love with *Rachel*, Leah's younger sister, who was the more attractive of the two. Jacob worked for Laban for seven years in order to marry Rachel, but Laban substituted Leah for her sister on their wedding night, because he said it was improper for the younger sister to be married first. Jacob was angry, but agreed to marry both sisters in return for another seven years of work.

Jacob did not love Leah, but in recompense the Lord gave her children and did not give Rachel any at first. Leah had four sons, *Reuben, Simeon, Levi* and *Judah*. Leah thought then that her childbearing days were over and, as Jacob had already had children by Rachel's maid, *Bilhah*, Leah in turn gave him her maid, *Zilpah*. Jacob and Zilpah had two sons, *Gad* and *Asher*. According to the custom of the times these two were also considered to be legally the sons of Leah.

Later Leah gave Rachel some mandrakes that Reuben had collected, in order to be allowed to sleep with Jacob again, and she had two further sons, *Issachar* and *Zebulun*, and a daughter, *Dinah*.

When Jacob moved back to his homeland because of his treatment by Laban, Leah and her sister both went with him, agreeing that their father had acted badly. Later, when she died, Jacob buried her in the family tomb at Machpelah.

Levi

Levi was the third son of *Jacob* and *Leah*, his first wife. He and his brother, *Simeon*, were the leaders in taking the family's revenge on *Shechem* for the rape of their sister, *Dinah*. Like his brothers and half-brothers, Levi joined in selling *Joseph* into slavery in Egypt, later visited Joseph there, and finally settled in Egypt with his family at Joseph's invitation. Levi and Simeon are both described as being excessively prone to violence in the so-called Jacob's Blessing, delivered by the patriarch on his deathbed.

Moses and *Aaron* both traced their ancestry from Levi, as did all the Levites who came to have various priestly and ritual functions. Levi is not consistently included in the list of names of the tribes of Israel, which were otherwise variously named for his brothers and half-brothers.

Lot

Lot was the nephew of *Abraham*, and traveled with him during his migrations. Eventually they reached Canaan, by which time both had large flocks. Clashes developed between their followers and herders, which Abraham resolved by allowing Lot to choose where he wanted to live. Lot settled near the city of Sodom and was captured there by an invading Mesopotamian army which carried him off. Abraham, however, released him.

Later the Lord decided to destroy Sodom because of the wickedness of its inhabitants, and told Abraham of this. Two angels came to Sodom, appearing as men, and Lot gave them hospitality. The people of Sodom came to his house that night, demanding to be allowed to have sexual relations with the men, but Lot refused, offering his two virgin daughters to the people instead. Lot and his family were protected by the angels, who urged them to leave in the morning, which they did. Lot's wife, however, looked back as the city was being destroyed by the Lord, and was turned into a pillar of salt.

Below: A fourteenth-century miniature depicting Abraham sharing his property with Lot.

Lot and his daughters took refuge in a cave in the hills where Lot was made drunk and seduced by his daughters in turn because they believed that he was the only man left alive from the destruction, and they wished to have children. The elder daughter had a son called *Moab*, ancestor of the Moabites, and the younger a son, Ben-ammi, ancestor of the Ammonites.

The devastation left by the destruction of Sodom, and the pillar of salt into which Lot's wife was turned, are commonly identified with aspects of the landscape in the Dead Sea area.

Magog

Magog was a grandson of *Noah*, and son of *Japheth*. Like various of Noah's descendants, he came to be regarded as the forefather of a group of peoples, in Magog's case a vaguely-defined grouping, possibly living on the south coast of the Black Sea. Magog is usually associated with *Gog* but, in the prophecy of *Ezekiel* concerning Gog, Magog is said to be the name of the land ruled by Gog, and not a particular individual. Together Gog and Magog have come to symbolize heathen attackers who would unsuccessfully try to destroy the kingdom of Israel.

Mahalath

Two personalities named Mahalath appear in the Old Testament. One, also known as *Basemath*, was one of the wives of *Esau*. The other, a granddaughter of *David*, was a wife of *Rehoboam*. The naming of Esau's wives is not consistent in the various parts of Genesis in which they appear (see the entry on Esau).

Left: Lot and his Daughters, a painting attributed to Lucas Van Leyden.

Below: A statue of Magog in the Guildhall in the City of London.

Malachi

Since the Hebrew word *malachi* means "my messenger," many students of the Bible believe that it is not a personal name at all, but rather a description of an anonymous prophet. No personal details relating to its author or authors are given in the Book of Malachi, but it is possible to deduce that it was probably written *c.* 500-450 B.C.

In the book, the people and the priests are condemned for their lack of attention to proper religious ritual: tithes are not paid, poor-quality animals are offered for sacrifice, and people openly say that there is little point in serving God when the wicked seem to prosper. The book concludes with a warning of the judgment to come, when the wicked shall be punished and the righteous rewarded if they have observed the law of *Moses*. *Elijah* will return to reconcile families, and to prepare for the "terrible day of the Lord."

Christian commentators make especial note of a verse in the first chapter, "For from the rising of the sun to its setting my name is great among the nations, and in every place incense is offered to my name, and a pure offering; for my name is great among the nations, says the Lord of hosts." This is construed as predicting the universal church of Christ which is to come.

Manasseh

1. Manasseh was the elder son of *Joseph* and his Egyptian wife, *Asenath*. Genesis 48 records how Joseph brought Manasseh and his younger brother, *Ephraim*, to see their grandfather, *Jacob*, near the end of his life. Jacob's eyesight was failing, and when he gave the brothers his blessing, he laid his left hand on Manasseh, the elder of the two. Joseph was angry at this at first, thinking that his father had made a mistake, but Jacob said that it was no mistake, and that Manasseh's descendants would be great, but would be surpassed by Ephraim's.

Like their uncles, Ephraim and Manasseh came to be regarded as the forefathers of tribes of Israel, although, as with their uncles, their inclusion in the various listings of the tribes is not consistent throughout the Old Testament. The situation of the younger inheriting more than the elder was a common theme in the family: Joseph, Jacob, and *Isaac* among their immediate forebears all having followed this pattern. The story of Jacob's blessing may reflect the relative power of the two tribes in later events, rather than being an authentic episode in the patriarchal history.

2. Manasseh was the son and successor of *Hezekiah* as king of Judah. His mother was Hephzibah. He had a long and seemingly peaceful reign from the time he succeeded his father at the age of 12 until his death, probably in 642 B.C. The date of his accession is less certain, but both Kings and Chronicles say that his reign lasted 55 years.

He is bitterly condemned in both accounts for his encouragement of idolatrous practices. Kings adds that this wickedness was the final cause of the Lord's decision to destroy the kingdom of Judah. Chronicles, perhaps in an attempt to explain why Manasseh could remain on the throne for so long in the face of such evident vice, explains that he was taken off to Babylon by the Assyrians and, while he was a prisoner, repented of his wicked ways, so that when he returned to Jerusalem

he removed the foreign gods and went some way toward restoring correct religious observance.

Assyrian records suggest that Manasseh may indeed have gone to Mesopotamia, but on a visit as a subject-king. Seen in this light, his religious policy can perhaps be regarded as being a largely successful attempt to keep the peace with his overlords. The king Pul, to whom Menasseh paid tribute, was otherwise known as *Tiglath-pileser*.

Another **Manasseh** was the husband of *Judith* who died of sunstroke. She remained faithful to his memory, and did not remarry.

Manoah

Manoah was the father of *Samson*. He and his wife, who is not named, were both involved in miraculous events before the birth of their son. Manoah belonged to the tribe of Dan and lived at Zorah. He and his wife had no children for some time, until an angel appeared to the wife foretelling the birth of a son. She was not to drink alcohol during the pregnancy, and was to be careful to avoid anything unclean.

Above: Mattathias kills the defiler of the temple; a woodcut by Doré.

Left: King Manasseh of Judah, whose reign lasted for 55 years.

The boy, she was told, would be a nazirite, and accordingly was never to have his hair cut.

She told her husband what had happened, and he prayed for further guidance regarding their son. The wife then had another meeting with what she thought was a man of God. This time Manoah joined them and offered hospitality to the man. The man said that instead they should make the kid that they proposed to eat into a burnt offering to the Lord, and when they did so they realized that the man was indeed an angel. Manoah was worried that they would immediately die because they had seen God, but his wife reassured him that they would not have been shown what they had seen if this was not intended. In due course Samson was born.

The only additional role that Manoah and his wife then played was initially to object to Samson's marriage to a Philistine woman.

Mattathias

Mattathias was a priest in the town of Modin in the first half of the second century B.C. He appears in the deuterocanonical/apocryphal First Book of Maccabees. He was the father of five sons, including *Jonathan, Judas* and *Simon*. Antiochus IV, the ruler of Judea at the time, was trying to impose various non-Jewish customs, including sacrifices to other gods, and in 167 B.C. Mattathias killed one of the king's officers and one of his townspeople who was trying to perform such a sacrifice. This was the signal for Mattathias and his sons to rouse the country and take to the hills, thus beginning the Maccabean revolt. Mattathias died the following year, but he committed the leadership to Judas and Simon.

Melchizedek

Melchizedek was a priest and king of Salem (believed to be Jerusalem) in the time of *Abraham*. Melchizedek met Abraham after Abraham returned from his military expedition to rescue *Lot*, gave Abraham bread and wine, and blessed him. In return Abraham gave him a tenth of everything he had. This payment by the patriarch Abraham to a priest is discussed by St. Paul in Hebrews 7 in the New Testament, where it is said also to demonstrate Christ's supremacy.

Menahem

Menahem was king of Israel from *c.* 745-738 B.C. He succeeded the usurper, *Shallum*, by assassinating him. He put down resistance to his rule brutally, even having pregnant women killed. He paid tribute to the Assyrian king, Pul (better known as *Tiglath-pileser*), by taxing every wealthy man in the kingdom 50 shekels. Menahem's reign is briefly described in II Kings 15, and he and the tribute he paid are also mentioned in Assyrian records. His father's name was Gadi, and he was succeeded as king by his son, *Pekahiah*.

Mephibosheth

Mephibosheth was the son of *Jonathan* who survived his father, and despite his disability, was adopted by King *David*. Mephibosheth was five years old when his father and grandfather, *Saul*, were killed in battle.

When the news of this came, his nurse picked him up to run away, but she dropped him and he became lame after the fall. Subsequently, David was told of Mephibosheth's survival by *Ziba*, who had been a member of Saul's household. David returned the family property to Mephibosheth, and gave him the privilege of always eating at the king's own table. Ziba became the head of Mephibosheth's household.

During the rebellion of *Absalom*, Ziba accused Mephibosheth of disloyalty to David, and David gave all Mephibosheth's property to Ziba. However, when Absalom had been defeated, Mephibosheth came to David proclaiming his loyalty, and said that he had only been prevented from coming to David before then by his disability and Ziba's failure to arrange for a donkey to carry him on the journey. David evidently did not completely believe either story, and divided the property in half between the two.

Mephibosheth also appears in genealogies in I Chronicles, where his name is given as Merib-baal.

A second **Mephibosheth** also belonged to Saul's family and was one

Above: The priest-king Melchizedek.

Below: The stela from Dibon, dated *c.* 830 B.C., commemorating Mesha's victories.

of Saul's sons by his concubine, *Rizpah*. He and his brother and five of their cousins were handed over to the Gibeonites by David to be killed in recompense for Saul's attacks on the Gibeonites. Rizpah ensured that all were given proper burial.

Merab

Merab was the elder daughter of *Saul* by his wife Ahinoam. She was first promised in marriage to *David*, but Saul had become jealous of David and decided instead to marry Merab to Adriel the Meholathite. Saul hoped that David would be killed in battle, but he survived to marry *Michal*, Saul's younger daughter.

Mesha

Mesha was a king of Moab, a small kingdom east of the Dead Sea known for its good grazing land. During the reigns of *Omri* and *Ahab* of Judah, Moab had been a tributary state but, after Ahab's death, Mesha rebelled. He was attacked by *Jehoram (1)* of Israel and *Jehosaphat* of Judah, and was at first defeated. However, when he came to be besieged in his last stronghold, Mesha sacrificed his eldest son, which frightened his opponents into retreating back to their own lands (II Kings 3).

Mesha is also known from his own record of events, the so-called "Moabite stone," which was discovered in 1868, and was eventually brought to the Louvre in Paris. The inscription describes the retaking of Moabite lands from Israel, and building works that Mesha undertook in his towns, and especially in his capital, Dibon. Mesha attributed his success to the Moabite deity, Chemosh.

Meshach

See *Abednego*.

Methuselah

Methuselah appears in Genesis 4 & 5 and in the genealogy in I Chronicles 1. His father was *Enoch*, and his grandson *Noah*. Noah was the son of Lamech, Methuselah's eldest son, who was born, we are told, when his father was 187 years old. Methuselah went on to live for 969 years, the longest of the many long life spans noted in the Old Testament.

Micah

1. The first personality of the name Micah to appear in the Old Testament is found in Judges 17 & 18. His first recorded act was to return 1100 pieces of silver that he had previously stolen to his mother. She used some of the money to make an idol, and Micah made a shrine for it, and persuaded a Levite to act as priest at the shrine.

At this time the tribe of Dan sent scouts to search for new land and, after an encounter with Micah's priest, these decided to attack Laish. When the full-scale expedition began, the army stopped at Micah's house and took away the idol, despite the protests of Micah and his neighbors. The expedition was successful, the captured town was renamed Dan, and the idol was set up there instead.

No explanation for this unusual story is provided, and there is no hint of the usual condemnation of such idolatrous practices.

2. According to the first verse of the Book of Micah, the prophet of that name came from the town of Moresheth in Judah and lived in the days of kings *Jotham, Ahaz* and *Hezekiah*, that is to say, the second half of the eighth century B.C. Although it is likely that this verse was added by a later editor of the text, as indeed other substantial parts of the book seem to have been, its information about the original prophet is likely to be accurate.

Micah's outlook seems to have been that of a countryman despairing of the iniquities introduced and increasingly practised by the peoples of the cities. He complained that priests and judges were motivated alike by money, tradesmen gave short measure, and all were covetous of land and property. He was not content with existing forms of religious observance, but instead emphasized personal morality: "what does the Lord require of you but to do justice, and to love kindness, and to walk humbly with your God?" The

Above: Micah (2) urges the Israelites to repent; a Doré woodcut.

Left: Methuselah, as portrayed in a stained-glass window in Canterbury Cathedral.

Book of Micah also looks forward to a future Messianic kingdom, where: "they shall beat their swords into plowshares, and their spears into pruning hooks; nation shall not lift up sword against nation, neither shall they learn war any more." This famous passage (which also appears in Isaiah) is, however, believed to have been a later addition to the text, dating from after the return of the Jews from the exile in Babylon, rather than being the work of Micah himself.

Micah is also the name of four other personalities in the Old Testament.

Micaiah

Micaiah was a prophet in Israel in the time of King *Ahab*. When Ahab formed an alliance with *Jehosaphat* for a

Left: Sir Edward Burne-Jones's design of 1882 for a portrait of the archangel Michael, seen here in a stained-glass window at Cattistock, Dorset.

quarrel with Zedekiah. Ahab decided to go ahead with the war despite this warning, but gave orders to have Micaiah put in prison on bread and water until he returned. Ahab did heed the warning sufficiently to disguise himself in the subsequent battle, but was shot by an enemy archer and died. No information on what happened to Micaiah afterward is given.

Michael

Angels appear in various places in the Old Testament, but are not often named. Michael, traditionally regarded as one of the four archangels, is, however, named in the Book of Daniel as appearing to *Daniel* in a vision, and as having been appointed as the guardian angel of the Israelites.

Michal

Michal was the younger daughter of King *Saul*. When *David* was making his reputation as a military commander against the Philistines, Saul first promised him the hand of his elder daughter, *Merab*, before allowing her to marry someone else. Saul then heard that Michal had fallen in love with David, and offered David the chance to marry her. To qualify, however, David had first to kill 100 Philistines, and Saul hoped that David would himself be killed in the attempt. David was successful (killing 200, according to some translations), and Saul became increasingly jealous.

Some time later Saul decided to kill David himself. Michal helped David escape from their house and concealed his absence until he was safely gone. During David's period as an outlaw, Saul made Michal marry a man called Palti. After Saul died, his son *Ishbaal* was supported at first by a general called *Abner*. Abner and Ishbaal quarreled, and Abner tried to become reconciled with David. David insisted that Abner help him obtain the return of Michal, to which Ishbaal was compelled to agree.

After David had taken control of Jerusalem, he had the Ark of the Covenant brought into the city. In his celebration of this David danced in front of

campaign east of the Jordan, Jehosaphat wished to be reassured that the move had divine approval. The two kings consulted a group of some 400 prophets who, led by *Zedekiah*, all agreed that the war would be successful. Jehosaphat was unconvinced, and asked if there might be another prophet who could be consulted. Ahab replied: "'There is still one other by whom we may enquire of the Lord, Micaiah son of Imlah; but I hate him,

for he never prophesies anything favorable about me, but only disaster.'" Nonetheless Micaiah was summoned, and at first agreed, presumably sarcastically, with what the other prophets had said, but then changed his tune and foretold that "all Israel" would be "scattered on the mountains".

Micaiah went on to explain that the other prophets had been misled by a lying spirit sent by the Lord to entice Ahab to disaster. This provoked a the Ark in what Michal thought was an unseemly manner. She reprimanded him for making a fool of himself in public. David replied that he had been chosen as king by the Lord, and that his dancing was also performed before the Lord. This incident seems to have brought their marriage effectively to an end, for the account adds simply that "Michal the daughter of Saul had no child to the day of her death."

Miriam

Miriam was the sister of *Aaron* and *Moses*. Their parents were *Amram* and *Jochebed*.

Moses is described as having been watched over by an unnamed elder sister when he was hidden in his basket among the reeds in Exodus 2. The sister was quick-thinking enough, when the child was discovered by pharaoh's daughter [*Pharaoh (3)*], to offer to find a nurse for him, conveniently choosing their mother. This sister could obviously have been Miriam.

Miriam led the Israelite women in a song of rejoicing after the pursuing Egyptian army had been swallowed up in the Sea of Reeds. Miriam is described as being a prophet in this passage.

The principal episode in which Miriam is involved appears in Numbers 12, in which she and Aaron are described as being critical of Moses for his marriage to a Cushite or Ethiopian woman (*Zipporah* may be meant by this, although she is more usually described as a Midianite). The two complain, "'Has the Lord spoken only through Moses? Has he not spoken through us also?'" implying that the three had together held some joint leadership role. However, following this the Lord appeared to them in a cloud, and confirmed Moses's supremacy. When the vision was over, Miriam was struck with a skin disease and, after Moses's intercession on her behalf, had to leave the camp for seven days to be cured.

Miriam died during the Exodus and was buried at Kadesh.

A second **Miriam** is mentioned in a genealogy in I Chronicles.

Mishael

See *Abednego*.

Moab

Moab was the son of *Lot* and his elder daughter following their incestuous relationship after the destruction of Sodom and Gomorrah. He was regarded as being the ancestor of the Moabites who lived in lands east of the Jordan and the Dead Sea.

Below: Miriam celebrates the deliverance of Israel from the Egyptian army; an illustration after the Flemish painter, Jacob Jordaens.

Molech

Molech was a god worshiped by various Semitic peoples, particularly the Ammonites, under a variety of similar names, and at times also worshiped by the Israelites, despite a specific prohibition of this in Leviticus. The worship of Molech is said to have involved devotees sacrificing their children by ''passing them through the fire,'' but some scholars believe that this is a misunderstanding of the ancient texts, and that human sacrifice did not take place.

Solomon allowed altars to be built to Molech, but in his later religious reforms *Josiah* defiled the sites used for the worship of Molech.

Below: The Triumph of Mordecai; an etching by Rembrandt, 1640. The deliverance of the Jewish people from certain death is still celebrated in the Feast of Purim.

Mordecai

Mordecai was an official in the court of the Persian king, *Ahasuerus*, and the adoptive father of *Esther*. He served the king by detecting an assassination plot mounted by two of the king's eunuchs. After the king had quarreled with Queen Vashti and divorced her, Esther was selected to join the royal harem. Mordecai told her that she should not reveal that she was a Jew. Esther was very beautiful and the king made her his queen.

Later, after *Haman* had been promoted to become chief minister, Mordecai refused to bow down before him, which angered Haman against Mordecai and, by extension, against all the Jews living anywhere in the kingdom. Haman therefore persuaded the king to issue an edict providing for all the Jews to be killed on a certain date to satisfy his hatred.

Mordecai, however, explained to Esther what was planned, and she agreed to try to convince the king to change his mind. During this process the king remembered how Mordecai had been loyal during the previous assassination plot, and gave him high honors. Haman was also soon discredited and executed, and Mordecai appointed in his place. Since the king's initial order, like all royal decrees of the Persian kingdom, could not be cancelled, Mordecai was allowed to send out a second order allowing the Jews to take up arms against their enemies, which they did successfully. Mordecai and Esther instructed the Jewish community that they should commemorate this deliverance in the Feast of Purim, which is still an important festival in the Jewish calendar.

See *Esther* for a brief discussion of the historicity of the characters and the events of their lives.

Above: *Crossing the Red Sea*; a painting from the Flemish School.

Right: The baby Moses is rescued – a painting by Simeon Solomon.

Moses

Moses was the most important figure in the history of the Israelite people. If *David* is remembered for uniting the people politically and giving them security in their land, Moses is regarded as leading the people to their religious identity as followers of the Lord God. Worship of the God of Israel not only directed the people in every aspect of their lives, it established their separate and distinctive character. Moses is described as being unique among the prophets in the intimacy of his relationship with the Lord.

The books of the Pentateuch, the first five in the traditional order of the Old Testament, are known as the Books of Moses. They make up the most important section of the Jewish scriptures, the *Torah*. Moses is regarded as being the law-giver, and traditionally as the author of the *Torah*.

Other strands of biblical study suggest that the books of the Pentateuch reached their present form some time around 400 B.C., and that the disparate elements of which it is composed date back perhaps 500 years before this (although these in turn may derive from earlier records now lost). Moses, however, must have lived several hundred years before even the earliest of these writings, and their earliest sources must have been various oral traditions. There is little doubt that a historical figure with at least some of the characteristics of Moses must have existed, although no mention of Moses has been found in any source outside the Bible, but many of the stories now related concerning his life may not originally have pertained to him. This, too, would account for the seeming contradictions and uncertainties in the account. That being said, it has also

Below: Moses comes down from Mount Sinai bearing the Ten Commandments, according to a Doré woodcut.

been pointed out that the picture that emerges of Moses is a generally consistent one. Above all, his determination and steadfastness of purpose shine through from his overcoming of pharaoh's [*Pharaoh (4)*] obstinacy, to his continued dragging back of the people to the righteous path throughout the difficult years of the Exodus.

Moses's parents were *Amram* and *Jochebed*, his sister was *Miriam*, and his brother *Aaron*. Moses was born at a time when the tribes of Israel were living in Egypt and were being oppressed there. He was saved from execution as a baby by the cleverness of his mother and sister, but was raised by pharaoh's daughter [*Pharaoh (3)*]. When he was a young man he killed an Egyptian foreman who was beating an Israelite, and had to leave the country.

In his exile he met a priest from a nomadic tribe, *Jethro*, and married his daughter, *Zipporah*. While he was living with them, Moses had the vision of the burning bush in which the Lord commissioned him to lead his people out of Egypt to the land of Canaan. Moses was uncertain of his fitness for this task, but was given powers to help him achieve it, and was told to work with Aaron in doing so.

Moses returned to Egypt and explained to Aaron and then the Israelite elders what was to occur. The two went to see pharaoh, and initially suggested that the Israelites should be allowed to travel three days' journey into the wilderness to perform sacrifices. Pharaoh refused, and instead increased the labor quota imposed on his Israelite slaves. The Egyptians then suffered from a series of dreadful plagues, put into effect by Moses and Aaron, which, despite some wavering, did not convince pharaoh to allow the Israelites to leave.

The final plague was the most dreadful: the killing of all the Egyptians' eldest children and their finest animals. The Lord instructed Moses and Aaron on the rituals that each Israelite family was to observe which would protect them. This is the origin of the Jewish feast of the Passover. After this horrible punishment, pharaoh relented and permitted the Israelites to leave. They took with them the remains of *Joseph* for eventual burial in the Promised Land.

During their journey the people were led by a "pillar of cloud by day" and a "pillar of fire by night". Pharaoh changed his mind and set out in pursuit. Moses miraculously led the people across the Sea of Reeds, but all of pharaoh's army was bogged down and drowned. (The traditional description, "Red Sea," is generally believed to have been a mistranslation, and a marshy area of the Nile Delta would fit well with other aspects of the story.)

Moses had to cope with repeated complaints from the people during the first stages of their journey into the wilderness. He made water sources drinkable and foretold the arrival of food in the form of quails and then the manna from heaven; he chose *Joshua* to lead the people in battle with the Amalekites, and performed a necessary ritual to ensure his victory over them; he was reunited with his family and, at the suggestion of his father-in-law, appointed judges to assist him in governing the people.

Next came Moses's summons to Mount Sinai, in which God pronounced to him the Ten Commandments. The first and most important of the commandments was the injunction "you shall have no other gods before me."

The first tablets of the Law that Moses was given were broken when he returned from the mountain to find that Aaron had permitted and assisted the people in making a golden calf, which they were now worshiping. Moses had many of the wrongdoers executed, destroyed the idol, and received a new copy of the commandments. Many other laws were received also, along with detailed instructions for the construction of the tabernacle and the Ark of the Law that was to be its centerpiece.

Before the people moved on, Aaron and his family were ordained as priests, and a census was taken. The people still complained, particularly at the monotony of their diet of manna. Moses met more personal complaints from Miriam and Aaron about his foreign wife, and about the dominant role that he insisted on keeping for himself. Moses's position was confirmed by signs from the Lord, and later a rebellion led by *Korah* was crushed by divine intervention.

When the Israelites reached the land of Canaan, one man from each tribe was sent ahead by Moses to scout the territory and assess its value and the strength of its inhabitants. All correctly reported on the richness of the land, but only Joshua and *Caleb* advised an immediate advance to take it. The people refused to follow this advice, and the Lord told them that, because of the lack of faith that this implied, He would make them wander for another 40 years in the desert. Only Joshua and Caleb would survive that period to enter the Promised Land.

After most of the 40 years had passed, Moses again led the people toward the Promised Land, but this time planned to enter Canaan via Jordan. Aaron died on the way at Mount Hor, and Moses invested Aaron's son, *Eleazar*, as Aaron's successor as leading priest. There were various further battles on the way and other trials also. The Lord sent poisonous snakes among the people because of their continuing moaning against Moses. Many were bitten and died until Moses arranged to mitigate the punishment. Further immorality and divine punishment occurred when Israelites began to sleep with Moabite women and worshiped their false god.

Moses also set in train the process by which the land to be captured would be divided between the tribes, setting out too how various towns were to be set aside for the Levites and others as cities of refuge. He also allotted land east of the Jordan to the tribes of Reuben, Gad and part of Manasseh, provided that they participated in the conquest of territory to the west.

Moses was now near death, and delivered a series of farewell speeches to the people. The second of these begins in Deuteronomy 5, with the formula "Hear O Israel," which is the opening of one of the most important formal prayers in Judaism. These addresses outlined the Law to the people once more (much of Deuteronomy 5 is a recapitulation of the Ten Commandments), and gave Moses's blessing to the various tribes in turn. Joshua was appointed as Moses's successor in a ceremony in the tabernacle.

Moses was granted a brief view of the Promised Land from the top of Mount Nebo, but there he died. He was aged 120 and was much mourned: "Never since has there arisen a prophet in Israel like Moses, whom the Lord knew face to face."

See also *Aaron, Abihu, Amram, Bezalel, Caleb, Cozbi, Eleazar, Eliezer, Gershom, Ithamar, Jethro, Jochebed, Joshua, Korah, Miriam, Nadab, Nahash, Og, Oholiab, Pharaoh (3 & 4), Phinehas (1), Zimri, Zipporah.*

Left: Naaman bathes in the River Jordan, seeking a cure for his skin disease.

Naaman

Naaman was the successful commander of the army of Damascus, probably in the time of *Ben-hadad (2)*, although this is not specifically stated. He is described as having contracted leprosy and to have heard, via a young Israelite girl who had been captured in one of his raids into Israel and taken to be his wife's slave, that a prophet in Samaria would be able to cure him. Modern commentators believe that the term in the Bible usually translated as leprosy does not only mean the illness known to the modern world by that name (or more correctly as Hansen's disease), but was a general term for various skin diseases.

Whatever his problem, Naaman consulted his master, the king, and was given permission to go to Samaria and a letter of introduction to the king of Israel stating why he had come. The king of Israel is also not named, but was probably *Jehoram (1)*. The Israelite king was at first concerned that Naaman's quest for a cure would be fruitless, and that this would provoke war with Damascus, but *Elisha* heard of Naaman's arrival and sent a message to the king telling him to send Naaman to Elisha's house. Elisha did not bother to go out and see Naaman when he arrived, sending a message instead that Naaman should bathe seven times in the Jordan and would

be cured. Naaman stormed off, angry at being treated in this off-hand manner, but was persuaded to try the remedy by his servants, and it naturally worked.

Naaman returned to offer Elisha a reward for what had been done, but this was refused. Naaman then asked to take away two mule-loads of earth, presumably so that he could stand on this during worship, to signify his new devotion to the Lord, Elisha's God. He also asked Elisha if he would be forgiven if he still went through the forms of worship of the gods of Damascus when this was required by his king. Elisha told him to go in peace. When Naaman was on his way home he was overtaken by Elisha's servant, Gehazi, who invented a story concerning two other needy priests. Naaman gave him money and clothing for them but, when Gehazi returned to Elisha's house, Elisha knew what had happened, and he told Gehazi that he would contract Naaman's disease.

Naaman was also the name of one of the near descendants of *Benjamin*, variously described as being his son or grandson.

Nabal

Nabal appears in I Samuel 25. He is described as "very rich" and "surly and mean", and his name may mean "fool". His wife *Abigail* was "clever and

beautiful". While *David* was an outlaw in the wilderness, he heard of Nabal and sent some of his men to Nabal to extort supplies, saying that they had protected Nabal's men and his sheep and had ensured that nothing was stolen from them. Nabal turned David's emissaries rudely away and, when David heard of this, he was sufficiently angered to determine to attack Nabal in force. Abigail discovered what had happened, and decided that it would be better to buy David off, which she did without telling her husband. When she told him later, he had a seizure and died. David then married Abigail.

Naboth

Naboth owned a vineyard near the royal palace of *Ahab*. Ahab wished to acquire the vineyard to make it into a vegetable garden, but Naboth refused the king's offer of a better vineyard or a cash settlement. Queen *Jezebel* therefore contrived to have Naboth falsely accused of blasphemy and stoned to death for this offense. Ahab was thus able to take possession of the vineyard, but both he and his queen were cursed by *Elijah* for their role in this judicial murder.

The crime was regarded as particularly serious because Naboth was acting virtuously, by the standards of the day, in refusing to sell the land, as it was part of his family's inheritance.

Nadab

1. Nadab was the eldest son of *Aaron* and, like his father and his brothers, *Abihu, Eleazar* and *Ithamar*, was also a priest. Nadab and Abihu burned incense before the Lord when they should not have, and were burned to death. Aaron and their brothers were forbidden to mourn for them.

2. A personality named Nadab was the second king of Israel after the division of the monarchy between Israel and Judah. He was the son of *Jeroboam (1)*, and succeeded his father. I Kings 15 tells us that he reigned for two years, and historically these are believed to have been *c.* 909 B.C. Nadab was conspired against by *Baasha* while he was besieging the Philistine town of Gibbethon, and Baasha killed Nadab and all his family. The reason, we are told, was because of Nadab's continuation of the idolatrous practices of Jeroboam.

Nadab is also the name of two other personalities in the Old Testament, who both appear in I Chronicles, and were respectively members of the tribes of Judah and Benjamin. A further **Nadab**, brother of *Ahikar*, appears in the deuterocanonical/apocryphal Book of Tobit.

Nahash

Nahash was a king of the Ammonites in the time of *Saul*. He fought and oppressed the people of the tribes of Gad and Reuben. He besieged their city of Jabesh-gilead and, when they tried to make a truce, he agreed, on the condition that he could have the right eyes of all the people of the city gouged out. Nahash allowed the city to have seven days' grace to call for help, which they did successfully from the newly chosen King Saul. Saul raised an army and attacked and defeated the Ammonites.

Both II Samuel and I Chronicles record that, after Nahash died, *David* sent envoys to console his son and successor, Hanun, because Nahash had been kind to David in some unspecified manner. This may imply that Nahash gave David help when he was outlawed by Saul.

The name Nahash is also used in some translations of II Samuel 17 for *Jesse*, David's father.

Nahum

Like others of the so-called minor prophets, Nahum appears only in the short book of the Old Testament named after him, and within it no personal information about him is found (other than that he came from an otherwise unknown town or region called Elkosh). The Book of Nahum is described in its first verse as being "An oracle concerning Nineveh." Nineveh was the principal city of the Assyrian Empire up until its fall in 612 B.C. The book seems to have been written shortly before Nineveh fell, and foretells in vivid, not to say gory, detail, what is going to happen to the city. The destruction of Nineveh is described as resulting from a divine judgment on the city and punishment for wickedness.

Naomi

Naomi is one of the central characters of the Book of Ruth. She and her husband, Elimelech, were from Bethlehem, but went to live in Moab during a famine. While they were there, Elimelech died and, although their two sons took Moabite wives, the sons died without children ten years later. Naomi decided to return to Bethlehem, but urged her daughters-in-law to go back to their own families. One of them, Orpah, reluctantly agreed to do so, but the other, *Ruth*, refused. Ruth said, "'Do not press me to leave you or to turn back from following you! Where you go, I will go; where you lodge, I will lodge; your people shall be my people and your God my God.'"

Below: Ruth and Naomi, by Evelyn de Morgan. Ruth was so devoted to Naomi that she refused to leave her after the death of their menfolk.

As widows, Naomi and Ruth were poor when they returned to Bethlehem, so Naomi encouraged Ruth to go gleaning behind the harvesters in a field belonging to a relative called *Boaz*. He was kind to Ruth, so that she returned home to Naomi with an unexpectedly large amount of grain on that first day, and continued to work in Boaz's fields until the end of the harvest. Naomi hoped to find a new husband for Ruth and, since custom dictated that he should be a close relative, she encouraged Ruth to go to see Boaz again, but told her to wash and perfume herself and put on her best clothes.

Boaz was attracted to Ruth and arranged to marry her. In due course Boaz and Ruth had a son called Obed, whom Naomi was delighted to care for. Obed was the father of *Jesse* and grandfather of *David*.

Naphtali

Naphtali was the sixth son of *Jacob*, the second borne by *Bilhah*, maid to *Rachel*, his second wife. Like his brother and half-brothers, he was involved in the selling of *Joseph* into slavery and the subsequent journey to Egypt to buy food when they met Joseph again. Naphtali's family joined the rest of the clan in settling in Egypt later at Joseph's request.

The name Naphtali, like those of his brother and half-brothers, was given to one of the tribes of Israel.

Nathan

Nathan was the leading prophet at the court of King *David*.

Nathan first appears in II Samuel 7 (and in virtually identical terms in I Chronicles 17), where he first encouraged David in his project to build a temple but then, after a dream, told David that this was not the Lord's wish. He told David of the Lord's covenant with him, that David would establish a dynasty, and that it would have the Lord's favor forever.

Later, after David had committed adultery with *Bathsheba* and had caused the death of *Uriah*, Nathan conveyed the Lord's anger to him in a parable of a rich and a poor man, and told David that he would be punished by the death of his son by Bathsheba. When another son, *Solomon*, was born, Nathan passed on the message that the Lord loved Solomon.

Nathan finally appears in I Kings 1, when he persuaded Bathsheba to join him in urging Solomon's right to the succession ahead of *Adonijah*. Two of Nathan's sons, *Azariah* and Zabud, appear in lists of Solomon's officers.

Nebaioth

Nebaioth was the eldest son of *Ishmael (1)*, and the traditional forefather of a tribe resident in the Arabian Peninsula.

Nebuchadnezzar

Nebuchadnezzar was the King of Babylon 605/4-562 B.C. His name is also, but less commonly, spelled Nebuchadrezzar in the Bible, and this is believed to have been a more accurate rendering of it. On behalf of his elderly father, Nabopolassar, he commanded the army that achieved a decisive victory over the Egyptians at the Battle of Carchemish in 605, before returning home to secure his succession to the throne when his father died. The success at Carchemish confirmed the Babylonians as the dominant power throughout the Middle East, inheriting the position formerly held by the Assyrians, who had finally been defeated a few years before.

The biblical account describes various of his campaigns in and around the Holy Land. *Jehoiakim* of Judah paid him tribute for a time, either following the victory at Carchemish, or during Nebuchadnezzar's campaigns in the region in the years immediately after. Jehoiakim then rebelled, and the Babylonians moved against Jerusalem. Jehoiakim died shortly before their attack developed fully, and his son, *Jehoiachin*, briefly succeeded him before being forced to surrender in 597. Nebuchadnezzar took Jehoiachin off to Babylon as a prisoner, deported many of the people of Judah, and took away treasure from the temple. Nebuchadnezzar appointed *Zedekiah* as his puppet king of Judah.

Zedekiah, too, eventually rebelled and, after a long siege, Jerusalem was captured. Zedekiah and all his family were brutally treated; much of the city

Left: Nathan rebukes David; a fourteenth-century panel in the French church of St. Etienne in Mulhouse.

was destroyed; and an even greater proportion of the population was deported to Babylon. Judah became part of the Babylonian Empire.

The Book of Daniel describes a period of madness that Nebuchadnezzar suffered at some point, but there is no other evidence for this. In addition, Nebuchadnezzar appears in the deuterocanonical/apocryphal Book of Judith, where he is described incorrectly as being an Assyrian king, but this is also not believed to be a historically accurate account of his actions.

Neco, Pharaoh

Neco, or Necho II, as he is usually described in secular historical works, reigned in Egypt *c.* 609-594 B.C. In the Old Testament he appears chiefly as a deposer and kingmaker of the rulers of Judah. He defeated and killed King *Josiah* of Judah at Megiddo. Then he imprisoned the next king, *Jehoahaz*, who eventually died in Egypt. His successor, *Jehoiakim*, continued to pay heavy taxes to Neco for a time. From non-biblical sources, and the Book of Jeremiah, it appears that Neco was decisively defeated by *Nebuchadnezzar* in 605 in a battle at Carchemish.

Left: Nebuchadnezzar the captor, in *The Daughters of Judah in Babylon*, by Herbert Gustave Schmalz.

Below: Nebuchadnezzar is thought to have suffered from lycanthropy, at times believing himself to be a wild beast.

Nehemiah

Nehemiah was a member of the exiled Israelite community in Babylon, and reached the important position of royal cupbearer to *Artaxerxes* (Artaxerxes I, reigned 464-423 B.C.). From other sources, not contradicted by any information in the Old Testament, this implies that he would have been a eunuch. The Book of Nehemiah, in which he chiefly appears, describes two periods that he spent as governor of Judea for Artaxerxes, *c.* 445-434 and *c.* 430. Nehemiah was the son of Hecaliah.

The Books of Ezra and Nehemiah were once regarded as being a single entity, and have only been divided in the present way since the third century A.D. Modern opinion is that this "Book" was written at the same time as Chronicles, probably in the fourth century B.C., and possibly by the same author or authors.

Nehemiah used his privileged position to tell his royal master of difficult times in Jerusalem, and was accordingly appointed governor, commissioned to rebuild the city, and given an armed escort and other facilities to see him on his way. Immediately on his arrival he inspected the city walls and mobilized the high priest, Eliashib, and others to start work. Leaders of various nearby communities complained about what was happening and then, as the work quickly proceeded, threatened an armed attack. Nehemiah arranged for some of the work force always to be on guard, and building continued, as it did also in the face of threats of a personal attack on Nehemiah. The walls were finished in 52 days.

Nehemiah arranged a system of gatekeepers and so on, to ensure that the walls were properly guarded. He also took steps to bring people into the city from the country to restore its population to an appropriate level.

In religious affairs Nehemiah was concerned, like *Ezra*, by the number of the people who had married foreign wives. (It is not clear from the chronology of Ezra and Nehemiah whether the changes in this matter instituted by the two were on separate occasions or part of a single reform.) Nehemiah instituted a covenant to put an end to this practice, and to raise funds to support the operation of the temple.

Nehemiah also improved the condition of the people in other ways. Many had suffered at the hands of rich lenders, having to sell their children as slaves when they could not keep up payments. Nehemiah persuaded the nobles and officials that this was wrong, and they returned property on which they had foreclosed. He set an example personally by not collecting his full salary but living frugally instead.

On his second stay in Jerusalem, Nehemiah discovered that Eliashib had allowed an Ammonite called Tobiah, one of those who had opposed Nehemiah's earlier building work, to use a room in the temple, although entry to the temple was forbidden to foreigners. Nehemiah threw him out. He also corrected other abuses, ensuring that tithes were collected and paid over to the Levites, and that trading on the Sabbath, particularly by merchants from Tyre, did not continue. Finally, he again took steps to put a stop to foreign marriages. The book ends abruptly with a brief prayer, "Remember me, O my God, for good."

Nimrod

According to Genesis 10, Nimrod was one of the sons of Cush, grandson of *Noah*, and was "a mighty hunter before the Lord" and a great warrior. There may be a confusion in the ancient texts between Cush, ancestor of the Ethiopians, and a personality of similar name from Mesopotamia. Nimrod is said to have ruled a powerful kingdom in what is now Iraq.

Left: Nehemiah inspects the walls of Jerusalem.

Below: Nimrod, the mighty hunter.

Noah

The story of Noah is told in Genesis 6-9. Noah was the son of Lamech, the tenth generation in descent from *Adam* through *Seth*. Noah was righteous in a time of corruption and violence, which caused the Lord to decide to make a great flood and destroy all living creatures.

He ordered Noah, however, to build a great ship – the ark – and to stock it with breeding pairs of all the birds, animals, and "creeping things," as well as appropriate food. Heavy rain then fell for 40 days and nights, totally flooding the earth and drowning everything not in the safety of the ark. After five months the waters began to recede; after seven the ark grounded on Mount Ararat; later Noah sent out birds to try to find dry land, which they did on the second and third attempts. After a year Noah, his family, and the animals were able to emerge and to begin to repopulate the earth. Noah built an altar and made sacrifices in thanks for his deliverance.

The Lord then made a covenant with Noah that He would not repeat the flood or totally disrupt the pattern of the seasons. As a token of this promise, rainbows were created. Noah and his descendants were also permitted specifically to eat meat, but only once the blood had been removed. Humans and animals were also forbidden to kill their own kinds and, if they did, were to be punished by the loss of their own lives.

Noah, we are told, was the first vintner. He drank his own wine, and was seen lying drunk and naked in his tent by his second son, *Ham*. Ham told his brothers, *Shem* and *Japheth*, and they covered their father up respectfully. When Noah awoke he cursed Ham's son, *Canaan*, saying that his descendants would be slaves to his uncles' families.

The flood is said to have taken place when Noah was 600 years old, and he lived to be 950.

Stories of a great flood are very common in the ancient folklore of many different cultures. The biblical version is particularly similar to the Babylonian Atrahasis and Gilgamesh legends, and it is likely that there is a connection of some sort between at least the older Atrahasis account and the Old Testament story. It is also possible that

Below: A woodcut from *The Schedel World Chronicle*, 1493, showing Noah and his family building the ark.

Noah, the hero of the flood, and Noah, the drunkard, may originally have been different characters later combined into one. The listing of the descent of various nations and peoples from Noah's three sons seems to have been derived from the political conditions in force when the account was compiled, and the placing of Canaan as the recipient of the curse in the drunkenness story probably also relates to this.

Obadiah

1. Obadiah was a senior officer of *Ahab*, king of Israel. When *Jezebel* was killing prophets of the Lord in support of her adherence to *Baal*, Obadiah arranged to hide 100 of them in caves, because he was righteous. Later, during the drought foretold by *Elijah* and caused by Ahab's and Jezebel's wickedness, Obadiah was sent by Ahab to travel round the country to find water. On his way he met Elijah, who

had been hiding from Ahab. Elijah instructed Obadiah to go to Ahab and tell the king that he had found the prophet. Obadiah was unwilling to do so at first, thinking that Ahab would be angry that he had spoken to Elijah at all, but Elijah persuaded him, and the meeting of prophet and king took place.

2. The Book of Obadiah is the shortest in the Old Testament. No personal information is given concerning the life of Obadiah, and the name itself means simply "servant of God." The Book of Obadiah consists almost entirely of a condemnation of the Edomites for joining in the looting of Judah "on the day of his calamity" despite the ancient kinship of the Edomites and the Israelites through their forefathers *Esau* and *Jacob*. The day of calamity presumably refers to the fall of Jerusalem in 587 B.C., with the book being composed at some time after this.

Obadiah is the name of 11 minor personalities in the Old Testament.

Above: Animals Assembled by Noah before the Ark, by Jan Breughel The Younger. Noah collected pairs of animals from which to breed.

Og

Og was a king of Bashan who was defeated by the Israelites. Numbers and Deuteronomy describe how *Moses* overcame him in a battle at Edrei, killing Og, and wiping out his whole family. Bashan was east of the Jordan, in the lands allocated to the tribes of Reuben, Gad and Manasseh, and, according to Deuteronomy 3, was well defended.

Oholiab

Oholiab was one of the craftsmen employed at the Lord's direction by *Moses* in the making of the tabernacle. He was the son of Ahisamach, of the tribe of Dan. The account in Genesis 35-39 is not specific as to which parts of the construction were made by

Bezalel, the chief craftsman, which by Oholiab, and which by the many others employed, but in Genesis 38 Oholiab's particular skills are described as: "engraver, designer, and embroiderer in blue, purple, and crimson yarns, and in fine linen." He may, therefore, have been responsible for the curtains and hangings, and the priestly vestments which were important parts of the scheme.

Oholibamah

Oholibamah was one of the wives of *Esau*, whom he married to his parents' displeasure because they were not of Israelite descent. She is said in the genealogy in Genesis 36 to have been the daughter of Zibeon the Hivite. The naming of Esau's wives is not consistent in the various parts of Genesis in which they appear (see the entry on Esau).

Omri

Omri was a commander in the army of Israel when King *Elah* was assassinated by *Zimri*. Omri was serving in a siege of Gibbethon when the assassination took place, and he was acclaimed king by the army. He attacked Zimri, defeated him, and took the capital, Tirzah, where Zimri died. Omri then had a further struggle for the succession with Tibni, son of Ginath, but he, too, was defeated and killed.

Omri was king of Israel for 12 years, and only one other incident from his reign is related in the Old Testament. After six years he bought land from a man called Shemer and built a new capital city at Samaria. Like his predecessors, Omri was condemned for his idolatry by the compiler of the account in I Kings 16 in which his story appears.

From non-biblical sources, Omri seems to have been a more impressive ruler than the biblical account suggests. For many years after his death Assyrian records refer to Israel as "of the house of Omri." Another record describes how Omri reconquered the area of Moab, east of the Jordan, that had been lost by his predecessors during their struggles with Judah following the division of the kingdoms. Omri's son and successor, *Ahab*, married *Jezebel*, daughter of Ethbaal, king of Sidon. This may have been a political marriage arranged by Omri.

Onan

Onan was the second son of *Judah*. After the Lord had put Onan's elder brother, Er, to death because of his wickedness, Judah instructed Onan, according to the law of the time, that he should marry his brother's widow, *Tamar (1)*, since she had no children by Er. "But Onan knew that the offspring would not count as his; so whenever he lay with his brother's wife, he spilled his seed on the ground so as not to raise up offspring for his brother" (R.E.B.). This angered the Lord, and he killed Onan also.

The term onanism has now come to mean masturbation rather than the *coitus interruptus* which Onan seems to have employed. Both practices are regarded as being sinful by many religious groups. However, it should be noted that the biblical condemnation of Onan is not because of his sexual practices, but for his failure to fulfill his familial obligation to his dead brother to give Tamar a child to carry on Er's line and inherit property.

Ornan

Ornan is also known as Araunah, and was the owner of a threshing floor purchased by *David* which became the site of *Solomon*'s Temple. Two versions of the story appear: one, in which he is named Araunah, is in II Samuel 24; the second, as Ornan, is in I Chronicles 21.

In both cases David's decision to compile a census was the cause of the Lord sending a pestilence to Israel. In the version in Samuel, David was originally prompted by the Lord to make the census, and the Lord had already decided to halt the pestilence as his angel was poised at Araunah's threshing floor. In Chronicles, the census was inspired by Satan, and the disease was still spreading when David was advised by *Gad*, his seer, to make an altar on Ornan's threshing floor, where the angel was waiting, ready to move against Jerusalem. In both versions, Araunah/Ornan offered his property and his oxen free of charge for a sacrifice, but David insisted on paying, albeit a different price (50 shekels of silver in Samuel and 600 shekels of gold in Chronicles). The altar was built in both cases, and the sacrifices were accepted by the Lord.

The Chronicles story then has David beginning preparations for the building of the Temple, which Solomon later took forward and completed.

Pekah

Pekah, son of Remaliah, was a leading soldier of King *Pekahiah* of Israel, but assassinated him and seized the throne from him. The text of II Kings 15 tells us that he reigned for 20 years, but more modern researches suggest a shorter period, *c.* 737-32 B.C.

Pekah allied with King Rezin of Aram-Damascus to attack Judah. They won a victory, but could not capture Jerusalem. Many prisoners were carried off but were later released after the intervention of a prophet called Oded.

By this stage both Israel and Judah were coming under increasing threat from the aggressive expansion of the Assyrian Empire; Israel and Pekah lost substantial territory to the attacks of *Tiglath-pileser*. Following this defeat, Pekah was assassinated and succeeded by *Hoshea*. The Assyrian records confirm the territorial gains recorded in the Old Testament, and add that Tiglath-pileser supported Hoshea's claim to the Israelite throne.

Pekahiah

Pekahiah succeeded his father, *Menahem*, as king of Israel, and reigned *c.* 738-37 B.C. He is ritually condemned in Kings, like his predecessors, for continuing the idolatrous practices set in train by *Jeroboam (1)*. No other information is given about his brief reign, but it is believed that he continued the policy of appeasement of the Assyrians that his father had begun. He was assassinated by *Pekah*, one of his generals, thus ending his short reign. Pekah succeeded Pekahiah as king.

Perez

Perez was one of the twin sons born of the incestuous relationship between *Judah* and *Tamar (1)*. During the birth his brother *Zerah*'s arm emerged from the womb first, and the midwife tied a red cord round it to identify which child was the elder, but after she had done this Zerah pulled his arm back and Perez emerged first. Genealogies describe *David* as being one of his descendants.

Pharaoh

Pharaoh was a title, not a personal name, of the kings of Egypt.

1. An unnamed pharaoh appears in the story of *Abraham*, taking his wife, *Sarah*, into his harem when they visit Egypt, believing her to be Abraham's sister. However, pharaoh sent her and Abraham away after the Lord had afflicted his household with plagues and he discovered the truth.

2. An unnamed pharaoh appears in the story of *Joseph* in Egypt. After pharaoh dreamed of the seven fat and seven thin cows and the seven plump ears of grain and the seven poor, his priests and magicians were unable to interpret the dream for him. Pharaoh learned from his cupbearer, who had been imprisoned with Joseph for a time, of Joseph's abilities to interpret dreams, and had him brought to him. Joseph correctly interpreted the dream as foretelling seven years of bumper harvests to be followed by seven years of famine. Pharaoh was impressed, and appointed Joseph as one of his chief ministers, charged with making provision for the famine.

When Joseph was visited by his brothers during the famine and invited them to live in Egypt, pharaoh provided transport for them, their families and goods, and their father, *Jacob*. Pharaoh welcomed them when they arrived and gave them land. Jacob died 17 years later, and pharaoh helped Joseph keep his promise to Jacob to bury him in the same tomb as *Abraham* and *Isaac*, sending many of his people to accompany them on the journey.

3. A further unnamed pharaoh set in train the events leading to the Exodus. His fears of the growing numbers and wealth of the Israelite people caused him to order all their male children to be killed. *Moses* escaped this ban, and was adopted by pharaoh's daughter. This pharaoh died after Moses had left Egypt, but while the Israelites were still being oppressed.

4. When Moses returned to Egypt he and *Aaron* went to the ruling pharaoh to ask, "Thus says the Lord, the God of Israel, 'Let my people go, so that they may celebrate a festival to me in the wilderness.'" But pharaoh said, "'Who is the Lord, that I should heed him and let Israel go? I do not know the Lord and I will not let Israel go.'" Instead he gave orders to make the Israelites' labors more arduous.

Right: The mummy case of an Egyptian pharoah.

Below: A twelfth-century Byzantine illustration depicts pharoah (2) with Jacob, Joseph, and his brothers.

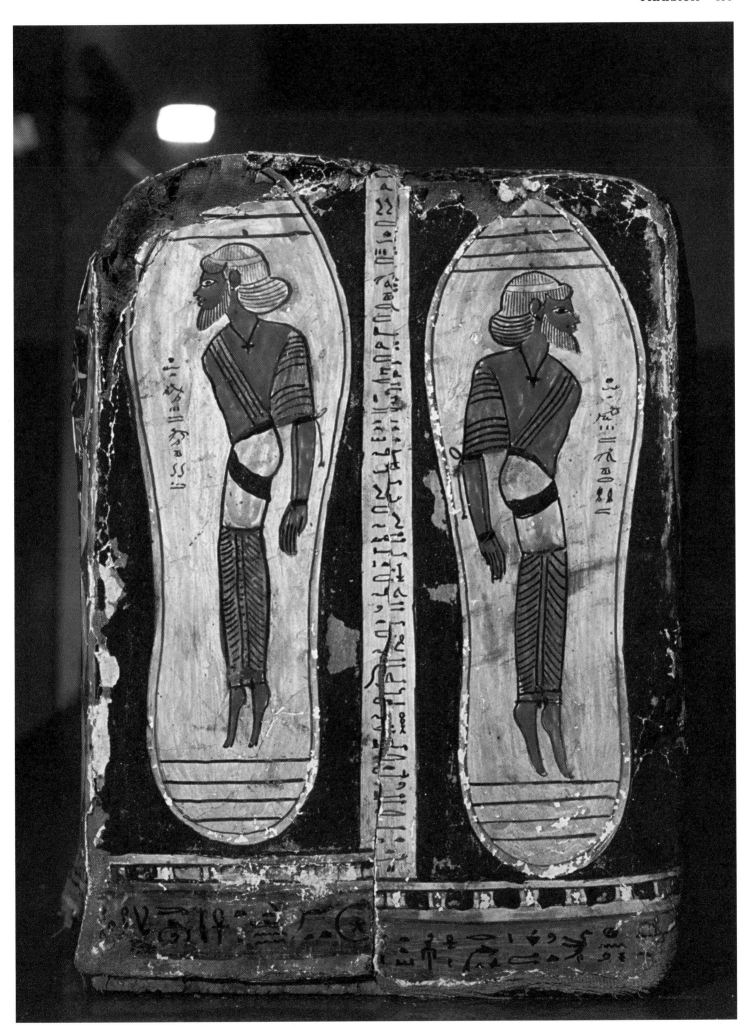

The Lord promised Moses that he would remember the covenant He had made with *Abraham*, and would compel pharaoh to allow them to leave. Moses and Aaron then joined in demonstrating various miracles to pharaoh, and then followed these by a series of plagues. Pharaoh remained stubborn, however, only offering to allow the Israelites to perform their sacrifices in Egypt. After the early crops of the Egyptians had been ruined in a hail storm, pharaoh relented, and said that the Israelites could go but changed his mind almost immediately. Pharaoh's next offer was to allow the Israelite men only to go, but this inadequate response was followed by the plague of locusts. Further miseries followed, and only after the eldest child of every Egyptian household had been killed did pharaoh finally relent and allow the Exodus to begin. Even then he had second thoughts, and led his army after the Israelites, but this venture ended in disaster when all his forces were drowned in the Sea of Reeds.

See also *Neco, Shishak*.

Phinehas

1. Phinehas was the son of *Eleazar*, and was a priest who became high priest when his father died.

Two principal incidents in his life are described. He executed *Zimri* and his Midianite concubine, *Cozbi*, when the sexual attraction of the Midianite women had helped seduce the people into worshiping the false god, *Baal*. After this incident the Lord halted the plague by which He was punishing the people. This passage appears in Numbers 25 and, according to Numbers 31, Phinehas was with the vengeful army which Moses sent against the Midianites.

Later, after the Promised Land had been conquered, Phinehas headed a party sent to investigate the building of an altar by the Israelite tribes who had settled to the east of the Jordan. It was agreed that this should not be regarded as usurping the position of the true tabernacle, provided it was not used for sacrifice.

Phinehas was given the town of Gibeah as his residence.

2. A second Phinehas was one of the immoral sons of the high priest, *Eli*. He and his brother, *Hophni*, were also

priests in the sanctuary, but they were accustomed to abuse the rites of sacrifice and to seduce women at the temple. After a defeat for the Israelites during a campaign against the Philistines, Phinehas and his brother brought the sacred Ark from the sanctuary to the army in an attempt to restore the army's morale. This failed, and a second defeat followed in which the Ark was captured and Phinehas and his brother were killed. When she heard the news, Phinehas's wife went into labor and gave birth to a son, whom she called Ichabod. She died immediately after giving birth.

A further personality called **Phinehas** appears in the Book of Ezra.

Potiphar

Potiphar was the captain of pharoah's [*Pharaoh (2)*] guard who bought *Joseph* when he was brought as a slave to Egypt. Potiphar promoted Joseph to serve in his household, and then made him overseer of all his property because Joseph served him so well. Potiphar's wife, however, became attracted to Joseph, and, when he refused to sleep with her, falsely accused him of attempting to rape her. Potiphar had Joseph put in prison (Genesis 39).

A personality named **Potiphera** is described in other passages (Genesis 46 & 50) as being Joseph's Egyptian father-in-law. The similarity in names suggests that there may be some

confusion between the two in the traditional story.

Rachel

Rachel was the younger daughter of *Laban*, and the second wife of *Jacob*. When Jacob arrived to live with Laban and his family, and to look for a wife, he met and fell in love with Rachel, who was more attractive than her elder sister, *Leah*. Jacob worked for Laban for seven years in order to marry Rachel, but Laban substituted Leah for her sister on their wedding night because he said it was improper for the younger sister to be married first. Jacob was angry, but agreed to marry both sisters in return for another seven years of work.

Rachel had no children at first, although Jacob loved her and not Leah. She accordingly gave Jacob her maid, *Bilhah*, as his concubine. According to the custom of the times, any children that Bilhah might have would legally be Rachel's. Bilhah had two sons, *Dan* and *Naphtali*. Eventually Rachel had a child of her own, *Joseph*.

When Jacob subsequently decided to move back to his homeland, because of his treatment by Laban, Rachel and her sister both went with him,

Below: The meeting of Jacob and Rachel – a bas-relief in stone at Salisbury Cathedral. Jacob worked for Laban through his love for Rachel, but he was tricked into marrying Leah.

agreeing that their father had acted badly. Rachel also stole the images which represented Laban's household gods. Possession of these indicated the family headship, and they should accordingly have been left with Laban for him to pass to his sons. When Laban caught up with Jacob and his wives, Jacob offered to have the thief of the gods executed, if they could be found. Rachel had not told Jacob what she had done, and successfully concealed the images when her father searched for them.

Rachel and her sister were with Jacob when he made his elaborate preparations to meet *Esau* once again. Later still in the family's travels, Rachel gave birth to a second son, whom she called Ben-oni. Rachel died immediately after the birth, and Jacob changed the child's name to *Benjamin*. Jacob buried her and erected a monument over her grave.

Raguel

Raguel was a kinsman of *Tobit*. He and his wife, *Edna*, and their daughter, *Sarah (2)*, lived in the city of Ectabana. Sarah was afflicted with a demon who had killed seven previous husbands on their wedding nights. Tobias, Tobit's son, arrived to visit Raguel and his family and, as was his right as a kinsman, asked if he could marry Sarah, with whom he had fallen in love.

Raguel warned Tobias of what had happened to the men who had previously tried to marry Sarah, but allowed the marriage to go ahead. The couple duly retired to bed and, assisted by the angel Raphael, exorcised the demon. Raguel did not know that this was happening, and in the meantime prepared a grave for Tobias. However, when he discovered that no harm had come to Tobias, he organized a lavish wedding feast instead.

Tobias and his new wife lived with Tobit until Tobit's death, and then returned to take care of Raguel and Edna.

Rahab

When *Joshua* was planning to attack Jericho, he sent spies to the city. They found refuge in the house of a prostitute called Rahab, who hid them when the king of Jericho sent men to look for them. In return they promised that Rahab and all her family would be spared when Jericho was captured,

provided that her house was marked by a red cord hung in the window. Rahab's motive is described as being due to her fear of the Lord because of her knowledge of the miracles with which He had aided Israel in the flight from Egypt. After the fall of the city, Joshua duly ensured that Rahab escaped unharmed (Joshua 2, 6).

Rebekah

Rebekah was the wife of *Isaac*, the daughter of Bethuel, and the granddaughter of Nahor, brother of *Abraham*.

When Isaac was growing old and was nearly blind, Rebekah overheard him telling *Esau* that he would give him his blessing after Esau had returned from a hunting trip. She therefore instigated the deception in which *Jacob* impersonated his elder brother to gain the blessing, and she devised the disguise that enabled it to be successful. Subsequently, to protect Jacob from Esau's anger, she arranged to send him away to live with her brother *Laban*, so that Jacob could also find a wife among his own people.

No information is given of the time or manner of Rebekah's death, but we are told that she was buried in the family tomb at Machpelah.

Rechab

Rechab and his brother, Baanah, were soldiers in the service of *Ishbaal*, *Saul*'s ineffective son. Their father was Rimmon, from the tribe of Benjamin. They decided to kill Ishbaal and switch their allegiance to *David*. They came to Ishbaal's house one day, seemingly to accept his hospitality, but when they had come into his private rooms they killed him, cut off his head, and made their escape with it. They took the head to David, but he was shocked at what they had done, to kill "a righteous man on his bed in his own house!" and had them executed in turn.

An earlier **Rechab** was the ancestor of an Israelite clan who clung to a nomadic way of life as much as possible, and did not drink wine. The best-known occasion on which they maintained their policy of temperance was during the siege of Jerusalem described in Jeremiah 35, when they refused to allow the prophet to sway them from the promise that their forefather had made.

Above: Rebekah gives water to Eliezer; a fourteenth-century illustration.

Rehoboam

Rehoboam was the son and successor of *Solomon*. Initially, he was set to rule the united kingdom of Judah and Israel, but the harshness with which he treated the delegates at an assembly at Shechem convened to confirm his right to the throne alienated many of them. Later, the royal official in charge of organizing forced labor was stoned to death, and Rehoboam had to flee to Jerusalem. This led to the establishment of the northern kingdom of Israel, with *Jeroboam (1)* as king, while Rehoboam became king of the southern kingdom of Judah.

Rehoboam initially planned to recover his lost kingdom by force, but was persuaded not to by the prophet, Shemaiah. Five years after he came to the throne, Rehoboam was attacked in turn by the Egyptian pharaoh, *Shishak*, who captured a number of towns and took valuable booty from the royal palace and temple at Jerusalem, presumably in return for not actually capturing the city. This is described in both II Kings and II Chronicles as a divine punishment for immorality, specifically in Kings for following other gods and employing male prostitutes in the temples.

Following Shishak's invasion, Rehoboam built a number of fortified cities in his territory. We are told that he was 41 years old when he came to the

Left: King Rehoboam, as seen in a stained-glass window of 1533 in St. Dyfnog's Church, Llanrhaeadr, in North Wales.

famine. They did not recognize that Joseph was the official in charge of the sale, and when he was awkward and obstructive Reuben reprimanded his brothers, saying that they should have listened to him and not harmed Joseph, and that their current predicament was a consequence of that earlier crime.

Like his brothers and half-brothers, Reuben and his family settled in Egypt subsequently and, like them, he became regarded as the forefather of the tribe of Israel named after him.

Reuel

See *Jethro*.

Reuel is also the name of two minor personalities in the Old Testament. One was a son of *Esau*, and the other appears in a genealogical list in I Chronicles.

Rizpah

Rizpah was one of the concubines of *Saul*. After Saul's death, *Abner* was accused by Saul's son, *Ishbaal*, of having sexual relations with her (association with a royal concubine was a strictly royal privilege, and could be treasonable – see *Abishag* and *Adonijah*). This caused a quarrel between Abner and Ishbaal, and was one of the factors which caused Abner to make peace with *David*.

Rizpah also appears later, in II Samuel 21. David was by then king, and decided to mitigate the punishment of a famine by handing over various of Saul's descendants to the people of the town of Gibeon, who had been wronged by Saul, thus bringing about divine disapproval. Rizpah's two sons and five of Saul's grandsons were accordingly handed over and executed. Executed men would normally have had their bodies exposed to the beasts and the elements, but Rizpah watched over the bodies until David decided that they should be given proper burial.

Ruth

Ruth is the central character of the Book of Ruth. She was the daughter-in-law of Elimelech and *Naomi*, and the

throne, and that he reigned for 17 years. Throughout his reign, Israel and Judah were often at war. His mother was Naamah, an Ammonite. Rehoboam himself had 18 wives, 60 concubines, 28 sons, and 60 daughters. He was succeeded by *Abijah*, his son by his favorite wife, Maacah.

Reuben

Reuben was the eldest son of *Jacob*, by his first wife *Leah*. Jacob preferred his second wife, *Rachel*. When Reuben was a young man he brought home some mandrakes to his mother (mandrake is a plant with supposed narcotic and magical properties). Leah gave these to Rachel in return for Rachel allowing Jacob to sleep with her (Leah) again. This led to the birth of *Issachar*.

Subsequently, Reuben angered his father by having an illicit incestuous affair with his father's concubine, *Bilhah*. When his brothers and half-brothers later became jealous of *Joseph*, Reuben tried to trick them into putting Joseph in a pit from which he could later rescue him. Instead, unknown to Reuben, *Judah* persuaded the rest of the brothers to sell Joseph to some passing Midianite traders as a slave. These took Joseph to Egypt. Reuben was dismayed, but did not demur when the brothers joined in deceiving Jacob that Joseph had been killed by a wild animal.

Later the ten brothers and half-brothers went to Egypt, where Joseph had prospered, to buy grain in time of

great-grandmother of *David*. Ruth's mother- and father-in-law were from Bethlehem but went to live in Moab during a famine. Elimelech died there, but both of his sons, Mahlon and Chilion, found Moabite wives, Orpah and Ruth. Mahlon and Chilion died some time later, leaving Naomi and her daughters-in-law as widows. Naomi decided to return to Bethlehem, but urged Orpah and Ruth to go back to their own families instead. Orpah reluctantly agreed to do so, but Ruth refused to be parted from Naomi.

When they returned to Bethlehem it was harvest time. One of the ways in which widows could support themselves was by gleaning behind the harvesters, which Ruth began to do. She happened to chose a field belonging to *Boaz*, who was a relative of Naomi's late husband. Boaz found out who she was, and was kind to her, giving her food and drink during the day, and ensuring that she was able to pick up a substantial quantity of grain. This continued throughout the harvest.

Above: Landscape with Ruth and Boaz, by Josef Anton Koch.

Left: An engraving of Ruth by J. H. Baker, based on a statue by W. Theed.

When the threshing time came, Naomi told Ruth to put on her best clothes and perfume and go to see Boaz once again. Ruth did so, and Boaz was attracted to her but explained that he was not her nearest male relative, and so could not perform the family duty and marry her unless the nearest relative first declined. The following day Boaz spoke to the nearest relative before witnesses. The relative wanted to acquire some land that Naomi had, but declined when he realized that he would have to marry Ruth to get it. He therefore passed on his rights to Boaz, who immediately announced that he would marry Ruth. Ruth and Boaz had a son called Obed. His son was *Jesse*, father of David.

One theme of the story of Ruth is clearly a discussion of the proper ways in which to care for the underprivileged in society, as widows very definitely were in ancient times. Another may perhaps have been to comment, at the time the book was composed, against trends in Jewish society hostile to mixed marriages with Gentiles. The book clearly portrays Ruth, the Moabite, as a righteous woman and, furthermore, as one of the ancestors of David, Israel's greatest hero.

Samson

The various stories attached to the life of Samson, the so-called strongest man in the Bible, appear in Judges 13-16. It is likely that the episodes describing the not-always-hostile relationship between the Israelites and the Philistines have been drawn together from a number of sources, and may not originally have related to a single individual. Samson became a folk hero to the members of his own tribe of Dan and to the Israelite people as a whole and, as with folk heroes, it is to be expected that the tales have exaggerated his various feats of heroism and strength.

Before his birth, his father, *Manoah*, and his mother had miraculous encounters with an angel, who foretold the birth, and said that Samson was to become a nazirite. (A nazirite was an individual who had made a special devotion to divine service, either for life or for a more limited period, and who was obliged not to have hair cut by a razor and to avoid alcohol and contact with dead bodies. The vow could be made by parents on behalf of a child.) Samson later acknowledged that he was indeed a nazirite in the final scene with *Delilah*, when he told her the secret of his hair. Despite this religious commitment and the three occasions on which we are told that "the spirit of the Lord rushed on him", Samson seems to have been a hot-tempered and lustful man, who specifically broke the nazirite vows.

The stories of Samson's adult life begin when he fell in love with a Philistine woman. His parents disapproved at first, but then agreed to the marriage. On the way to see the woman, Samson killed a lion bare-handed and, when he came past the spot later, he found that bees had made a hive inside the lion's carcass. Samson took their honey, ate some himself, and gave some to his parents. Samson then used this incident to set a riddle and make a bet with the other guests at his wedding. When they could not solve the riddle, they threatened Samson's new wife, saying that her family would be hurt unless she found out the answer from Samson. She nagged Samson until he told her; Samson was furious when he then had to pay up on the bet. The wager had been for 30 sets of fine clothing, so Samson accordingly killed 30 men of the town to get the required garments, and returned in anger to his parents, leaving his wife behind.

Samson later went back, only to find that his wife had married someone else. Samson was again very angry, and burned down the Philistines' crops. In reprisal, they killed his wife and father-in-law, and Samson in turn "struck them down hip and thigh with great slaughter." This escalation of what had been a family dispute caused the Philistines to raid into Judah, and rather than face this, the men of Judah came to Samson to capture him and hand him over to the Philistines. Samson allowed them to tie him up. When the Philistines arrived to capture him, Samson broke the bonds, picked up the

Left: Samson and the Lion, by Albrecht Dürer.

Right: Samson destroys the Philistine temple.

Left: Samuel stands before Eli, after having heard the voice of the Lord.

Samuel

The story of Samuel is related in what is now known as the First Book of Samuel. In the Hebrew text, I Samuel and II Samuel are a single compilation, and since Samuel dies substantially before the end of II Samuel, there can be no question of him having been the original author. In fact, biblical scholars generally believe that the material in the Books of Samuel was compiled from a number of different sources with different viewpoints. This provides an explanation for the seeming contradictions and inconsistencies on the one hand, and the apparent duplication of other items on the other. However, a consequence of this is that, although a reasonably coherent narrative of what is recorded of Samuel's life can be produced, its historical value is clearly uncertain.

Samuel was born following special prayers offered by his mother, *Hannah*, whose marriage to *Elkanah* had, up until then, been childless. Samuel was her first child, and in thanks he was brought to the temple at Shiloh and entered into the service of the priest there, who was called *Eli*.

One night, when he was still a boy, Samuel thought three times that he heard Eli calling him from his bed. After the third occasion, Eli realized that the Lord was talking to Samuel, and told him to return to his bed, but to reply to the voice on the next occasion. The Lord told Samuel of the punishment to come for the wickedness of Eli's sons, *Hophni* and *Phinehas (2)*. They duly died in battle with the Philistines, and Eli fell over in shock when he heard the news, breaking his neck. This was the first event that marked out Samuel to the people as a potential leader.

Some 20 years later, Samuel was able to begin leading the Israelites back to their faith, persuading them to set aside the foreign gods that they had been worshiping. Samuel summoned a gathering of the people to Mizpah, where they were threatened by a Philistine attack. Samuel offered a sacrifice, and the Lord helped drive the Philistines away. Samuel continued his career as a judge (seemingly in something like the modern legal sense),

jawbone of a donkey which happened to be lying nearby, and with it killed 1000 men. Then, as further proof of the divine favor with which Samson was viewed, the Lord made a spring so that Samson could quench his great thirst.

Samson's next opportunity to display his strength came when he was visiting a prostitute in Gaza and the local people closed the town gates to try and capture him. Instead Samson uprooted the gates and carried them away.

Finally, he fell in love with Delilah, and she accepted bribes from the Philistine leaders to try and find out the secret of his strength. Three times he suggested different ways in which he could be tied up and subdued. She tried each of these in turn, but none

worked. Finally, after she had nagged him for a long time, he gave in, and told her that he would lose his strength if his head was shaved with a razor. Delilah told the Philistines and arranged for someone to shave Samson while he was sleeping. The Philistines arrived, captured him, put out his eyes, and threw him into prison in Gaza.

Later the Philistines were celebrating a festival of their god *Dagon* and brought Samson out of prison to mock him. They did not realize that while he had been in prison his hair had grown again. Samson had himself led to the pillars that supported the Philistine temple and, calling on the Lord to help him, pulled them down and the building with them, thus killing over 3000 Philistines.

Right: Samuel is blessed by Eli, as depicted in a painting by W. W. Topham.

traveling around the country from his home at Ramah, where he also built an altar.

Following this, the account provides two versions of *Saul's* selection as king, and Samuel's role in this. The first, antimonarchical, version begins with the people calling on Samuel to choose a king for them because, now that he was old, they needed another ruler, as Samuel's sons, *Joel* and *Abijah*, had been proven to be corrupt. The Lord told Samuel that the real reason was different: "'they have not rejected you, but they have rejected me from being king over them. Just as they have done to me, from the day I brought them up out of Egypt to this day, forsaking me and serving other gods.'" The Lord told Samuel to warn the people that a king would be a burden to them, demanding taxes, military service and slaves, but they insisted that they wanted a king, and the Lord told Samuel to appoint one. This version of events was completed when Samuel summoned the people to a meeting at Mizpah and arranged to choose the new monarch by drawing lots. When the choice was eventually narrowed down to Saul, he was found to have tried to hide among the baggage, but was brought out and hailed as king.

The alternative version tells how Saul came to visit Samuel when he was searching for some straying donkeys belonging to his father. Samuel honored him with lavish hospitality and, before they parted, privately anointed him as king. Saul began to act as king in a successful campaign against the Ammonites, and his position as king was confirmed by Samuel at an assembly at Gilgal.

The account then resumes its antimonarchical tone, setting the scene for the conflict between Samuel and Saul that was to follow. Samuel summed up his career and the history of the Israelite people, pointing out how the Lord had delivered them in the past when they were faithful. His warning was: "'if both you and the king who reigns over you will follow the Lord your God, it will be well; but if you will not heed the voice of the Lord, but rebel against the commandment of the Lord, then the hand of the Lord will be against you and your king.'"

Some time later, Saul planned to undertake a campaign against the Philistines. Samuel had arranged to join Saul and his troops but, when he did not come at the agreed time, Saul took it on himself to offer a preparatory sacrifice. Samuel finally turned up shortly afterward, and told Saul that, because he had usurped the priest's proper role, his kingdom would not last, and he would be replaced by another.

Despite this, Saul continued to be successful in a variety of military efforts. Eventually Samuel told him to attack the Amalekites and, when he was victorious, to kill them all and slaughter all their animals. Instead Saul took the Amalekite king, *Agag*, prisoner, and he and his men brought back the best of the Amelekites' livestock also, intending to offer the animals as sacrifices. Samuel was furious that his instructions had not been carried out to the letter, saying that Saul's failure to obey meant that he rejected the Lord and that the Lord would accordingly reject him. Samuel insisted that Agag be brought to him, and when he was, Samuel "hewed Agag in pieces."

Samuel was then called upon to anoint Saul's successor. Samuel was told to go to Bethlehem and examine the sons of *Jesse* to find the new king. *David* was the youngest of the family, and Samuel first examined and rejected all his older brothers before anointing David in the presence of the rest of his family. In due course David entered Saul's service (see *David* for the variant accounts of how this came about), and Saul became jealous of him and tried to kill him. David fled for his life and took refuge with Samuel at Ramah. Saul's messengers caught up with him there, but first they, and then Saul when he arrived personally, were thrown into an ecstatic prophetic frenzy before Samuel. David again made his escape.

Some time after this Samuel died, was much mourned, and was buried at Ramah, but this was not the end of his encounters with Saul. Before what transpired to be his final battle, Saul was worried enough to consult a medium, the witch of Endor. He asked her to summon up the spirit of Samuel, which she did, only for Samuel correctly to predict that Saul would lose the coming battle, and that he and his sons would be killed.

Below: Samuel anoints Saul king of the Israelites. This interpretation is clearly the promonarchical version.

Sarah

1. Sarah (also known as Sarai) was the wife of *Abraham*, and mother of *Isaac*. She was Abraham's half-sister, but became his wife and accompanied him on his various travels. She was very beautiful, and to avoid danger to himself Abraham agreed with her that she should be passed off as his sister so that he would be safe if other men found her attractive. This led to two similar episodes. In Egypt she was taken into pharaoh's [*Pharaoh (1)*] household. The Lord then afflicted pharaoh and his house with plagues, he learned the truth, and sent Abraham and Sarah away. Later she was taken by *Abimelech*, king of Gerar, but he was warned of the truth by the Lord in a dream, and returned her immediately.

Because she was childless, Sarah arranged that one of her slaves, *Hagar*, should have a child with Abraham (which was evidently an acceptable practice at the time). Sarah became jealous, but Hagar had a son, *Ishmael*. Despite Abraham's and Sarah's very advanced age, there followed several divine promises, which neither initially wished to believe, that they would have a child. Sarah at this time was over 90, and Abraham nearly 100. Their son, *Isaac*, was born shortly afterward, however. When Isaac was a small baby, Sarah had Hagar and Ishmael sent away to protect Isaac's inheritance. Sarah died when she was 127, and was buried by Abraham in the cave of Machpelah, near Hebron, which he bought for this purpose.

2. Sarah was the daughter and only child of *Raguel* and *Edna*, and became the husband of Tobias in the Book of Tobit. She had been married seven times but, before any of the weddings could be consummated, the demon Asmodeus had killed each of her husbands. When Tobias, who was a relative, arrived to visit her family, he fell in love with her and asked to marry her. Her father warned Tobias, who in fact already knew, what had happened to her previous husbands, but allowed the marriage to go ahead. Tobias had been shown how to drive off the demon by his traveling companion, who was the angel Raphael in disguise, and this was successfully done. She and Tobias lived happily thereafter, first with *Tobit*, Tobias's father, and later with Sarah's parents.

Below: Pharoah (1) returns Sarah (1) to Abraham once he discovers that she is Abraham's wife, not sister. A miniature from a fourteenth-century Bible.

Sargon

Sargon was an Assyrian king who is believed to have ruled 722-704 B.C. His predecessor, Shalmaneser, died during the final siege of Samaria that completed the overthrow of the kingdom of Israel, and Sargon finished the job. This is not, however, clear from the biblical account in II Kings 17, which merely uses the expression "the Assyrian king". After the siege was over, the Assyrian king arranged the deportation of a large proportion of the Israelite population, and brought in settlers from other parts of his empire. Judah was not annexed at this time, but was essentially a subject nation.

Sargon is mentioned by name in the Old Testament only in a single verse of Isaiah 20, which describes how one of his armies attacked Ashdod. This campaign seems to have been mounted to put down a rebellion, and it has been suggested that the prophecy in Isaiah was delivered at the time to try to prevent *Hezekiah* joining this revolt against the Assyrians. Sargon was succeeded in turn as king by his son, *Sennacherib*.

Saul

Saul was the first king of the Israelites. His father's name was Kish, and he was a Benjaminite. His reign is usually dated to some time in the period 1050-1000 B.C. The text of the passage in I Samuel 13 which describes the length of his reign is clearly incomplete, and so this cannot be precisely stated.

The kingship is described as having been instituted by popular demand for a single leader who could unite the people to defend themselves against the increasingly serious attacks of the Philistines and others. It seemed all the more necessary because, not long before this, the succession from the judge *Eli* had been jeopardized by his corrupt sons, and the sons of *Samuel* were clearly no better. Samuel, however, was bitterly opposed to establishing a king, arguing that perceiving the need for such a temporal ruler detracted from belief in the Lord and His power to protect the people from harm. Nonetheless, the Lord told Samuel to select a king.

The Old Testament has two versions of the story of Saul's selection. The more favorable to the monarchical position has him visit Saul by chance

during a search for some strayed donkeys, only to be offered abundant hospitality and then, as he was leaving, being taken aside and anointed as king. The less favorable has Samuel summon a gathering of the people and proceed to select Saul by lot, only to have to drag him out from hiding among the baggage to complete the job. In both versions, Saul's reign was not immediately effective until he intervened, shortly after, in a siege of the town of Jabesh by *Nahash* the Ammonite. Saul mustered a relieving force and successfully drove the attackers off.

Much of Saul's reign was devoted to war: "There was hard fighting against

Above: An Assyrian relief representing King Sargon and his vizier (a high official in the hierarchy of courtiers).

the Philistines all the days of Saul; and when Saul saw any strong or valiant warrior, he took him into his service." Saul's principal military subordinate in his early days was, in fact, his son, *Jonathan.* Jonathan won a victory at Geba, and was instrumental in the larger defeat of the Philistines that followed at Michmash. However, at the start of the campaign, Saul clashed with Samuel when he took it upon himself to offer a sacrifice when the prophet did not arrive to do so at the appointed time. Saul argued that this

Left: Saul dies at the battle at Mount Gilboa by falling onto his sword following the calamitous defeat of his army.

a skillful musician, was brought to the king to play to him soothingly when his mood was bad. The second version has David's rise to prominence begin with the killing of *Goliath.*

However their relationship began, David soon became an important military commander, popularly acclaimed for his many successes. Saul became jealous, and in one of his fits of depression even tried to kill David. David avoided this, so instead Saul sent him on increasingly dangerous missions, hoping that he would die, and even offered David his daughter *Michal* in marriage if he killed 100 Philistines, which David easily did.

Saul's jealousy grew, and he discussed killing David with Jonathan. Jonathan was David's friend, and persuaded his father to change his mind for a time about this, but also warned David what was afoot. Again, in one of his black moods, Saul tried to kill David himself, and then sent men to David's house to do the job. David fled with the help of Michal, and escaped when the king caught up with him when he had taken refuge with Samuel. When Saul came to see Samuel in pursuit of David, Saul became drawn into the atmosphere of religious testimony surrounding the prophet and he, too, fell into a prophetic frenzy, during which David fled.

Saul's enmity toward David is also confirmed in a parallel account, in which Jonathan again interceded with Saul at a feast, only for his father in his anger to attack him. Saul told him that David would prevent him ever becoming king, and that he intended to kill David. Jonathan remained loyal to his friend, and passed the news on to David.

David began to live as an outlaw, traveling from place to place and gathering a band of sympathizers. Saul heard that he had had help from *Ahimelech* and the priests of Nob, so he had *Doeg* kill them all and destroy their town. Later Saul nearly trapped David in the town of Keilah, but David left just in time.

There then followed two incidents in which David had every opportunity to kill Saul, but declined to do so. On both occasions they parted amicably, with Saul offering good wishes to David.

was necessary to steady the morale of his troops, but Samuel accused him of impiety, and said that, as a consequence, he would be supplanted by another king. This military success did, however, give Saul a breathing space in which to attack some others of Israel's enemies and deter them from raids into Israel.

A major campaign was fought against the Amalekites, and became the occasion of another clash with Samuel. Before the fighting began, Samuel had told Saul to kill every Amalekite he could, and to slaughter all their livestock. Saul instead took King *Agag* prisoner and brought back the best of the Amalekites' animals to offer them in sacrifice. Samuel was outraged at this disobedience, and pronounced a harsh and uncompromising judgement: "'For rebellion is no less a sin than divination, and stubbornness is like iniquity and idolatry. Because you have rejected the word of the Lord, he has also rejected you from being king.'" Samuel then proceeded secretly to anoint the young *David* as Saul's successor.

There are again two versions of how David next came to Saul's notice and was taken into his service. The first describes how Saul became subject to some form of depression, because "an evil spirit from God" was tormenting him, and David, who was known to be

Neither fully trusted the other, evidently, because David then went and took service with the Philistine king, *Achish* of Gath.

Saul fought one final battle against the Philistines, but before it took place he became worried by the apparent strength of their army, and decided to consult a medium for advice. He went to the witch of Endor, and she raised the spirit of Samuel at Saul's request. Saul could hardly have expected good news from Samuel, but the prediction was grim. Saul and his sons would be killed the next day in the battle, which would be a dreadful defeat for Israel. This, according to Samuel, would take place as a punishment for Saul's disobedience regarding Agag and the Amalekites.

The battle at Mount Gilboa duly went badly for the Israelites. Jonathan and two others of Saul's sons were killed, and Saul himself was badly wounded. He asked his armor-bearer to finish him off, but the armor-bearer refused, so he had to fall on his own sword. The Philistines found the corpse, hacked off the head, and displayed the body on the walls of Bethshan. However, the men of Jabesh, scene of Saul's first victory, came and removed the body, and buried it properly in their town.

"Second Isaiah"

The Book of Isaiah is commonly divided by scholars into at least three sections. Most, but not all, of the first 39 chapters relate to the life and times of the great prophet and, although probably composed by a number of authors, are believed accurately to reflect his teaching. It is now generally accepted that the other, later chapters of the book, along with 13-14 and 24-27, do not have the same authorship as the first section. Chapters 40-55 are now usually described as making up a second section of the book, and chapters 56-66 a third. Like the earlier material, these are likely to have been the products of multiple authors but, in something of an oversimplification of a difficult subject, these supposed authors are sometimes referred to as "Second Isaiah" and "Third Isaiah."

Sennacherib

Sennacherib succeeded his father, *Sargon*, as king of Assyria, and reigned 705-681 B.C. When he came to the throne he was faced with a rebellion across much of his extensive empire, notably in Babylon, but also in Syria/Palestine (with Egyptian involvement). In 701 he came to Palestine to restore his ally, Padi, king of the Philistine city of Ekron, to his throne. In the course of this campaign he carried out a successful siege of the city of Lachish in Judah, an event which is depicted in great detail in reliefs found at Sennacherib's capital, Nineveh. Sennacherib also defeated Egyptian forces supporting the rebellion in a battle at Eltekeh. Only some of this emerges clearly in the biblical account.

In the Old Testament, Sennacherib is discussed in three sections: II Kings 18 & 19, II Chronicles 32, and Isaiah 36 & 37. The description of his doings in all three versions is generally similar. Sennacherib is said to have come to Judah in the fifteenth year of *Hezekiah*'s reign, and to have captured "all the fortified cities". Hezekiah then sent messengers to him at Lachish in an attempt to make peace, and Sennacherib demanded, and was paid, a substantial tribute in gold and silver. Perhaps to enforce this, Sennacherib then

Left: Saul consults the witch of Endor as to the result of the battle with the Philistines; a painting by Salvator Rosa.

Above: A relief from Sennacherib's palace at Nineveh shows soldiers with slings at the siege of Lachish.

Seth

Seth was the third son of *Adam* and *Eve*, and was born after the fatal quarrel between his brothers, *Cain* and *Abel*. Seth was born when Adam was 130 years old. No personal details of Seth's life are recorded, other than that the eldest of his unspecified number of children was a son called Enosh, and that Seth himself lived for 912 years.

Shadrach

See *Abednego*.

Shallum

Shallum is a common name in the Old Testament, being borne by 14, mainly minor, personalities. The best known of the name was the son of Jabesh, who assassinated King *Zechariah* of Israel and reigned in his place for one month, before being killed in his turn by *Menahem*. Shallum was also an alternative name of *Jehoahaz (2)*.

Below: Doré's interpretation of the destruction of Sennacherib's army by a divine angel.

sent an army to Jerusalem under one of his generals. Hezekiah refused to surrender the city, heartened by a prophecy from *Isaiah*, and, after suffering severe casualties inflicted by a divine angel, the Assyrians left. This may indicate that the Assyrians were struck by some form of epidemic. All the accounts conclude their descriptions of Sennacherib by mentioning his assassination by his sons, which did indeed take place.

There is some ambiguity in the texts and the non-biblical records that suggests that the episode when Hezekiah paid tribute, and the tale of the abortive attack on Jerusalem, may relate to separate Assyrian expeditions, but most historians believe that the whole account relates to 701.

II Kings 20 records a visit of an envoy from Babylon to Hezekiah. Although this is placed later in the text than the events of 701, it may, in fact, predate this, and relate to an attempt by the Babylonians to bring Hezekiah into the rebellion that they were organizing at the time of Sennacherib's accession.

Sheba, Queen of

The Queen of Sheba appears in I Kings 10 and II Chronicles 9. These references describe in almost identical terms how she visited *Solomon* and was deeply impressed by his orderly, rich and pious court. She and Solomon exchanged lavish gifts. Historically, Sheba seems to have been situated in southern Arabia in the area of modern Yemen. Other Old Testament references and ancient Assyrian sources also refer to Sheba as being a trading nation. Passages in Kings and Chronicles mention Solomon's use of a Red Sea port, so it would be highly plausible to regard the embassy of the queen as some sort of trade mission.

Sheba was also the name of a leader who briefly mounted a revolt against *David*.

Shechem

Shechem was the son of *Hamor*, ruler of the town of Shechem in the time of *Jacob*. He raped *Dinah*, Jacob's daughter, and subsequently asked his father to arrange for him to marry Dinah. Her brothers at first pretended to go along with the idea, provided that all the men of Shechem agreed to be circumcised. While they were all still weak from this procedure, Dinah's brothers, *Simeon* and *Levi*, led an attack on the town in which both Shechem and his father were killed and Dinah taken away to safety (Genesis 34).

Shem

Shem was the eldest son of *Noah*. He and his family were saved in the ark. Afterward, he and his brother, *Japheth*, covered up their father's nakedness after he had been seen lying drunk in his tent by their other brother, *Ham*. Shem and his descendants were blessed by Noah for this. Shem was regarded as being the ancestor of the Semitic peoples, including the Israelites, and Noah's blessing was held to support their superiority over the descendants of Japheth, and especially also of Ham.

Above: A Persian miniature portraying a seductive Queen of Sheba.

Below: Shem and his brothers discover a drunken Noah; a fresco at St. Savin in Vienna.

Shishak, Pharaoh

The Egyptian pharaoh described in the Old Testament as Shishak, is known in other sources as Shoshenk. He ruled from *c.* 935-914 B.C. His own record of his actions appears in inscriptions on a temple wall at Karnak, and includes an account of his invasion of the Holy Land.

In the Bible he appears in I Kings and II Chronicles in precisely this role of invader. *Jeroboam (1)* fled to Egypt after his quarrel with *Solomon*, and took refuge at Shishak's court. Later, in the fifth year of *Rehoboam*'s rule over Judah, Shishak attacked. He captured the cities of Judah and took valuable booty from the temple and the royal palace at Jerusalem. The biblical account does not say that he captured Jerusalem (nor is Jerusalem included in the long list of captures noted at Karnak), which suggests that the attack may have been bought off.

Simeon

Simeon was the second son of *Jacob* and *Leah*, his first wife. He and his brother, *Levi*, were the leaders in taking the family's revenge on *Shechem* for the rape of their sister, *Dinah*. Like his brothers and half-brothers, Simeon joined in selling *Joseph* into slavery in Egypt, later visited Joseph there, and finally settled in Egypt with his family at Joseph's invitation. During the negotiations with Joseph to buy grain during the famine, Simeon was kept as hostage by Joseph to ensure that the brothers would return with *Benjamin* as Joseph wished. Simeon and Levi are both described as being excessively prone to violence in the so-called Jacob's Blessing, delivered by the patriarch on his deathbed.

Simeon was the name given to one of the tribes on Israel, as was the case with his brothers and half-brothers. However, Simeon's name does not consistently appear in the various listings of the tribes.

Simon the Maccabee

Simon was one of the sons of *Mattathias*, and succeeded his brothers, *Judas* and *Jonathan*, as the Jewish leader in the later stages of the Maccabean revolt. He was an important commander in many of the campaigns fought under his brothers' overall leadership and, when he himself took charge, he effectively completed the task that they had begun. Like Jonathan particularly, he continued to exploit divisions between contestants for the Seleucid throne. With his support for Demetrius II, he received in return recognition of the *de facto* independence of Judea. He continued his campaigns to extend his power, capturing the town of Gazara, and winning a victory over the forces of the new Seleucid ruler, Antiochus VII. However, following this, Simon and two of his sons were assassinated by his son-in-law, Ptolemy, who in turn was killed by Simon's eldest son, who became the leader of the Jews.

Sisera

According to Judges 4, Sisera was a Canaanite general in the service of King Jabin of Hazor, who was defeated by the Israelites under *Barak* at Mount Tabor. Sisera lived at Harosheth-hagoiim. His military power was based around a force of 900 "chariots of iron." He deployed his whole force against Barak, but the Lord put Sisera and all his army into a panic, so that they ran away. Sisera tried to find refuge with *Jael*, but she first pretended to give him hospitality, and then killed him by driving a tent peg into his skull while he slept.

In Judges 5, which may be an older version of the story, Jabin is not mentioned, and Sisera appears to be king in his own right. The defeat of Sisera's army is attributed here to difficulties with the waters of the River Kishon. Jael is particularly commended for the killing of Sisera, even though this seems to have violated the usual customs of giving hospitality.

Below: A seventeenth-century roundel in Begbroke, Oxfordshire, showing Jael killing Sisera.

Solomon

Solomon was the son of *David* and *Bathsheba*, and succeeded his father as king of Israel. Whereas David was generally a violent man of action, Solomon was an intellectual, diplomat and judge. He was famed for his sagacity: "God gave Solomon very great wisdom, discernment, and breadth of understanding as vast as the sand on the seashore, so that Solomon's wisdom surpassed the wisdom of all the people of the east, and all the wisdom of Egypt." His greatest physical achievement was the building of the temple in Jerusalem.

Traditionally, Solomon has been regarded as being the author of the Books of Proverbs, Ecclesiastes, Song of Solomon and Wisdom of Solomon, as well as two of the psalms. The material in Proverbs cannot be directly credited to Solomon, other than by the brief attributions at the head of some chapters, but the age of Solomon seems to have seen the development of substantial literary activity in Israel, and it is very possible that parts of the existing Book of Proverbs, although collected considerably later, may originally date to that earlier time. Ecclesiastes is definitely of a substantially more recent date than Solomon's reign. The Song of Solomon (or Song of Songs) seems to have been attributed to Solomon, and is in some way connected to his reputation as a great lover. Much of its content consists of poems of love, often of an erotic nature. Analysis of the text has found words and expressions that date from several centuries after the time of Solomon, though again it is possible that some older material was preserved.

The main narrative of Solomon's life and reign is given in I Kings 1-11 and II Chronicles 1-9.

When David was old, the eldest of his surviving sons, *Adonijah*, began to take steps to secure the succession for himself. Solomon's mother, Bathsheba, was David's favorite wife and, assisted by the prophet *Nathan*, she persuaded David to nominate Solomon to the crown. This halted the claims of Adonijah's party.

Right: An engraving made after a painting by Rubens of the judgment of Solomon, in which he decided who was really the baby's mother by initially decreeing that the baby should be cut in half.

Before David died, he advised Solomon of the importance of obeying the divine law, and also asked him to take final revenge on two of David's enemies, which Solomon did. Solomon even sent *Benaiah* into the sanctuary by an altar to kill *Joab* as David had asked. Adonijah was also killed for asking to be given David's former servant, *Abishag*, as his wife.

Having thus established his succession, Solomon offered sacrifice in thanks. The Lord then appeared to him in a dream, and asked him what Solomon wanted to be given. Solomon asked for wisdom to undertake the difficult task of governing his people. The Lord replied that, since Solomon's request was so modest, he would also be given riches, honor and a long life, provided always that he obeyed the commandments as David had done. The wisdom granted to Solomon was then demonstrated in the case in which he decided which of two women was really the mother of a baby.

The great work of Solomon's reign was, of course, the building of the temple, and a substantial part of the text of the accounts in both Kings and Chronicles is a detailed description of its design and construction, and of the

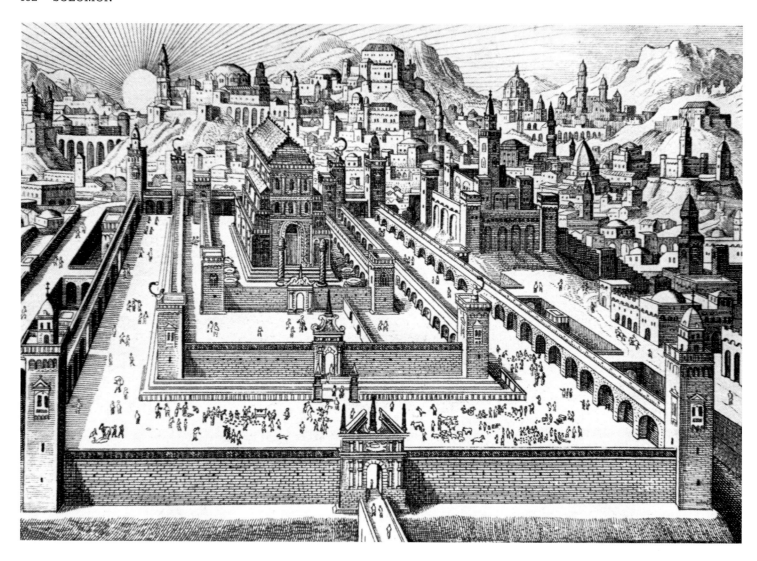

various elaborate, and obviously costly, furnishings and ritual items made and installed therein. Many of the materials were bought by treaty from King *Hiram* of Tyre, and much of the fine metalwork was done by another Hiram, who also came from Tyre.

Once the temple was finished, it was dedicated in an elaborate service in which Solomon himself offered a long prayer for divine favor and forgiveness to be directed toward Israel. After the conclusion of this, the Lord appeared to Solomon, confirmed that he had heard Solomon's prayer, and said that he would indeed bless Solomon and his line for as long as they obeyed the commandments and did not worship other gods.

Solomon's building works were not confined to the temple. He constructed a palace for himself, another for his Egyptian wife, built other major buildings in Jerusalem, and improved the city walls there. Away from the capital, he fortified other towns, and constructed barracks and storehouses to support his military and administrative developments.

It is also clear from the lists of Solomon's officials, the goods he sent to Hiram to pay for the wood and other materials for the temple, and the labor force he organized to transport the materials and carry out his massive building program, that Solomon's administrative system was elaborate and thorough. His marriages to a daughter of the ruling pharaoh, and to other foreign women, seem to have been dynastic and diplomatic alliances. He co-operated with Hiram of Tyre in various trade ventures too, and worked as the middleman in a lucrative traffic of chariots and horses. The most famous of his diplomatic and trade contacts with a foreign monarch was with the Queen of Sheba (see *Sheba, Queen of*).

The conspicuous wealth of Solomon's court, and the huge expense of his program of public works, came at a price, however. The demands of forced labor led to considerable discontent, although there is some doubt as to whether this imposition was made only on the native Canaanites, or on the Israelites too. Tribal divisions also

Above: A copper engraving of Solomon's Temple, dated 1650.

Right: King Solomon's many wives; an illustration from a Nuremberg reliquary of 1491.

seem to have been maintained, and all this was probably a factor in the unsuccessful rebellion and exile of *Jeroboam (1)*.

Among the extravagances was a huge harem of 700 wives and 300 concubines. Solomon's foreign wives were eventually a source of trouble: "For when Solomon was old, his wives turned away his heart after other gods; and his heart was not true to the Lord his God, as was the heart of his father David." "He did the same for all his foreign wives, who offered incense and sacrificed to their gods." The Lord was angered, but promised to reserve punishment until after Solomon's death, because of what He had promised to David.

Kings tells us that Solomon died after a reign of 40 years. Biblical commentators place his reign in the middle part of the tenth century B.C., perhaps around 970-930.

Susanna

Susanna appears in a deuterocanonical/apocryphal section of the Book of Daniel. She was the wife of a man called Joakim, and was very beautiful. Two of the elders of the community were accustomed to see Susanna when she was taking her regular walk in the gardens of her home. They lusted after her, and one day surprised her while she was bathing and tried to persuade her to sleep with them. She refused, even though they threatened that, if she did not submit, they would falsely accuse her of adultery, which was a capital crime. They brought her to trial, and she would have been convicted if *Daniel* had not intervened. He arranged for the elders to be questioned separately, and contradictions in their stories proved that they were lying. They were then executed instead of Susanna.

Tamar

1. Tamar appears in Genesis 38, initially as the wife of Er, eldest son of *Judah*. Er was quickly put to death by the Lord because of his wickedness. According to the so-called Levirate Law, as a widow, Tamar was entitled to marry her *levir* (the brother of her deceased husband), in order that she could have a son by him who would be regarded as her first husband's descendant and would inherit his position and property. Er's brother, *Onan*, refused to perform his duty properly, spilling his semen on the ground to avoid making her pregnant. The Lord killed him for failing her in this way.

Judah should then have arranged to marry her to his third son, Shelah, but did not do so in case Shelah also died, giving Tamar the excuse that Shelah was too young. Some time later, Tamar saw that Shelah had grown up and, in attempt to secure the child to whom she was entitled, dressed as a prostitute and solicited Judah. She became pregnant, and at first Judah was outraged when he heard of this but, when she proved that he was the father, he accepted that he was more in the wrong than Tamar, and acknowledged the twin children, *Perez* and *Zerah*, as his own when they were later born.

Left: Susanna and the Elders, by Tintoretto. The lovely and virtuous Susanna was a popular subject for many great painters.

Above: Tamar (l) and Judah, by Vernet.

2. Tamar was the beautiful daughter of *David* and Maacah, and sister to *Absalom*. David's eldest son, her half-brother Amnon, fell in love with her, and, by pretending to be ill, had David give permission for her to visit him in his private rooms. He tried to seduce her when they were alone, but she refused him unless they first asked David's consent for a marriage. Amnon would not listen, and raped her. Amnon's love then changed immediately to revulsion, and he threw her out of his house. In distress she went to live with Absalom. David did nothing to punish Amnon, and neither did Absalom at first, but two years later he invited Amnon to a feast and killed him.

Tamar was also the name of a daughter of Absalom.

Tiglath-pileser

The Tiglath-pileser mentioned in the Bible is better known to secular historians as Tiglath-pileser III, ruler of Assyria. In the Old Testament he is also known by the names Pul, or Tiglath-pilneser. Tiglath-pileser was a very successful monarch, reversing a long period of Assyrian decline in a variety of military campaigns. The Old Testament mentions his campaigns in Syria and Palestine in 734-32 B.C.

Tiglath-pileser received tribute from *Menahem* of Israel, presumably to buy off a threatened attack, since the account in II Kings 15 adds "So the king of Assyria turned back, and did not stay there in the land." This might refer to an earlier expedition that Tiglath-pileser may have made in 738.

His later campaign destroyed the kingdom of Aram-Damascus, and occupied much of the territory of Israel.

Above: An Assyrian relief showing a besieged fortress in the reign of Tiglath-pileser III.

The biblical account describes this as being at the behest of King *Ahaz* of Judah, in order to free him from attacks by Israel and Damascus. *Pekah*, Menahem's successor as king of Israel, was killed in the course of this campaign by *Hoshea*. Tiglath-pileser deported a substantial proportion of the population of the captured territory to Babylon. Ahaz subsequently paid tribute to Tiglath-pileser, and also copied an altar that Tiglath-pileser had built in Damascus, and installed it in the temple in Jerusalem.

Tobit

Tobit is the principal personality in the book of the same name. The Book of Tobit is regarded as being apocryphal by Protestants and Jews, but is included in the Old Testament by some Orthodox churches, and as a deutero-canonical book by Roman Catholics. The Book of Tobit was originally written in either Aramaic or Hebrew, not Greek, as once was thought. It is not

Above: Jan van Hemmessen's painting of Tobias restoring Tobit's sight.

certain when or where it was written; it may possibly have been in Egypt, Palestine or Mesopotamia, and the likeliest date is approximately 200-175 B.C. Most scholars suggest that it should be regarded as being wisdom literature rather than as a strictly historical account. It cannot be entirely accurate in historical terms in any case, since Tobit himself is described as having been a young man when the kingdom split between Israel and Judah (*c.* 931 B.C.) while his son, Tobias, is said to have died after the fall of Nineveh (612 B.C.).

Tubal-cain

Tubal-cain appears in Genesis 4 in the genealogy of the descendants of *Cain*. He is described as being the ancestor of all who work with metals. His cousins, *Jabal* and *Jubal*, are similarly described as being the first herdsman and musician respectively.

Uriah

Uriah the Hittite was the unfortunate first husband of *Bathsheba*. He was one of the leaders of the army of *David*. David fell in love with Bathsheba, and seduced her while Uriah was absent with the army at the siege of Rabbah. Bathsheba became pregnant, and David had Uriah recalled from the campaign, supposedly to report to him, but actually in the hope that he would spend time with his wife and that the paternity of the child would thereby be obscured. After Uriah had made his report, David suggested to him that he ought to go home, but Uriah refused because he did not think it proper to do so while the battle was still going on.

Even after David had made him drunk he was not tempted to go home, but slept in the royal palace.

When Uriah returned to the army the next day, David gave him a letter for the commander-in-chief, *Joab*, which gave orders for Uriah to be sent on a dangerous mission, and then not properly supported so that he would be killed. Uriah was duly killed in this way, and David married Bathsheba, but the child she was carrying died.

Uriah was also the name of four other personalities in the Old Testa-

Left: Andrea Pisano's metalworker, of which Tubal-cain was the first.

Below: King Uzziah; a stained-glass window in St. Dyfnog's Church, Llanrahaeadr, North Wales.

ment. Of these, the most prominent was a priest in the reign of *Ahaz*, who was associated with the king in building a new altar for the temple, following an Assyrian pattern. Another was a prophet in the time of *Jeremiah* and *Jehoiakim*, who was killed by the king for his unwelcome prophecies.

Uzziah

Uzziah was the son and successor of *Amaziah* as king of Israel. He came to the throne at the age of 16, after his father was assassinated. His mother was Jecoliah, and he reigned *c.* 783-742 B.C. (although it should be noted that the dates here are less certain than for most of the other kings of Israel and Judah).

Uzziah's long reign seems to have been a time of prosperity and modest military success for his kingdom, and also for Israel under *Jeroboam (2)*, to the north. He was able to rebuild the port of Elath (Eilat) on the Red Sea, presumably following unspecified victories over the Edomites. He also waged successful campaigns against the Philistines on the coastal plain to the west of Judah, and against the Ammonites to the east. At home he rebuilt the fortifications of Jerusalem, and installed stone-throwing and other weapons on the walls. All this was achieved on the back of a more efficiently organized army. In civil affairs his own herds seem to have prospered, and he built cisterns to assist in watering them, and for crop irrigation.

Below: Zadok the priest anoints Solomon, for which he was rewarded by being appointed a high priest.

His religious policy is generally praised in both Kings and Chronicles, but Kings mentions that he did not put an end to idolatrous practices among the people, and Chronicles describes an incident in which he personally burned incense on the altar in the temple, contrary to the Mosaic Law, which reserved this rite for the Levites. For this he was immediately rebuked by the high priest *Azariah*. According to Chronicles, he was also immediately struck down with leprosy as a punishment. Both Kings and Chronicles agree that he was a leper for a number of years before his death, and that during this period much of the work of government was done by his son, *Jotham*, who became his successor.

Uzziah is also known as Azariah in certain passages, and it has been suggested that Uzziah was, in fact, a ruling name given after he succeeded to the throne, with Azariah being his original family name.

Zadok

Zadok was one of the two high priests during the reign of King *David*. Zadok appears chiefly in Samuel, Kings, and Chronicles. He was the son of Ahitub, and claimed descent from *Aaron* through his son and successor, *Eleazar*.

Zadok and the other high priest, *Abiathar*, took the Ark of the Covenant out of Jerusalem, ready to follow David into exile, at the time of *Absalom's* uprising. David sent them back, but asked them to spy on Absalom and use their sons as the couriers for any information, which they did when they had news of Absalom's plans, warning David not to remain in the plains but to cross the Jordan to safety. After Absalom's death, Zadok was a spokesman to the elders, urging them to ask David to come back.

When the succession was again disputed, Zadok and the prophet *Nathan*

were involved in the anointing of *Solomon* rather than *Adonijah*, who was supported by Abiathar, the other leading priest. For his help in this, Zadok and then his son, *Azariah*, were appointed as high priests by Solomon. For centuries thereafter, all the high priests were drawn from their descendants. Passages in Ezekiel refer to the legitimacy of the family alone among the Levites.

Some biblical students suggest that Zadok may not have been truly descended from Aaron, but that the passages (particularly in I Chronicles) which describe this were inserted at a later date to connect the actual Zadokite priests, who definitely held the office, with the traditional genealogy, when in fact the Zadokites had an entirely different descent.

There are seven other minor personalities of the name **Zadok** in other sections of the Old Testament.

Zaphenath-paneah

Zaphenath-paneah was the Egyptian name given to *Joseph* when he was appointed as pharaoh's chief minister [see *Pharaoh (2)*].

Zebulun

Zebulun was the sixth son of *Jacob* and his first wife, *Leah*, and the tenth of Jacob's sons to be named in Genesis. Like his brothers, he was involved in selling *Joseph* into slavery in Egypt, and later visited Joseph with his brothers and half-brothers to try to buy corn. When Jacob subsequently took his whole clan to settle in Egypt, Zebulun and his family are named as being with him.

Zebulun is also the name of one of the tribes of Israel who were supposedly descended from him.

Zechariah

The prophet Zechariah was active during the rebuilding of the temple in Jerusalem, which took place 520-515 B.C., although Zechariah's preaching seems to have been confined to the first two of these years. He is very briefly mentioned in the Books of Ezra and Nehemiah, but appears chiefly in the Book of Zechariah. Biblical scholars are almost all agreed that only

Chapters 1-8 of the book relate to the prophet, and that the other chapters were written much later, perhaps in the third century B.C.

Zechariah, like *Haggai*, urged the community to proceed with the work on the temple, and also argued for them to maintain the highest standards of moral conduct. Much of the language of the Book of Zechariah is obscure, and the imagery and symbolism fantastic and bizarre. Nonetheless, some points are clear. The high priest, Joshua (see *Jeshua*), is commended, as is the people's secular leader, *Zerubbabel*. Chapter 8 alludes to a coming restoration of the true Kingdom of Israel, when the Lord will save his people and bring them once

Above: Detail of the prophet Zechariah from Michaelangelo's fresco paintings of the ceiling of the Sistine Chapel in the Vatican.

again to Jerusalem. This leads into the chapters in the second section of the book which discuss aspects of the Messianic age.

Zechariah is an extremely common name in the Old Testament, used by almost 30 others, in addition to the important prophet discussed above. Of these, the best known were a king of Israel who reigned for six months *c.* 745 B.C., succeeding his father *Jeroboam (2)*; and a priest, the son of Jehoiada, who was stoned by the order of *Joash (1)*.

Zedekiah

Zedekiah was the last king of Judah. He was a younger brother of *Jehoiakim*, and succeeded Jehoiakim's son, *Jehoiachin*, as king. He reigned 597-587 B.C. Jehoiachin was deposed by *Nebuchadnezzar* of Babylon, and was taken off to Babylon as a prisoner; Zedekiah was put on the throne by Nebuchadnezzar in his place. Zedekiah's given name was Mattaniah; his throne name, by which he is much better known, was chosen by the Babylonians. His mother's name was Hamutal.

Zedekiah seems to have been in an unenviable position, trying to achieve some sort of independence from Babylonian control, as he was being urged to do by some of his supporters, without antagonizing his overlord, which too much emphasis on the exclusive Israelite God Yahweh might do, while all the time being badgered by the gloomy predictions of the great prophet *Jeremiah*. He is said to have continued the evil religious policies of Jehoiakim, restoring false gods and so on. It is, however, interesting to note, that in Chronicles he is criticized for breaking his vows of allegiance to Nebuchadnezzar.

He rebelled against Nebuchadnezzar finally in 589. The Babylonians attacked and, after a long siege, captured Jerusalem. Zedekiah escaped for a brief time, but was captured. His end was unpleasant: "They slaughtered the sons of Zedekiah before his eyes, then put out the eyes of Zedekiah; they bound him in fetters and took him to Babylon." Jerusalem was devastated, the temple destroyed, and many of the people taken off into exile in Babylon.

The above account comes essentially from II Kings 24 & 25 and II Chronicles 36, and is confirmed in Jeremiah 52. Zedekiah is also mentioned in numerous other places in the Book of Jeremiah. The text of Jeremiah does not present a clear chronological sequence, but certain events involving the prophet and the king can be highlighted. Zedekiah was consistently advised not to rebel, and was warned during the rebellion that, if he surrendered, he would be spared, but, if not, he would be killed, and Jerusalem destroyed. At some point Jeremiah rebuked the king for first encouraging the people to free their slaves and then taking them back. Zedekiah

imprisoned Jeremiah to try and halt his unwelcome flow of advice, but then consulted him and apparently believed the prophecy, but was unable to act upon it. Zedekiah seems to have been well-meaning but personally weak – and to have been placed by events in a very difficult situation.

Zedekiah was the name of one of the prophets who gave *Ahab* the incorrect advice to attack Ramoth-gilead and had an angry encounter with *Micaiah* when this mistake was revealed.

Zephaniah

Like most of the other "minor prophets," little is recorded of the life of Zephaniah, even in the book of the Old Testament that bears his name. A brief note of his descent is recorded in the first verse of the book, but no other personal details appear. This verse names his father as being Cushi, and his great-great grandfather as Hezekiah, usually presumed to be the same person as the noted King *Hezekiah*, although this is not specifically stated. The book is said to have been written in the reign of *Josiah*, and the content suggests the earlier part of his reign (i.e., *c.* 640-621 B.C), before the religious reforms which Josiah undertook.

The Book of Zephaniah is cast in the form of a dialog between the Lord and the prophet. The majority of the book is concerned with various oracles against the wickedness of Jerusalem and Judah and the surrounding nations. The possibility of salvation is admitted, however, especially if the sin of pride is avoided: "Seek the Lord, all you humble of the land, who do his commands: seek righteousness, seek humility; perhaps you may be hidden on the day of the Lord's wrath." Finally comes a promise of deliverance, offered to people of all nations, but especially to the righteous "remnant of Israel."

Zerah

Zerah was one of the twin sons born of the incestuous relationship between *Judah* and *Tamar (1)*. During the birth, Zerah's arm emerged from the womb and the midwife tied a red cord round it to identify which child was born first but, after she had done this, he pulled his arm back, and his brother *Perez* emerged. *Achan* was one of Zerah's descendants.

Zeresh

Zeresh was the wife of *Haman*, and was associated with him in his attempts to have *Mordecai* disgraced. She and some of Haman's friends suggested to him that he advise King *Ahasuerus* to build a large gallows and hang Mordecai on it. When Haman's plot went wrong, he was hanged on it instead.

Above: Zerubbabel's image in St. Dyfnog's Church at Llanrhaeadr, North Wales.

Zerubbabel

Zerubbabel, son of Shealtiel, was one of the leaders of the Israelite people in the early years of the return from Babylonian exile. He was descended, through *Jehoiachin* of Judah, from *David*, and is described in Messianic terms in both the Books of Haggai and Zechariah. He seems to have been crowned in some way by *Zechariah*, as described in Zechariah 6, but with *Jeshua*'s name substituted by a later editor. Zerubbabel may then have been regarded in or around his own time as somehow restoring the realm of David, but this does not clearly appear in the surviving account of his life in the Bible.

Zerubbabel is named in the list of the leaders of the first group of Israelite returnees from exile in 538 B.C. The overall leader of this group is named as being Sheshbazzar, and some commentators have suggested that he and Zerubbabel were the same person.

Little work was done to rebuild the temple at that time, but Zerubbabel had an important role when this project was revived in 520, following the accession of *Darius* as Persian emperor. Partly inspired by promptings from *Haggai* and Zechariah, Zerubbabel and Jeshua, the high priest, began work. Some local people, who would in time develop into the distinct Samaritan sect within the Israelite/Jewish religion, wished to join in the rebuilding, but Zerubbabel would not allow this. Their complaints and obstruction delayed the work. Permission to continue with it was confirmed by Tattenai, the regional governor, who consulted the imperial administration before allowing the project to proceed. The temple was finished in 515, but Zerubbabel is not named as being present at its dedication or at any subsequent event. What happened in his later life in unknown.

Ziba

Ziba was a member of King *Saul*'s household, but only came to prominence after the death of Saul. He was wealthy in his own right, owning 20 slaves. After Saul and *Jonathan* had died, *David* looked for any survivors from the family, and Ziba told him that *Mephibosheth*, Jonathan's son, was still alive. David adopted Mephibosheth, who was somehow disabled in his

Below: Zophar and his companions lament with Job; an illustration by William Blake.

feet, returned to him all the family's property, and put Ziba in charge of his household.

Later, when David left Jerusalem at the start of *Absalom*'s rebellion, Ziba came to him, bringing supplies and alleging that his master was disloyal to David. David was angry, and promised Ziba all his master's estates and goods. After David's victory over Absalom, Ziba was quick to meet the returning king and tried to ingratiate himself with him. However, Mephibosheth also came to meet David, and denied the charge of disloyalty. David cannot have completely believed either one, for he returned half of the confiscated property to Mephibosheth.

Zilpah

Zilpah was one of the concubines of *Jacob*, and the mother of his sons *Asher* and *Gad*. She was originally given as a slave by *Laban* to his elder daughter, *Leah*, Jacob's first and unloved wife. When Leah thought that she could no longer have children, she gave Zilpah to Jacob.

Zimri

Zimri was King of Israel for seven days, the fifth monarch after the split with Judah. During the reign of his

predecessor, *Elah*, Zimri is described as being the "commander of half his chariots". Zimri's brief rule began when he murdered Elah and others of Elah's family. He was quickly attacked and defeated by *Omri*, commander of the army, and retreated into the royal palace and burned it down over his own head. The killing of Elah's family and the almost immediate death of Zimri are both described as punishments for idolatry.

A further personality called **Zimri** appears in Numbers 25. He and his lover, *Cozbi*, were killed by the priest *Phinehas (1)*. The name is also used twice more in the Old Testament.

Zipporah

Zipporah was one of the seven daughters of *Jethro*, and became *Moses*'s wife. When Moses ran away from Egypt after killing an Egyptian, he met Zipporah and her sisters trying to water their father's flocks at a well, but being obstructed by other shepherds. Moses helped them, met their father, and was given Zipporah in marriage. They had two sons, *Gershom* and, later, *Eliezer*.

When Moses later returned to Egypt he became ill, and Zipporah hurriedly circumcised Gershom, believing that failure to carry out this important rite was the cause of the divine punishment being inflicted on her husband. It is not made clear whether Zipporah went to Egypt with Moses, but she was certainly separated from him at some point, only to be reunited with him in the desert during the journey to the Promised Land.

Zophar

With his companions, *Bildad* and *Eliphaz*, Zophar visited *Job* after he had been tested by the Lord, and conducted a debate with him to try to stop his curses against the Lord. The debate occupies Job 3-31. Zophar made two contributions to the debate, first reminding Job "that God exacts less of you than your guilt deserves" and that the righteous have nothing to fear, and in his second contribution "that the exulting of the wicked is short and the joy of the godless is but for a moment." Finally, Zophar and his friends gave up their attempt to argue with Job, and they were later admonished by the Lord for this failing.

JOHNSTON PUBLIC LIBRARY
JOHNSTON, IOWA 50131

Acknowledgments

The publisher would like to thank Ron Callow of D23 for designing this book. The following individuals and agencies provided the pictures.

Agence Photographique de la Réunion des Musées Nationaux, Paris, © Photo R. M. N./Louvre, pages: 32, 114

The Barber Institute of Fine Arts, The University of Birmingham, page: 25 (top)

The Bettmann Archive, pages: 4, 12, 14, 15, 16, 19, 20, 21, 22, 23, 27, 29, 38, 40, 46, 48 (top), 49 (bottom), 50, 51, 55 (bottom), 57, 67 (both), 68, 71, 76 (bottom), 77, 78, 80, 81, 82, 84, 85, 93, 94, 97, 99, 103, 109 (both), 113, 116 (top), 117 (top), 121, 122, 124, 126, 129 (bottom), 130 (both), 131, 137, 141, 144 (both), 149 (top), 151, 152, 153 (bottom), 154 (bottom), 157

Bildarchiv Preussischer Kulturbesitz/ Photo Jürgen Liepe, 1992, page: 62

The Bridgeman Art Library/Russell-Cotes Art Gallery and Museum, Bournemouth, page: 24/Graf Harrach'sche Gemäldegalerie, Vienna, page: 34 (bottom)/Dulwich Picture Gallery, page: 47

C. M. Dixon, pages: 3 (top), 6, 11, 12 (top), 31, 43, 61, 66, 98, 105 (bottom), 106, 117 (bottom), 135, 145, 148 (top), 154 (top right)

e. t. archive, page: 111 (top)

Giraudon, page: 5 (bottom)

© Sonia Halliday Photographs, pages: 13 (bottom), 30, 52, 60 (top), 70, 88, 90, 128, 134, 136, 138, 158/Photo James Wellard: page 45

© Sonia Halliday and Laura Lushington, pages: 28, 39, 53, 56, 118, 120, 150, 155 (bottom)

Hulton Deutsch Collection, Ltd., pages: 1 (bottom three), 5 (top), 17, 26, 33, 34 (top), 35, 38, 44, 48 (bottom), 49 (top), 55 (top), 58, 59, 63, 65, 72, 74, 75, 79, 86, 87, 102, 104, 105 (top), 108, 110, 111 (bottom), 116 (bottom), 119, 122 (bottom), 139 (bottom), 140, 142, 143, 146, 147, 148 (bottom), 153 (top), 156, 159

Life File/Photo Stuart Norgrove, pages: 7, 8/Photo Barry Mayes, page: 18/Photo S. Kay, pages: 41, 65

John McNeill, page: 9

Private Collection, page: 42

© Roger-Viollet, pages: 1 (top), 95, 149 (bottom)

Scala, Florence, pages: 69, 76 (top), 155 (top)

The Society of Antiquaries, London, pages: 25 (bottom), 60 (bottom), 89, 100

Sotheby's, London, pages: 2, 3 (bottom), 10-11, 92, 112, 122 (top), 127, 129 (top), 132, 139 (top)

The Wallace Collection, page: 155 (top left)

Woodmansterne Picture Library, pages: 73, 115